THE GENESIS OF PERFECTION

Three Theses

1. *In Judaism, creation is understood through the revelation at Mount Sinai.*

   It was said in the name of Rabbi Samuel who in turn heard it said in the name of Rabbi Yishaq: "The idea of creating Israel preceded the idea of creating all else." [. . .] Rabbi Bannay said: "The world and all therein was not created except through the merit of the Torah."

   Genesis Rabbah

2. *In Christianity, creation is understood through the advent and passion of Christ.*

   On March 25, our Lord Jesus Christ was crucified, conceived, and the world was made.

   Martyrology of Jerome

3. *Adam and Eve did not thwart the designs of God but, paradoxically, advanced them.*

   [*Adam's words after the fall:*]
   O goodness infinite, goodness immense!
   That all this good of evil shall produce,
   And evil turn to good; more wonderful
   Than that which by creation first brought forth
   Light out of darkness! Full of doubt I stand,
   Whether I should repent me now of sin
   By me done and occasioned, or rejoice
   Much more, that much more good thereof shall spring,
   To God more glory, more good will to men
   From God, and over wrath, grace shall abound.

   John Milton, *Paradise Lost* XII:469–78

THE GENESIS OF PERFECTION

Adam and Eve
in Jewish and Christian Imagination

GARY A. ANDERSON

Westminster John Knox Press
LOUISVILLE • LONDON

© 2001 Gary A. Anderson

Scripture quotations from the New Revised Standard Version of the Bible are copyright © 1989 by the Division of Christian Education of the National Council of the Churches of Christ in the U.S.A. and are used by permission.

Book design by Sharon Adams
Cover design by Pam Poll Graphic Design

First edition
Published by Westminster John Knox Press
Louisville, Kentucky

This book is printed on acid-free paper that meets the American National Standards Institute Z39.48 standard. ∞

PRINTED IN THE UNITED STATES OF AMERICA

02 03 04 05 06 07 08 09 10 — 10 9 8 7 6 5 4 3 2

Library of Congress Cataloging-in-Publication Data

Anderson, Gary A., 1955–
    The genesis of perfection : Adam and Eve in Jewish and Christian imagination / Gary A. Anderson.
        p. cm.
    Includes bibliographical references and indexes.
    ISBN 0-664-22699-X (alk. paper)
    1. Adam (Biblical figure) 2. Eve (Biblical figure) 3. Bible O.T. Genesis I–III—Criticism, interpretation, etc.—History. I. Title.

BS580.A4 A57 2001
222'.110922—dc21   2001026107

For Lisa Marie, née Detlefs

Contents

List of Illustrations

Acknowledgments

Three individuals were instrumental in shaping this book. First is Moshe Goshen-Gottstein, the late professor of Semitic languages of the Hebrew University, Jerusalem, Israel. In my very first course as a graduate student at Harvard University in the fall of 1981, I enrolled in his course entitled "Targum and Midrash." Here I was tutored in the ways of Jewish interpretation from the beginnings to its flowering in the medieval period.

Whereas Prof. Gottstein put a premium on philology and semantics, my most able mentor in the field of biblical interpretation in its full hermeneutical complexity was James Kugel. He graciously gave of his time during my final days as a graduate student to read rabbinic texts privately. Ever since, he has been unstinting in his generosity of time and encouragement for my development as a scholar.

Finally, I must mention Professor Michael Stone. He has been a true mentor in the deepest sense of the word. I met him while a Fulbright fellow in Israel in 1988–89. He invited me to his seminar, and this was the beginning of countless conversations on Jewish Apocrypha and Pseudepigrapha. To my great surprise he arranged for me to give a paper at the Society for New Testament Studies meeting in Milan in the summer of 1990 on the *Life of Adam and Eve*.

This, of course, was the beginning of a decade of collaboration. It was as joyful a scholarly experience as one can imagine. Along the way we codirected two National Endowment for the Humanities seminars and participated in several joint conferences (twice at Hebrew University and once at the University of Leiden). It was from Professor Stone that I learned to take seriously the place of the *Life of Adam and Eve* in Late Antique Christian culture. And so resulted an irony only the late twentieth century could provide: as a Christian scholar, I argued for the prominence of Jewish exegetical sources; as a Jewish scholar, he constantly reminded me of the text's Christian transmission history. For all his many kindnesses, I owe Professor Stone a bill of indebtedness that cannot be repaid.

This book began solely as a Jewish venture. I have always been in love with Jewish sources and the living Jewish tradition; I hope this book reflects both these matters. But along the way, I took an interest in the early Christian usage of these materials. Here my tutors were three: Robert Wilken, Robin Young, and Sidney Griffith. To Professor Wilken I owe the joy of some ten years of being his junior colleague at the University of Virginia. Over that time I read patristic texts in Greek with him, Judy Kovacs, and a bevy of devoted graduate students. This was almost like a second graduate degree in early Christianity. My knowledge and confidence in patristic material is due in large to his intellectual generosity.

For nearly fifteen years I have read St. Ephrem with Robin Young and Sidney Griffith. This was an act of both scholarship and piety. In Charlottesville, Virginia, we would often end our reading sessions with a trip to the Trappestine monastery for evening vespers. Our discussion of Ephrem in the Syriac original never ended with the parsing of verbs or even the setting of the various texts in their proper historical ambit. We always ventured into territory more beloved to us three: the role of patristic thought in the life of the church.

And of course there are countless others to whom I owe my thanks. Among the institutions let me mention NEH, which funded two summer seminars (1993, 1996) and the production of an electronic edition of the *Life of Adam and Eve* [a project still in the making] (1994); the American Council of Learned Societies, which funded my travel to Milan in the summer of 1990; the University of Virginia, which gave numerous summer grants and an occasional sabbatical; and the Association for Theological Studies, which granted me a year's fellowship to be a Henry Luce III fellow (1997–98).

Among the other people I should thank, let me mention two exceptionally talented graduate assistants, Richard Layton (U. Va.) and Sergio La Porta (Harvard), as well as a host of faculty colleagues, in particular those Duke, Virginia, and University of North Carolina Chapel Hill faculty who were esteemed members of SCRAM (Society, Culture, and Religion of the Ancient Mediterranean): Marc Bregman, Nicholas Constas, Steven Fraade, Israel Knohl, Jon Levenson, Shlomo Naeh, Carol Newsome, James Nohrnberg, Luk van Rompey, and David Satran. I should also thank students at Virginia and Harvard who have helped me shape my argument in the classroom.

I would like to thank my agent, Donald Cutler, for the immense patience he showed as I tried, in draft after draft, to make my manuscript appeal to a wider audience than mere academic specialists; Mark Edington who provided numerous last-minute corrections; and also my editor Carey Newman of Westminster John Knox for his understanding and abiding interest in my project.

Two chapters in this book have appeared elsewhere, and I would like to thank the sources for their permission to republish. Chapter 5 appeared in *Theological Exegesis: Essays in Honor of Brevard S. Childs*, edited by Christopher Seitz; Eerdmans, 1998; and my appendix "Biblical Origins of the Fall" appeared in *Pro Ecclesia*, volume 10, 2001. In addition I would like to thank Scholars Press for the rights to republish a portion of Michael Stone's translation of the American version of the *Life of Adam and Eve*, a work that we coedited in 1999: *A Synopsis of the Books of Adam and Eve*, Atlanta: Scholars Press; and Westminster John Knox for the right to republished a portion of "The Gospel of Nicodemus." Finally, I would like to thank St. George's Greek Orthodox Church, Toronto, for the rights to print a photograph of the fresco of the *Anastasis* that adorns their church. The iconographers are the Pachomaioi brothers (that is, monks) who work out of Mount Athos, Greece; the photographer is Alexei Mezentzev.

Quotations from scripture are generally taken from the New Revised Standard Version, but as the argument required, I frequently translated them myself.

The book is dedicated to Lisa Marie, my beloved wife of almost twenty-five years. And let me thank my boys Christopher Michael and Matthew Tobias as well, who have borne patiently with their often absent-minded father as he slowly assembled the chapters that make up this book.

Preface

Like many biblical scholars, my interest in the academic study of the Bible originated from a very specific theological framework. I wanted to get at the core of what could be called "biblical religion." Being raised Protestant and educated in the historical method of the Enlightenment, I believed that the Bible's essential message could be cracked open by recovering its original historical setting. This required considerable familiarity with the history, languages, and culture of the ancient Near East out of which the Bible took its shape.

But a funny thing happened along the way. Already during my training as a Protestant seminarian at Duke, I was made aware of the immense importance of church and synagogue in shaping the very form of scripture. Trained by the church historians David Steinmetz, Robert Gregg, and Jill Raitt at Duke, I found my theological compass pointing in a new direction. Eventually, I emerged a Roman Catholic with the deepest and most abiding love for Judaism and the Jews.

While a graduate student at Harvard, I received the best historical and philological training one can get, under the tutelage of Frank Cross. But due to my growing interest in how Jewish and Christian tradition shaped the very form of the Bible, I was drawn to the persons of Moshe Goshen-Gottstein (a visitor from Israel during my first year at Harvard) and James Kugel (a scholar of Jewish biblical interpretation), and to the writings of Brevard Childs (a biblical scholar with strong interests in the history of interpretation). Ever since, I have embarked on what has been uncharted territory: I have sought a way of combining what we know about the Bible's *history of composition* (the historical-critical method proper) with its *history of reception* (the history of interpretation).

What I have found as I have worked these two different sides of the street is that there are real intellectual and theological gains to be

made from the combination. Those who work in the history of interpretation from the patristic or medievalist angle rarely see their
authors engaging in interpretation proper. Rather this interpreter or
that is doing what he or she does because of some contemporary (generally polemical) circumstance. Gregory of Nyssa, for example, waxes
eloquent on Adam and Eve's chaste state in the Garden not because it
is a biblical issue but because the fourth-century church values
celibacy. What looks like *exegesis* (teasing meaning *out* of the text) is
really just *eisogesis* (forcing one's pet theories *into* the text). Though
self-interest is never far from any interpreter—including us—there is
much more biblical interpretation going on in these writers than is
generally conceded. Biblical scholars are trained to recognize these
interpretive moves.

On the other hand, knowing the history of interpretation gives one
a whole new perspective on modern biblical criticism. Though this
movement began with very clear theological interests, those have
been left behind in the contemporary academy. Among those who
practice the academic study of the Bible today, there is almost no
knowledge of what the church or synagogue has taught about the
Bible. Students often take an introductory course to the Old or New
Testament in college or seminary thinking they will learn why Jews
and Christians revere this book. More often than not, the issue is
rarely engaged. The whole semester is spent dividing the book up
into its discrete literary pieces and tying each to some self-interested
circle from the past.

My book is by no means a solution to this near schizophrenic
divide. The crisis in biblical studies has been a long time in forming,
and it will take some time to overcome. This book's goal is more humble: it is an attempt to draw a comprehensive picture of how Jews and
Christians in the first few centuries of the Common Era *retold* and
relived the story of Adam and Eve.

Let me issue a couple of caveats. This book is not encyclopedic.
There are many lacunae that I am sure my reviewers will note. For
example, I have not engaged the work and influence of the Jewish-
Hellenistic Philo, and I have almost completely ignored second-
century heretical Gnostic sects. This is not because I think they are
unimportant; in my courses on the subject I regularly teach these
materials. Rather, my bias has been toward normative materials. My
interest has been to see what rabbinic Judaism and the church that
confesses the great creeds did with these materials.

My book is also unique in that it considers several different genres of interpretive materials. Everyone is familiar with the **commentary**. These large tomes that began in antiquity and continue to our present day cite a line or section of scripture and then comment on its linguistic, historical, and theological significance. In the early church, these commentaries are associated with the great theological thinkers (also known as "church fathers") such as Origen (Alexandria, Egypt; d. 215; his highly influential commentary on Genesis has been lost) and Augustine (North Africa, d. 430; he composed two (!) commentaries on Genesis 2–3). Named Jewish commentators on Genesis don't emerge until the medieval period (e.g., ibn Ezra, Rashi, and Nachmanides), but we have a variety books that collected different rabbinic dicta on Genesis and assembled them in commentary form, the most important of them being the third-century Palestinian work *Genesis Rabbah*.

In addition, this book takes special interest in the apocryphal or **retold Bible**. In these works, the author retells the biblical story in his or her own voice and works into this retelling dozens of complex interpretive decisions. Perhaps the most famous example of this genre would be the last great example of it: John Milton's *Paradise Lost*. We shall consider this great work along with retold Bibles of far greater antiquity, such as the book of *Jubilees* (second century B.C.E.) and the *Life of Adam and Eve* (fourth century C.E.). It will be my task to pull apart these complex narratives and reveal their interpretive substrate.

I have also taken considerable interest in how early **Christian art** interprets the story of Genesis. I have been surprised at what a wonderful resource early iconography has been. More careful scholars would not dare venture into these materials for fear of being exposed as gross amateurs by specialists in the field. I have been foolish enough to run this risk. But I suppose I have done so because, in reviewing much of the art-historical literature, I have been surprised time and again at how rare theological learning is among the specialists. There are exceptions of course (e.g., Anna Kartsonis, Henry Maguire, Thomas Mathews, and Leo Steinberg), and it is on these individuals that I have leaned heavily.

Finally, I should mention one more genre of materials that has proved immensely useful and really deserving of far more coverage than I could give it: **liturgical writings**. By this I mean the actual texts of liturgical rites such as baptism as well as the prayers that accompany them (such as the seven blessings said over the bride and groom in a Jewish wedding). If Adam and Eve are anything in early Judaism and Christianity, they are *living* figures whose being is not restricted to some prehistoric geological era. All of the most learned philological commentary in both traditions generally takes its point of origin from some aspect of the respective lived religion. This point should not be forgotten as we pore over the many subtle and complex turns in this enormous literature.

In the end, what has struck me over the course of researching this book is how complex yet organically interrelated the world of early biblical interpretation is. Each piece is carefully woven into the fabric of the other. It is often impossible to understand a particular sentence within a commentary without knowing how the interpretation in turn would be treated in a retold apocryphal story. Similarly it is difficult to understand a particular iconographic feature without recourse to a specific liturgical rite. When one reads early Jewish and Christian texts about Adam and Eve one is peering into an entire culture, a way of living that must be respected for what it was (and is).

This work has grown in deep respect to traditional Jewish and Christian learning about the Biblical text. I have tried, at every step along the way, to put myself in the position of a student and to listen attentively to what the great commentators have to say. Few paragraphs of this work will reflect my own personal voice. To the extent that I use the personal pronoun, it is to expose my efforts to uncover what *they* thought. This book is, I hope, a presentation of the world they have created.

The Eve of the Epiphany of Our Lord
6 January 2001

Chronological Table

Before the Common Era (B.C.E.)
Beginning of the First Temple Period

THE BIBLICAL PERIOD PROPER

1000–500   Composition of Genesis 1–3
                Reign of King Manasseh
                Jeremiah
                Ezekiel
587   Destruction of Jerusalem by King Nebuchad-
                    nezzar of Babylon
                Second Isaiah

Beginning of the Second Temple Period

FINAL EDITING OF THE JEWISH BIBLE

516   Dedication of rebuilt Temple
167   Maccabean Revolt
                Book of Jubilees
                Daniel
                Dead Sea Scrolls

Common Era (C.E.)
4 B.C.E.–30   Jesus of Nazareth
66–70   Roman siege of Jerusalem, destruction of
                    Temple
                Composition of the New Testament

Close of Second Temple Period

RISE OF RABBINIC MOVEMENT AND THE CHURCH FATHERS

200   Codification of the Mishnah
                Irenaeus of Lyon (d. 200?)
                Clement of Alexandria (d. 215)
                Tertullian (d. 225?)
                Origen (d. 254)

300   Composition of *Genesis Rabbah*
                Gregory of Nyssa (d. 394)
                St. Ephrem (d. 373)
                St. Chrysostom (d. 407)
                Life of Adam and Eve (mid-fourth century?)

400   St. Augustine (d. 430)
                Mary declared "Mother of God" at the Council
                    of Ephesus (431)

500   Composition of the Babylonian Talmud

Introduction

Was Adam Jewish? Was Eve Mary?

The end is always like the beginning: and therefore, as there is one
end to all things, so ought we to understand there was one beginning.
—Origen, *On First Things*

Everything needs a purpose or a goal, even a good story. And
somewhat paradoxically to understand how a good story begins
we need to have some knowledge of how the whole comes to clo-
sure. Because the end configures the beginning, there is a sense
in which we can say the end comes first. This idea has some
rather dramatic consequences for how Jews and Christians have
interpreted Genesis. They do not so much read it as it stands as
re-read it in light of its proper end or goal.

Everyone knows what it is like to be in the presence of a master.
A good cook, a sensitive musician, a loving mother all conjure
within us a feeling of admiration. As they practice their respective
crafts we are almost magically drawn into their orbit—at first just to
observe but eventually to understand and, perhaps, to learn. This
book is just such an exercise. We will be peering over the shoulders of
some of the greatest and most influential biblical intepreters in
Judaism and Christianity. Over the course of these pages, we will
observe and learn how these great scholars practiced their craft. What
did Adam and Eve become, and who are they for us? These are the
questions I have asked as I have peeked over their shoulders.

The story of Adam and Eve has been told and retold in many different media. Textual scholars have puzzled over, at times, thorny
grammar; poets have given expression to the subtle inner voices that
resonate between the lines; and artists have rendered mere words visible. Over the course of this book I will consider each of these. Let me
begin with art.

An Innocent Eve

Michelangelo's depiction of the temptation and fall of Adam and Eve, on the ceiling of the Sistine Chapel, is as familiar as it is unusual (fig. 1). Adam is portrayed almost entirely in the shadows; his whole appearance takes on a somber, almost morbid hue. Is this a being created in the image of God? And even more peculiar, Adam seems to be aggressively grabbing the main branch of the tree with his left hand in order to get leverage to reach with his right. Mirroring him, the serpent to the side of Adam maintains a tight grip on the trunk of the tree so that he (or she?) can reach forward and extend a piece of fruit to Eve.

And Eve? She is the only relaxed figure in this particular panel. Bathed in light, she reclines like a noble Roman matron at dinner. Her posture is turned away from the tree as though indifferent to it. The

Figure 1
Temptation and Fall of Adam and Eve, by Michelangelo, Sistine Chapel, Vatican Palace. (Vatican Museum)

snake has to thrust himself forward to place the fruit in her passive hand. Eve can hardly be the source of humanity's fall.

But the book of Genesis implies that Eve was the culprit. It was she who first took the fruit and then shared some with Adam. Why, then, is Adam the overeager one here? And what gave Michelangelo the freedom to depart from the biblical story?

Eve's Rigid Finger

Yet another detail does not quite fit. Eve's whole posture exudes a feeling of repose: her legs are gently folded; her toes lightly stretch across the ground; even her arm and neck, which turn backward, do so without strain or care, save one detail: the middle finger of her right hand, located directly below Adam's male organ, is stiff and rigid. This clear phallic allusion points directly at her vulva. Surely, one must conclude, it foreshadows the moment of original sin. Adam and Eve will eat the fruit and awaken to the rising temperature of bodily lust.

John Milton, the great Puritan poet of seventeenth-century England, provides perhaps the most detailed and surely the most prurient description of what happens next—a tale missing from the canonical account but plainly obvious to him just the same. For in Milton's eyes (and he is just borrowing from St. Augustine, but that's a story for a subsequent chapter), Adam and Eve consummate their sin with carnal pleasure. Just after eating the fruit, Adam expects that his eyes will be opened to god-like knowledge. "But that false fruit," Milton observes,

> Far other operation first displayed,
> Carnal desire inflaming, he on Eve
> Began to cast lascivious eyes, she him
> As wantonly repaid; in lust they burn.
> (*Paradise Lost* 9:1011–15)

Milton then motions the reader to a shady bower where Adam has just escorted Eve. There they took "their fill of love and love's disport." And sadly for them, the amorous display quickened not their love, but sealed "their mutual guilt." Soon they found "their eyes how opened, [but] their minds how darkened."

Yet, as evocative as Milton's poetry may be, I cannot believe that this is all that went on in Michelangelo's mind. There is another way of reading that rigid finger that will take us in a very different direction, a direction that is lost on nearly everyone who has gazed on the ceiling of that chapel. To get some grasp on this larger frame of meaning we must step back from this panel and take a look at Michelangelo's larger design for the ceiling as a whole. Let's not miss the forest for the trees.

Was Eve Mary?

Eve's stiff middle finger marks a line that cuts across all three panels (panels 4, 5, and 6) dedicated to Adam and Eve. Beginning in panel 6 with the *Temptation*, it proceeds diagonally across the scene (fig. 2). One can follow this line to the bottom of the panel and into the top portion of the adjacent image, that of the *Creation of Eve* (panel 5). From there, the line traverses the midsection of Eve's body and continues into the next panel (4), the *Creation of Adam*.

In the (chronologically) first of the three panels (panel 4) dedicated to this couple, our oblique line comes to rest on a depiction of Eve (or is it Mary?), who looks longingly at Adam while at the same time being wrapped in the embrace of God the Father's left arm. Just to the right of Eve sits an infant who is also held by God the Father, though this time with just the thumb and index finger. The extension of his fingers corresponds exactly to the way a priest would grasp the eucharistic wafer. In other words, this child is *Mary's* boy, the Christ child. Strikingly, he is the only figure on the entire ceiling who looks directly down into the gaze of the viewer. And so our question as we ponder the women in these three panels: Are they Eve, the first woman and spouse of Adam, or Mary, the Mother of Jesus and symbol of the Church? Or perhaps more accurately, are these women in truth both Eve and Mary?

To get a better purchase on this, let's leave this larger frame and focus for a moment on the middle panel, the *Creation of Eve*. Indeed this image is also the *center point* of the entire ceiling: being the fifth image in a series of nine, it cuts the ceiling into two equal parts, four images preceding it and four following. The chapel below is also marked by a similar symmetrical division. The eastern half of the building was designated for lay and clerical observers. The western half, on the other hand, was raised one step higher and was reserved for the papal elite. It was, to use biblical language about the Temple, the *sanctum sanctorum* or the "holy of holies." The *Creation of Eve* is at the very center point of the chapel's liturgical structure.

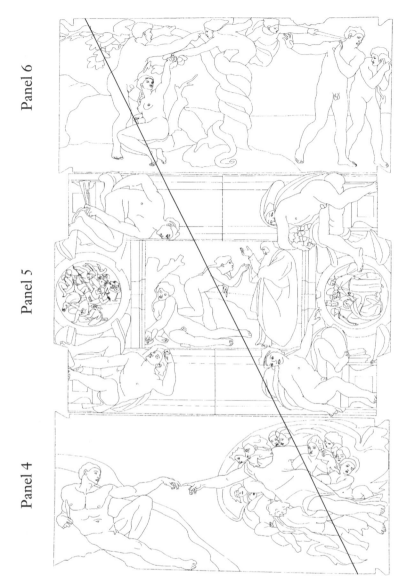

Figure 2

Panels 4, 5, and 6

Temptation, Creation of Eve, Creation of Adam, by Michelangelo, Sistine Ceiling. Line drawing from the Sistine Chapel. (*The Sistine Chapel,* Harry N. Abrams, Inc., 1995.)

These are the three middle panels of the nine that make up the Ceiling (1,2,3 = creation; 4,5,6 = Adam and Eve; 7,8,9 = Cain and Abel until Noah). The *Creation of Eve,* panel 5, sits at the *very center* of the whole composition. The line that bisects all three panels passes through Eve at temptation, at creation, and through Eve/Mary prior to creation.

In the image itself, Eve emerges from the side of Adam in a position of prayer and rises toward God the Father (fig. 3). Yet a couple of details are highly unusual.

Adam lies slumped around a *dead* tree, an odd sight for a luxuriant garden where death was, as of yet, unknown. The only way to understand this tired figure is to see him as a prefiguration of Christ, the "second Adam," who was destined to hang on a barren piece of wood. "The sleep of [Adam]," the fourth-century theologian St. Augustine observed, "clearly stood for the death of Christ" (*City of God* 22.17). The death of the "second Adam" has configured the way we understand the sleep of the first.

If this is how we are to read this image of Adam, perhaps a similar interpretation holds for Eve. To get our bearings on this we must bear in mind two facts. First, Mary as "second Eve" is she who gives birth to Christ. Second, Mary as the "symbol of the church" is she who emerges from the rib of Christ on the Cross. In this central panel of the Sistine ceiling, we see *both* the first and second Eve emerg-

Figure 3
Creation of Eve, by Michelangelo, Sistine Chapel. (Alinari/Art Resource, New York)

ing from the ribs of Adam. Not unlike those figure-ground illusions that psychologists are so fond of where an image changes its appearance on the basis of perceptual expectation, so here we can see either Adam and Eve or Christ and Mary depending on our vantage point.

Further support for this comes from the history of the chapel itself. It was built on the model of Solomon's Temple and was dedicated on August 15, 1483, the feast day of the Assumption and Coronation of the Virgin Mary in Heaven. A favored image of Mary in Christian devotional practice was Mary as the ark or tabernacle of God. Like the ark of the covenant in the Old Testament, the throne upon which God almighty took his seat, Mary was the seat in which God took human form. Like the Temple itself, she housed the *verum corpus* or "the true body" of God.

All of this makes our first understanding of Eve's fateful finger very uncertain. Is this phallic image a suggestion of the onset of original sin conceived of as unquenchable lust? Or does her finger point in the opposite direction altogether and indicate the organ of salvation, that is, the womb of Mary, that second Eve? Early Christian preachers were very fond of the notion that though humanity had fallen through the willful disobedience of Adam, it would be the shrewd obedience of Mary to the archangel Gabriel that would inaugurate the incarnation. "At the moment of Original Sin," the noted art historian Leo Steinberg observes, "as if by unconscious reflex or premonition, Eve designates her receptive womb." He continues, "The finger addresses that port of sin which, by grace of that other Eve, becomes the gate of redemption."

A Matter of Perspective

What do we see, then, when we gaze on this image? Are the private parts of these first humans the harbingers of our destruction or the necessary vehicles of our salvation? Is the story of Adam and Eve about human sin and degradation or human potential and perfection?

Everything depends on perspective. If we limit our gaze to the terms of Genesis 3, then that finger portends certain doom. Eve is the culprit and in her finger we see the outlines of reckless, wanton desire. Most appropriately, Adam and Eve were evicted from the Garden and condemned to a life of hard labor. End of story.

But if our perspective is broad enough to bring the first Eve under the wings of the second, then that rigid finger portends a very different sort of omen. For it is only through the womb of the second Eve that humankind will merit salvation. In that womb resides our sole hope, and Eve already indicates as much at the very point of transgression.

Jewish and Christian readers of the Bible had different notions about just what the end of the biblical story was. But they did not differ as to what the significance of that end was. For these readers of the Bible, the story of Adam and Eve is not an account of sin alone but a drama about becoming a being who fully reflects God's very own image. *Genesis is not only about the origins of sin; it is also about the foundations of human perfection.* The work that God has begun in creation, he will bring to completion.

And so our next question—why were early Jewish and Christian readers aware of this while most of their modern counterparts have not been?

A Sense for the Story

In order to understand with any depth how a story begins one must have some grasp of how it ends. Consider the film by Steven Spielberg *Saving Private Ryan.* It opens precisely where it ends, with Private Ryan kneeling before the grave of the man who died in battle in order to save him. As we watch this movie unfold, we can't make sense of the scene at first; the characters and the specific force of their actions remain unclear. It is the burden of the film's unfolding to lay bare the primal scene's significance.

A similar structure governs the Bible. We must have some sense of the whole in order to grasp how it opens. Countless readers have thought that if they simply pored over the first three chapters long enough they would be able to make sense of what is told therein. To read later details back into the beginning is thought of as a violation of the interpretive process. But such an assumption goes against a basic principle we all employ when we read any book. To understand the first chapter or two of any literary work requires one to size up the shape and scope of the whole.

And it is exactly this sort of preunderstanding that informs all theological interpretations of Adam and Eve. *Religious readers know where the story is heading before they have glossed even one word.* Reading early Jewish and Christian interpretations of the story of Adam and Eve is like eavesdropping on a circle of friends who have rewound *Saving*

Private Ryan and are watching its opening scene a second time. Their memories of the film's ending well up again and again to inform, and even overwhelm, the terse beginning.

Over the course of my book you will see how intertwined scripture's *brief* outline of the world's origin is with scripture's *far more detailed* account of why we are here and where we are headed. In every chapter we will see how the terse opening of the book of Genesis has grown over time under the careful supervision of countless Jewish and Christian readers. For Jewish and Christian readings of Genesis have not been so much a teasing out of a few new details as full-scale revisions of the whole. By the time we reach John Milton, these three small chapters have become twelve substantial books.

These chapters were pored over with such intensity because they were thought to reveal the answers to some of life's larger mysteries: What is the nature of sexual love? Whence does evil originate, and how can we protect ourselves from it? Are women or men more prone to temptation, and how should fault for the first sin be apportioned? For what end was human life created, and how can it be brought to perfection? These are the sort of questions that were put to our text.

A common modern prejudice has it that all of this additional material that has been added to the Bible over the centuries is something like useless clutter in an attic. Its sheer weight and volume has all but obliterated those precious family heirlooms that lie below. With the tools of biblical interpretation, it is held, we can remove the clutter and sweep away the cobwebs and by so doing recover the pristine form of the original.

I would prefer a different metaphor. The accumulation of interpretive glosses over the centuries is something like the slow filling out of a genealogical tree. At the beginning, we start with a simple human couple on their wedding day; in the end we have a substantial extended family. The meaning and significance of that founding relationship is not fully disclosed by the immediate circumstances that attended courtship. I would suggest that the bond woven among this initiating couple is more deeply revealed by what results from the children, the grandchildren, and all the nieces and nephews. Through the lives of these offspring we see reflected the full panoply of virtue and vice that lay hidden in that brief but tantalizing beginning.

The stories about Adam and Eve grow exponentially over time. Spurred on by the literary environment in which they have been set, these stories reach beyond the confines of their brief beginning. The first three chapters of Genesis open out into a far broader tale about the ways of God with his people. It is this larger story and its relationship to scripture's beginning on which we must keep our eye focused.

An Eye on the Goal

For those versed in the practice of literary criticism, what I have just said will come as no surprise. Aristotle, for example, came to the same set of conclusions some twenty-five hundred years ago in his *Poetics*. For him, each event in the unfolding of a plot appears to the reader as though at random. But once the climax of the tale has been reached and the purpose of the plot laid bare, each and every random incident along the way comes into focus as a necessary part of the story's unfolding. And there is no better place to see this principle illustrated than in Aristotle's favorite story, *Oedipus the King*. It would be impossible for the reader to know in advance that this tragic figure would blind himself, but once he has done so, the reader realizes that each and every turn in the plot has contributed in one way or another to this end.

Jean-Paul Sartre, the French philosopher and novelist, took this detail of the novel as emblematic of human life as a whole. For just as we read the various incidents within a narrative as hints of some final coherence, so in our own lives we try to situate what happens to us within a larger construal of what purpose our life serves. Walter Benjamin, the modern Jewish philosopher and literary critic, noted that we seek in a good novel the knowledge of death that eludes us in daily life. For who we are at death casts a long shadow of significance over who we have been along the way. To paraphrase Sartre, we become our obituary. Spiritual directors have long been aware of this insight and have counseled those under their charge to order their lives in view of how they wish to be remembered at death.

How the World Lost Its Story

The purpose and value of stories and storytelling is patent. They give us some purchase on the meaning of human life or, at the very least, of some key aspect of it. However, the twentieth century has not been kind to the idea of a story. Already in the nineteenth century, thinkers such as Friedrich Nietzsche had persuaded many that human life bears no inherent purpose and, considered on its own, makes no sense. All attempts to render human life in some overarching narrative were thought incapable of revealing some sort of fundamental and timeless truth; rather they were little more than veiled claims to power. The church may declare that scripture has this sense or that, but what it is really doing is compelling you to buckle under to its authority.

If, like Nietzsche, we presume life has no inherent meaning, it follows that any story that claims to make sense of life—however entertaining it might be—is patently false. A good plot line confers on human life a structure, a sense that life makes sense and can be rendered as such in story form. Much of twentieth-century literature and theatre has followed the lead of Nietzsche and sought different narrative conventions. Indeed, one of the hallmarks of a good amount of twentieth-century literature is its loss of any clear sense of plotted time. Compare the writings of James Joyce, Thomas Pynchon, or William Faulkner to those of Jane Austen or Charles Dickens and you will see what I mean.

The same dilemma also holds true in the field of biblical studies. It is hard to find scholars committed to the notion of scripture's narrative unity. Indeed quite the opposite view is more often the rule—that the Bible is a collection of fragmentary and self-contradictory pieces. So it follows that any reading of the Bible presuming a narrative integrity to the whole is a contested reading. It becomes an act of faith or even a Pascalian wager rather than a statement of objective fact. There are many who lament this fact and long for a return to yesteryear. I, on the other hand, do not believe that recent developments need be considered a total loss for religious readers. For me, the Bible's unity is not a self-evident proposition.

To a certain extent Nietzsche was correct; it was the culture of Christendom that propped up this notion of the Bible's unity as an objective fact. With the collapse of Christendom in the West, we can now see more clearly what was always the case: the affirmation of scripture's unity is a statement of faith not of science. To understand Jewish and Christian interpretation we have to respect the domain of the Creed as much as the territory of the dispassionate literary historian. My claim is not that faith should stand in place of historical method; rather, each type of inquiry should recognize its proper domain.

Christians confess the principle of scripture's integrity through the Creed. The Creed gives witness to the fact that it is one and the same divine author who stands behind creation ("I believe in God the Father Almighty, Creator of heaven and earth . . ."), incarnation (I believe in Jesus Christ the only son of God . . ."), and the foundation of the church ("I believe in the Holy Spirit . . . and the Holy Catholic Church"). It is important to note that this confession is not a roster of objective facts. It is a declaration of faith, that is, a profession that one intends to live on the presumption that it is true. By affirming God's stewardship of the entire created order through the words of this creed, the Christian also confesses an allegiance to a certain narrative pattern for all of creation. Because it is one and the same God who has created and redeemed the world, so we should live our lives according to the pattern of life he has laid down.

Though Jews are not as given to creeds as Christians are, they also claim the unity of scripture as an article of faith. This was well expressed by the most famous and influential of all Jewish philosophers in the medieval period, Moses Maimonides:

> We believe that the entire Torah presently in our possession is the one given to Moses our master (may he rest in peace), that it is all from the mouth of God, that is, that it was all given to him from the Lord (may he be blessed) in the manner that is metaphorically called "speaking.". . . And there is no difference between (insignificant) verses like "and the sons of Ham were Cush and Egypt" [Gen. 10:6]. [. . .] and [verses that sum up Israel's faith like] "Hear, O Israel" [Deut. 6:4]. For all of them come from the mouth of God.

For Maimonides, the implications of a monotheistic faith for the reading of the Bible is clear: just as there is one God who created and upholds the universe, so there is one divine voice behind Israel's scriptures who continues to guarantee their narrative integrity. It is a fundamental assertion of Judaism that the Bible is a unity, that each and every verse has equal value and integrity in the eyes of God—and because of this, each verse can be related, potentially, to all others.

What all this comes down to is a question of how one construes the Bible. And in this vein, I would like to emphasize how radical it is to conceive the entire scriptural witness as a single story. Many in the ancient world did not, and many still do not. Although this matter has become increasingly controversial in our day, it remains a primary element of nearly every ancient confession about the Bible's essential nature. Only by understanding this presupposition can we begin to fathom the ways classical Judaism and Christianity have read and reread the story of creation.

Was Adam Jewish?

I began this chapter with a turn toward Michelangelo and the Sistine Ceiling. In those magnificent frescoes the figure of Eve points toward Mary. To "read" this ceiling we need more than the text of Genesis. For Michelangelo, Eve was more than Eve. She was, to overstate the matter ever so slightly, Mary.

In Jewish tradition we do not find this same sort of tight symmetry because Adam and Eve do not point forward to two subsequent persons but to an entire nation. Adam is, in many rabbinic readings, Jewish.

According to the book of Genesis, Adam and Eve are ultimately responsible for giving birth to the entire world. So the first woman is aptly named "Eve," or the "mother of all living." Yet a detail not often noted, but extremely important, is the fact that Adam and Eve's progeny add up to seventy nations in total (Genesis 10). The number 70 is significant not merely because it symbolizes wholeness or completeness—early Jews and Christians believed that there were seventy guardian angels in heaven apportioned over the seventy nations—but because it points to the genealogy of Israel herself. When Jacob and his family descend into Egypt at the close of the book of Genesis, they do so as seventy persons (Genesis 46; Exodus 1). When Israel leaves Sinai, on her way to the Holy Land, she is made up of seventy families (Numbers 26). Israel is a microcosm of the whole world.

God had promised Abraham that he would not only grant his children the land of Canaan, but he added that the whole world would somehow in return derive blessing from this nation-to-be (Gen. 12:1–3). Through a careful calibration of numbers, our biblical writer fastens this theological detail deep into the heart of our text. What God does on behalf of the smaller seventy (Israel) will have enormous ramifications for the larger seventy (the world at large).

Because Israel's charter as a chosen people is established at Mt. Sinai where Israel is given God's Torah or commandments, Jewish interpreters have naturally seen the election of Israel at Mt. Sinai as the pinnacle of scripture. In regard to the tabernacle that Moses builds at the foot of Mt. Sinai, the learned medieval commentator Ibn Ezra said, "This is the beginning of the world and it is a mystery (*sod*)" (*Shorter Commentary to Exodus* 40.2). All creation remained unfinished until God descended upon that Mount and spoke to Moses face to face. Here Israel, according to some Jewish traditions, came as close as one can in this world to embodying God's very own image.

Sinai as a New Eden

The connection of Eden to Sinai is made explicit in *Genesis Rabbah*, a fourth-century Jewish work. Commenting on the verse "They heard God walking to and fro in the Garden at the cool of the day (Gen. 3:7)," Rabbi Abba ben Kahana said,

> "Walking" is not written here, but "walking *to and fro.*" This means that God repeatedly leapt skyward and ascended.
>
> The real home of the *Shekinah* (divine presence) was in the realm below, not the heavens above. When Adam sinned, it departed to the first level of the heavens. With Cain, it departed to the second; the generation of Enosh, to the third; the generation of the flood, to the fourth; the builders of the tower of Babel, to the fifth; with those of Sodom, to the sixth; and with the Egyptians in the days of Abraham, to the furthest remove possible, the seventh heaven.
>
> But over against these sinful generations, seven righteous persons arose: Abraham, Isaac, Jacob, Levi, Kohath, Amram, and Moses. They brought the *Shekinah* from the seventh heaven back to the realm of earth. (*Genesis Rabbah* 19:7)

The symbol of God's very presence, the *Shekinah*, undergoes a remarkable transformation. Fully present in the Garden, it is forced into exile by the sin of Adam and Eve. With each successive generation this exile becomes more and more severe as God moves from the first heaven to the seventh. Only with the appearance of Abraham do things change. Through Abraham and the chosen line he was to establish, the *Shekinah* gradually makes its way back to earth. With Moses, at the top of Mt. Sinai, the story line comes to closure. The divine presence again resides on earth. In one tradition, the power of the angel of death was removed from Israel. The effects of the fall were undone. Paradise had been regained.

Was Israel Driven from Eden?

Paradise was regained at Sinai, at least for a time. The biblical writer, however, was not so comfortable with prolonging Israel's moment of bliss. If paradise was in view, it was quickly removed. Israel built the golden calf, and God's wrath burned so hot that he nearly destroyed the entire nation, save Moses. The veneration of the calf, according to rabbinic thinking, brought Israel back to earth. Israel was no longer beyond the reach of the angel of death. She would, to quote a rabbinic reading of Psalm 82, "die just as Adam did."

The calf, in turn, became something of a cipher for the later tragic note on which Israel's history came to a momentary end. For just as the tribes of Israel violated their charter at Sinai by the construction of the calf, so the kingdom of Israel came to an abrupt end through the various apostasies she committed in the Promised Land. In the early sixth century B.C.E, armies from Babylon invaded, destroyed Jerusalem and her Temple, and carried the kings and the city's elite off into exile—an exile that Jews to this day still implore God to bring to an end.

It is against this national story that the lives of Adam and Eve are retold. The Bible's goal is the reception of the Torah and its full implementation in the Holy Land. In the Garden of Eden, this entire dramatic sequence is foreshadowed. One Jewish tradition, told by Rabbi Abbahu in the name of Rabbi Jose the son of Hanina, compared Adam's life to that of Israel. God declares that

> just as I led Adam into the Garden of Eden and gave him a commandment and he transgressed it, whereupon I punished him with dismissal and expulsion and bewailed him by crying *ekah*— how could this be!—so for the nation Israel. . . . And just as I brought Adam and Eve into Eden so I brought my people into the land of Israel and gave them commandments. [Like Adam and Eve] they too transgressed my commandments and I punished them with dismissal and expulsion and bewailed them crying *ekah* [Lam. 1:1], which means "how could this be." (*Genesis Rabbah* 19:9)

This highly imaginative and creative piece of interpretation, known as midrash, has tied the Hebrew word *ayekkah* from Genesis 3:9 to *ekah* in Lamentations 1:1. Although the words sound very similar, they have very different meanings. Genesis 3:9 is better translated "where are you" whereas Lamentation 1:1 simply means "how [on earth could this be!?]."

What is striking here is the instinct of our commentator to override the plain meaning of Genesis with the derived meaning he has drawn from the book of Lamentations. In the latter, God is weeping over his city Jerusalem after it had been ravaged by the Babylonians. The end of Israel's story now casts light back on her nascent beginnings. Adam becomes a forerunner of the Jewish people as a whole. In his experience in the Garden we see the history of God's relation to Israel worked out in miniature.

Rewriting Genesis

Over the course of this book, we shall follow in the footsteps of some of the greatest early Jewish and Christian readers of Genesis. As we watch them at work, three basic principles of interpretation will emerge. First is a sense of how the biblical story ends. Second is the relation of that story to the *lived* religious life. And third is an exceptionally keen eye for stumbling blocks in the text itself.

As an example, let us consider our first example, that of Mary as second Eve. There can be no question that reading Mary into Genesis 1–3 presumes a grasp of the entire scriptural story. Mary, according to the logic of early Christian exegesis, is the "end" toward which Eve points. As Eve's disobedience introduced death into the world, so Mary's obedience led to life.

It is also a well-known fact among scholars of early Christianity that the language of prayer is at the root of most creedal affirmations. This principle is summarized in the terse phrase *lex orandi, lex credendi*, which I could paraphrase "how we pray shapes how we believe." Because the story of the annunication—that is, the appearance of the archangel Gabriel to the Virgin Mary to announce the birth of the Messiah—became a paradigm of every Christian's devotion and obedience to God, it quickly became a form of theological shorthand for the entire biblical story. If our obedience is patterned on that of Mary, then our waywardness must be rooted in the figure of Eve. And so the development of Eve's person in the book of Genesis cannot be separated from the corresponding development in the cult of Mary.

Mary's role in shaping our portrait of Eve is not simply presumed by early Christian readers; it was *discovered* in the text of Genesis. Armed with their notion of a Marian typology that spanned both testaments, early Christian readers pored over the text of Genesis in search of some hint or clue of Mary's person. Their efforts were not in vain. They noticed the very unusual words spoken to the serpent just before the expulsion:

> "I will put enmity between you and the woman,
> and between your offspring and hers;
> he will strike your head,
> and you will strike his heel."
>
> (Gen. 3:15)

Difficulties abound in these few lines. What is meant by the enmity between the woman and the serpent? Does this refer to the common human abhorrence of snakes, or does it refer to the animosity between that evil power that animated the snake in the first place (a.k.a. "Satan") and the human beings who succumbed to it? The Hebrew word for offspring is literally "seed." Does the biblical writer have one particular person in mind who will rise up and strike the serpent's head, or is this a general statement about the power of all persons over the serpent?

Many early Christian readers answered these questions by reading these lines as a prophecy of Christ's victory over Satan at his resurrection. For he, as "the offspring" of the new Eve, would rise up and vanquish ("strike the head") of that ancient foe of humankind. During Holy Week, Jesus would descend into Hades, break down the doors of Satan's kingdom, and retrieve the figures of Adam and Eve. This verse, as a testimony to how last things inscribe first things, took on the name *protoevangelium* or "foreshadower of the gospel."

So popular did this interpretation become that many medieval Latin manuscripts of the Bible came to be read,

> I will put enmity between you and the woman,
> and between your offspring and hers;
> *she [ipsa]* will strike your head
> and you will strike *her* heel.
>
> (Gen. 3:15, italics added)

As we shall see ever so frequently in the course of this book, *the biblical text has been rewritten in conformity with an evolving interpretive tradition.* For premodern readers of the Bible, whether Jewish or Christian, it took great effort to distinguish between what was in the

Bible and what had grown up around it. The Bible was, in their eyes, a collage of original text and authoritative interpretation.

The Biblical Story

In each chapter of this book I will explore how early Jewish and Christian readers approached each crucial turn in the story and what conclusions they drew. My sources for this interpretive pilgrimage back in time will be drawn from the first several centuries of the Common Era. For it is during these centuries that the basic building blocks of the Jewish and Christian tradition are laid down and all subsequent interpreters will have to go through them. From time to time I will draw in later writers such as Milton and Dante to illustrate their ties to this classic period.

In addition, I should say something about the nature of my sources because they are rather untraditional. In addition to using classical line-by-line commentaries on Genesis, I will also employ both rewritten accounts of the Garden that weave interpretive traditions into the terse biblical original (*Paradise Lost* would be an example of this) and iconographic, that is, visual, representations of the same. Artists almost never portrayed the story "according to the letter"; mixed into every fresco or icon were the deep hues of earlier readings.

I have divided the biblical account into five different scenes. Each one poses a sort of textual puzzle that our early interpreters will try to solve. It will be important to bear in mind that the biblical narrative leaves us in the dark about a number of crucial pieces of information. It will be our interpreters' task to scan the rest of the Bible and their own religious lives and traditions in search of the answers.

The first scene is that of creation itself. According to the first chapter of Genesis this was an act that involved not only God but other members of the divine assembly. In Genesis 1:26 we read the famous lines "Let *us* create man in our image." Just who is being invoked by the plural subject "we"? we might ask. If it is the angelic host, one might wonder whether the archnemesis of Adam and Eve, Satan, was among this fold. And if this was so, was this story about the very creation of humankind instrumental in his fall from grace?

In our second scene, the biblical writer backtracks for a moment and retells the story of Adam's creation. Here the interest is not so much a divine image as the creation of a single person (*Adam*) from the dust of the earth (*adamah*) (Gen. 2:7). Only after this earthling,

Adam, has been animated by the divine breath and is introduced into Eden does God notice that something is not quite right. Adam is without a mate (2:18). Immediately God moves to rectify the situation; Eve is created and shown to Adam (2:21–23).

After Eve has been brought to Adam, we confront one of the oddest features of the entire story. The narrator pulls us aside to inform us that the joining of Eve to Adam will be a model for every subsequent human marriage: "Therefore a man leaves his father and his mother and clings to his wife, and they become one flesh" (2:24). Adam and Eve were married in Eden, we might conclude. But not so fast. The very next line draws us up short: "But the man and his wife were both naked and were not ashamed" (2:25). If this remark about lack of shame is an indication of their prepubescent state, then marriage would seem to be out of the question. What then is the relationship of Adam to Eve in the Garden? Are they just good friends, or man and wife?

Things don't get any clearer when we turn to our third scene, that of the temptation. No sooner is Eve joined to Adam than the snake draws near and questions her about the nature of God's command. His first words are a bald-faced lie: "Did God say, 'You shall not eat from any tree in the garden'?" (Gen. 3:1). The woman then responds with what appears to be a simple repetition of what God had told Adam earlier,

> "We may eat of the fruit of the trees in the garden; but God said,
> 'You shall not eat of the fruit of the tree that is in the middle of
> the garden, nor shall you touch it, or you shall die.'" (Gen. 3:2–3)

Yet appearances can deceive. Eve's version of the command is slightly different from that of Adam's. Earlier we read that God warned Adam not to eat of the tree (Gen. 2:16–17); but Eve believes the command had two parts: don't eat and don't touch. Which version is true? If Eve is correct, one puzzles over why Adam's version does not correspond. If Adam is correct, one must puzzle over why Eve has misstated the original. Did Adam misinform her, or did she willfully alter the wording? The answers to these questions are absolutely necessary in order to determine who is to blame for the fall.

Bible readers of all ages have puzzled over the climax of this tale. In our fourth scene God appears in the Garden "at the cool of the day" (3:8), questions Adam and Eve about their motives (3:9–13), and then turns to pronounce judgment on all three guilty partners. The snake loses his legs and is forced to eat dust; the woman is to suffer in child-birth; and the man is to toil on the earth (Gen. 3:14–19).

But something is amiss. Earlier in the story, God sternly warned Adam that *he would die* on the very day he ate of the forbidden fruit (2:16–17). Yet no such thing happens; the lives of Adam and Eve span nearly a millennium. Did God overstate his case at the beginning of the tale?

And finally, there is the expulsion of Adam and Eve from the Gar-den. According to the rhythm of Genesis, this would appear to be a punishment from which there was no turning back. After they leave Eden, neither Adam and Eve nor their progeny make any effort to return. God had placed fearsome cherubim at the entrance to the Gar-den (3:24) and evidently this was so effective that Eden is never heard from again. Yet the possibility of a return to Eden animated nearly every Jewish and Christian reader of this story. God's designs for human life could not be frustrated for an eternity. Somehow, these interpreters reasoned, the gates of Eden would be reopened and the descendants of this first couple would be allowed a return.

The story of Adam and Eve is very, very short. The story of Joseph and his brothers is easily ten times as long if not longer. Yet the very brevity of the tale, along with the knotty questions it leaves unan-swered, cries out for some sort of interpretive expansion. Jewish and Christian readers set about to fill in these gaps by correlating them to other parts of the biblical story.* Like readers returning to the open-ing pages of a novel, they reread—and eventually rewrote—the story of human beginnings in light of where they believed them to point.

---

*Because the Jewish and Christian Bibles differ both in the order and number of books they contain I will employ both Jewish and Christian terms to identify the collection in question. When speaking of Christian readings of the Bible I will employ the terms "Old" and "New Testament"; when speaking of Jewish readings I will simply use the term "Bible" or occasionally "Jewish Bible."

Chapter 1

The Fall of Satan and the Elevation of Adam

*But we are your people [Israel], the members of your covenant; . . .
the community of Jacob **your first-born son,** whom you named
Israel and Jeshurun because of your love for him and the delight you
took in him.*

—Jewish Daily Liturgy

*I [Satan] said, 'Go away, Michael! I shall not bow down to him who
was born after me, for **I am former.** Why is it proper for me to bow
down to him?*

—*Life of Adam and Eve*

*You might think the celestial hierarchy has always started with God
at the top, the angels just a little below, and us humans well below
that. But in some versions of the classic creation story, a dramatic
reversal takes place: we humans, by way of a divine degree, usurp
the privileged rank of the angels. For some angels the humiliation
is too much to bear—and there begins a little-known and less
understood interpretation of the meaning of the creation story. The
story of the rebel angels brings our ultimate human destiny into
focus: we humans will be glorified by and reunited with the God
who makes us out of love.*

You Made Him Little
Less than the Angels

God created man," our biblical writer observes, "in his image. In
the image of God he created them; male and female he created
them" (Gen. 1:27). Without any fanfare or further details, the Bible
introduces us to what will become one of its most important ideas in
the history of the West.

But what is meant by the phrase "image of God?" At the very least, the term conveys a special closeness between God and the human person. This same point is made clear by God's personal involvement in the making of humans. Whereas in the creation of all other things in Genesis 1, God acted in a more distant manner ("Let there be light . . . and there was light"), with the creation of human beings, God took a personal interest ("let *us* make man . . .").

Another hint can be teased from the brief notice made about the serpent. At the beginning of chapter 3 we are abruptly introduced to a snake who is said to be "more crafty than all the other animals" (3:1). It seems he is also envious of Adam and Eve, for as soon as our snake appears on the scene, he approaches Eve and proceeds to tempt her to do what God had strictly forbidden. Eve informs the snake that, for fear of death, fruit from the tree of knowledge was not to be eaten—whereupon the snake, from some mysterious font of knowledge, declares just the opposite. "You won't die," he promises confidently, "God knows that should you eat the fruit your eyes will become opened and you will be like God himself, knowing both good and evil" (3:4).

For many early Bible readers, the implications of all this was clear. The serpent did not simply tempt for the thrill of it; *something was at stake.* Someone must have envied the stature of Adam and Eve as the image of God. It was not logical to assume that a mere snake could have been the primary culprit. Most likely, the fallen angel Satan had put him up to it.

But this only shifts the question one step backward: Why did one of the angelic host envy Adam and Eve? One might suppose that their god-like attributes posed a threat to the position of the angels in heaven. Though the book of Genesis is mute on these questions, other narratives in the Bible can be pressed into service to help answer them.

Strikingly, Jewish and Christian readers followed similar paths toward their respective solutions. For both of these traditions, the mystery of God's salvific intentions are cloaked in the fabric of election. In the Jewish Bible, the focus centers on God's choosing or "electing" Israel as his very own people. In the New Testament, the focus shifts to the election of Jesus as God's Messiah. Chosenness is a theological concept around which a good percentage of the Bible turns. Time and again biblical writers try to define what it means to be chosen and how one can be faithful to such a vocation.

Because election is so deeply rooted in how Judaism and Christianity describe the "end" for which humans were created, it became a routine starting point for stories about Satan's rebellion. Without the elevation of Israel at Sinai or Jesus through the incarnation, there would have been no rebellion on the part of the angels in Judaism or Christianity.

But now I am getting ahead of myself. Before turning to early Jewish or Christian texts I would like to begin with a much later writer, John Milton. This choice is made with good reason. As many scholars have long noted, the account of Satan's fall in his *Paradise Lost* is not strictly Milton's own invention; he is dependent on early Christian writings for his own startling drama. Through his stirring narrative we will work our way back to the origins of the tradition itself.

God Made Thee Perfect, not Immutable

Satan's fall and the battle that ensues during which he is driven from heaven occupies the central section of *Paradise Lost*. The entire tale is introduced to the reader through a question Adam poses to archangel Raphael. Adam and Eve have just hosted this angelic guest at their bower in Eden, and, after a magnificent repast, Adam asks about the nature of such feasts in heaven. After Raphael answers, he adds that Adam too could become a denizen of the heavenly realm "if ye be found obedient." Adam takes offense at this suggestion of disobedience on his part. "But say," Adam interjects,

> "What meant that caution joined, *If ye be found*
> *obedient?* Can we want obedience then
> To him, or possibly his love desert
> Who formed us from the dust, and placed us here
> Full to the utmost measure of what bliss
> Human desires can seek or apprehend?"
>
> (*PL* 5:512–518)

Raphael uses this opportunity to recount the fall of Satan. And, quite important, this story is not told merely to entertain but to warn and instruct. "God made thee perfect," Raphael declares, but then adds, "not immutable"; perseverance has been left "in thy power."

Service to God is freely chosen, and so it can also be freely rejected. The account of Satan's fall is retold to warn Adam about his tempter but also to warn Adam about his own mutability. "Freely we serve, /

Because we freely love," Raphael declares, "as in our will / To love or not; in this we stand or fall" (5:538–40). And so Raphael proceeds to tell the story of Satan's fall.

Satan's Envy

It happened that one day in the midst of heaven, God the Father assembled the entire angelic host and said,

> Hear all ye angels, progeny of light,
> Thrones, dominations, princedoms, virtues, powers,
> Hear my decree, which unrevoked shall stand.
> This day I have begot whom I declare
> My only Son, and on this holy hill
> Him have anointed, whom ye now behold
> At my right hand; your head I him appoint;
> And by my self have sworn to him shall bow
> All knees in heaven, and shall confess him Lord.
> <div align="right">(<i>PL</i> 5:600–608)</div>

At the dawn of creation, God elevated his son before the entire angelic host. Because he is the perfect image of God, all are commanded to prostrate before him.

For most of the angelic host, this moment of exaltation became the cause for a majestic celebration. They feasted on delicacies that only heaven knew and spent that day reveling in song and dance. The festivities lingered into the wee hours of the night before the host of heaven saw fit to retire to their "celestial tabernacles" and sleep while fanned with "cool winds."

All slept save Satan. Brooding over the day's events, he found himself without repose. This angel, the "first archangel, great in power, / In favor and pre-eminence," was fraught "with envy against the Son of God." He roused his companion, Beelzebub, from his sleep and gave voice to his complaint. For Satan, the exaltation of the son was "a new law" and hence unfitting for the unchanging reign of God in heaven. A decree "so late [in time]" could portend nothing but woe to the archangels of the heavens.

But Satan is as resourceful as he is deceitful. Realizing that the joys of the past day do not provide a fit environment in which to advance his own case for rebellion, he concocts a ruse. He and Beelzebub will gather their bands of underlings and fly to the north with the stated intention of preparing "fit entertainment to receive our king."

The angels gather around Satan, and there, in the far northern reaches of heaven, he unveils his plot. We are Christ's equals, he contends, beings who "are ordained to govern, not to serve." Prostration before the divine Son is unthinkable. This discourse holds most of the angels in rapt attention.

Yet one angel, Abdiel, bristles at these seditious words. The act of genuflection, he contends, is not some craven act—"knee-tribute" in the idiom of Satan. Quite the contrary, *to realize the form of God in one's own person requires self-abasement.* Humiliation precedes exaltation.

Satan remains unmoved by this argument. For Satan, the elevation of the Son is a pure "power-grab" on the part of a johnny-come-lately among the angelic fold. The universe of honor is a closed system, a zero-sum economy. To laud and honor Christ will exact a high price— Satan's own dramatic diminishment. For Abdiel, the reverse is true. To render honor to the Son will redound to the greater glory of both parties—"all honour to him done returns our own." In heaven a superabundance of grace abounds; what you pay out to another is rendered back a hundredfold.

Before Adam was Born, I was

Milton's tale is both captivating and profound. With a palette of exquisite poetic colors, he has painted a theological picture of servanthood and exaltation worthy of careful study. Yet the reader must wonder where such a story could come from. The book of Genesis offers no hint of such a tradition. Most likely, Milton borrowed the description from an apocryphal tale; the *Life of Adam and Eve.*

This postbiblical narrative is quite ancient; some have claimed for it a Jewish origin and have dated it to the New Testament period. However this may be, the story was subsequently copied only by Christians, and it is this framework I will assume. The tale was very popular in the late antique world and was known in Greek and Latin versions as well as in such far-flung realms as classical Armenia and Georgia. The prophet Muhammad learned the story from his Jewish and Christian neighbors and cited it seven times in the Koran. So Milton was working with a tradition that had an impressive literary and theological pedigree.

In this tale, the story of Satan's fall is told retrospectively to Adam by Satan himself. The retelling occurs after Adam has learned of Satan's second successful temptation of Eve. Exasperated by this turn of events, Adam turns to Satan and angrily demands to know why he harbors such hostility toward him. Satan responds,

> "I came to this measure because of you, on the day on which you were created, for I went forth on that day. When God breathed his spirit into you, you received the likeness of his image. Thereupon, Michael came and made you bow down before God. God said to Michael, 'Behold I have made Adam in the likeness of my image.'
>
> Then Michael summoned all the angels, and God said to them, 'Come bow down to god whom I made.' Michael bowed first. He called me and said, 'You too, bow down to Adam.' I said, 'Go away, Michael! I shall not bow [down] to him who was born after me, for I am former. Why is it proper [for me] to bow down to him? The other angels, too, who were with me, heard this, and my words seemed pleasing to them and they did not prostrate themselves to you, Adam." (*Life of Adam and Eve* 13:1–14:3)

The story assumes that the angels are assembled just after Adam received the breath of life from God (Gen. 2:7). Adam is made to worship the Lord first; then Michael is told that Adam has been created "in the likeness of my image" (Gen. 1:26).

Next comes the surprise. As soon as Adam's identity as "the image of God" is revealed to the angels, they are commanded to bow before him.

The authority of Adam over the angels mimics that of God himself. This similarity is astonishing to some of the heavenly host. "I will not bow down to him who was born after me," Satan angrily protests. The Latin version of the tale adds, "I am prior to that creature. . . . He ought to worship me."

Because Satan persists in such insubordination, he is evicted from heaven and forced to wander the earth below. From this vantage point Satan constructs his stratagem to enter the serpent and deprive Adam and Eve of their glory. To be made in the image of God is to *be enthroned over the angels.* Such an indignity is unbearable for Satan.

The parallels of this story to Book 5 of *Paradise Lost* are patent. In both tales, God assembles the angels and demands that they bow their knees in homage to the image of God. In the *Life of Adam and Eve,*

Satan refuses on the grounds that he was created prior to that image; in *Paradise Lost* Satan claims to have known no beginning. He declares himself self-begotten. Both tales describe a fellow angel attempting, without success, to dissuade Satan from his rebellion. In the end, Satan must be cast from the heavenly realm.

Both Milton and the *Life of Adam and Eve* are interested in defining what it means to be created in "the image of God." Both come to a similar conclusion: *it means to be exalted over the angels.* And so we have answered at least one problem from the third chapter of Genesis. Satan incites the serpent to tempt Adam and Eve because he resents the authority they hold over him. And that anger had a rational ground, at least in the eyes of Satan: "I will not worship him who was born after me, for I am former. Why is it proper for me to bow down to him?"

The Elder Shall Serve the Younger

Satan's words of rebellion are hardly his alone. What we hear from his mouth is nothing other than the indignation of those who have been passed over by God elsewhere in the book of Genesis. When Rebecca, the wife of Isaac, becomes pregnant by the decree of the Lord, she is told by her God,

> "Two nations are in your womb,
> and two peoples born of you
> shall be divided;
> the one shall be stronger than the other,
> the elder shall serve the younger."
> (Gen. 25:23)

The key phrase here is "the elder shall serve the younger." God has chosen to redeem the world in a very peculiar way. The most unlikely son, Jacob, becomes the most favored. And the son who is passed over, Esau, reacts with rage.

The biblical writer is fond of this idea because it inscribes the very story of the people of Israel. Though arriving late in the historical process itself, long after the rise of the great civilizations of Egypt, Sumer, and Babylon, she was destined to be God's most favored nation. She would become the nation through whom all other nations were to derive blessing (Gen. 12:1–3).

Israel was, in the eyes of the Bible, the first-born child of God (Exod. 4:22). And just as this fact enraged Pharaoh to the point of wishing to do away with the entire nation, so also the estranged brothers in Genesis found this sort of favoritism unsettling: Jacob, the son who should have been favored, strived to eliminate Esau, the beloved sibling. Jacob had to flee from his brother Esau, and he spent many years in exile prior to reconciling himself to his estranged brother.

In Genesis, the question of who can lay claim to the rights of the "preferred son" is not based on birth order. The mysterious selection process of God always involves a reversal of human expectations. What comes last in historical time is really first in God's own reckoning.

Numerous biblical stories bear this out. Cain, though born first, found his sacrifice passed over in favor of that of his younger brother Abel. Rachel, the second daughter of Laban, became the preferred daughter in the eyes of Jacob. Joseph, the son of his father's old age, is more beloved than all his brothers put together.

Although the electing of a younger sibling over the elder is a commonplace in Genesis, the comprehension of its significance is not. Biblical characters remain surprised by this predilection of God to the very end. Consider, for example, the story of the blessing of Joseph's sons at the end of the book of Genesis. Through these two sons, Manasseh and Ephraim, Joseph is to receive the double share of the inheritance that rightfully should have belonged to the first born (Genesis 48). Joseph presents the sons before his father, Jacob, in the customary manner: The firstborn, Manasseh, is presented at Jacob's left so that Jacob can place his right hand on his head and offer him the fullest form of blessing.

Jacob, however, will have none of this. In obvious favoritism toward the latter-born son, Ephraim, he reverses his hands and places the right hand on Ephraim and his left on Manasseh. When Joseph saw this, he was astonished. He quickly tried to remedy the situation by moving his father's hands to the appropriate son, but Jacob refused. "I know, my son, I know," Jacob responded, "even Manasseh will become a nation; even he will become great, but his younger brother will become greater than he" (Gen. 48:19).

First Born of All Creation

It is worth pausing over this tale and letting its significance sink in. Not only is the second son chosen over the first, but Joseph, who has witnessed this very form of reversal in his own life, remains just as surprised at the end of the story as he was at its beginning. For us, the mystery of God's electing hand remains as difficult to understand at the end of Genesis as it was at the beginning.

In the *Life of Adam and Eve*, the story of reversed primogeniture is pushed one step back in time, from the era of the patriarchs to the creation of Adam himself. *God's electing activity is woven into the very fabric of creation itself.* And just as the election of Israel remains a troubling theme even in the twentieth century—consider the rage it aroused among the atheistic Nazi regime—so it enraged a certain sector of the angelic host at creation.

As the Jewish theologian Michael Wyschogrod has observed, God has made a special pact with humanity through his elected nation. "There are those who hate God [and so] they hate the God of Israel. They would like to kill the God of Israel. [But] this is difficult to do . . . the closest you can come to it is to kill Jews." And so for Satan. His rage toward what God has done through Adam leads to his rebellion in heaven. Having failed at the venture, he takes up a more realizable task: that of subverting the people God so dearly loves.

It is helpful to remember that these tales of election not only provide a rational grounding for Satan's rebellion but also reveal just what the phrase "image of God" means. When Christ, in *Paradise Lost*, bemoans the punishment Satan will bring upon the human race through temptation, he refers affectionately to man as "Thy creature *late* so loved, thy *youngest* son" (*PL* 3:150, italics added). The chosen son in Genesis, like the incarnate Son in the Gospels, is not really a son to be envied. His life is not an easy one.

To Be Chosen for Death

Each of the chosen sons in Genesis suffers. Isaac nearly dies on the altar at Mt. Moriah; Jacob flees the land of Canaan to live the life of an exile in Aramea; and Joseph is sold into slavery and forced "to descend into Egypt." As the modern Jewish biblical scholar Jon Levenson notes, the beloved son *must* undergo a near-death experience. *To be elected by God is to be elected to die.* This point was not lost on Jesus ("he who wishes to follow me, let him deny himself and take up his cross"), though the disciples found it beyond comprehension.

But the death of the elected son was never final, never a termination of life; obedience of this kind always leads to rebirth. Consider the words of God the Father in *Paradise Lost* when he hears his Son's desire to die in man's stead:

> because in thee
> Love hath abounded more than glory abounds,
> Therefore thy humiliation shall exalt
> With thee thy manhood also to this throne,
> Here shalt thou sit incarnate, here shalt reign
> Both God and man, Son both of God and man,
> Anointed universal king, all power
> I give thee, reign for ever, and assume
> Thy merits
>
> (*PL* 3:311–319)

The contemporary Catholic thinker Hans Urs von Balthasar comes closest to capturing the mystery of this pattern of election when he says, "in the Incarnation the triune God has not simply helped the world, but has disclosed himself in what is most deeply his own." By this he means God's *character* comes into clearest focus in the Son's decision to offer himself as a sacrifice on behalf of those he so deeply loves. Abdiel knew this aspect of God's ways with the world very well. Bending the knee portends exaltation not humiliation. The Satan of *Paradise Lost* and the *Life of Adam and Eve* does not understand this.

Angelic Reservations about the Creation of Man in Judaism

So far we have traced the story of Satan's fall back from *Paradise Lost* to the *Life of Adam and Eve* and ultimately to the patriarchs in Genesis. The theological trajectory that unites all these pieces is that of election. As God elected younger sons in Genesis to fulfill his purposes in creation, so he elected Adam at the beginning of creation to serve a similar function.

And just as elder sons were passed over in this process and were understandably enraged, so it was for the once-worthy figure of Satan. He too was passed over at the dawn of creation in an act of calculated favoritism shown toward human creation. "Let us make man in our image," God proposed to his divine assembly; "Not on your life," muttered this soon-to-be rebellious angel under his breath. "Before

Adam was made," Satan declared, "I had already been made. He ought to worship me."

The Rabbis also tell a story about the angels' disagreement with God's suggestion to create man; this story is frequently cited as a close parallel to the account of Satan's fall in the *Life of Adam and Eve*. And, as we will see, the continuities extend far beyond the external form of the story.

Until I Am Gray
I Will Bear with Them

This rabbinic tale has a certain light-hearted façade. But beneath the surface lies a profound reflection on the nature of the human person and God's commitment to him. When God proposes to create man, he does not announce his intention to create man in the form of a royal decree—"*Let us [now] make man in our image*"—but rather frames his intentions in the form of a question, "*Should we make man in our image?*" The angels are suspicious and, rather than give a hasty reply, decide to inquire further, "Lord of the Universe, what is the nature of his deeds?" God then answers the angels that man's deeds will be both good and bad (Babylonian Talmud, *Sanhedrin* 38b).

This response is particularly troubling to the angels, who are portrayed here as the phalanx within the divine kingdom appointed to maintain the principle of justice (*middat ha-din*). These angels feel the need to remind God that the universe could not bear the creation of such troublemakers. They immediately protest: "Lord of the universe, '*what is man that you mention him, the son of man that you take thought of him?*'" To this seemingly innocent inquiry God responds abruptly with punishment: the initial group of questioning angels are vaporized. This happens to a second group of angels as well. The third group of angels wises up and sees that God will not be persuaded on the matter. They assent to the plan.

But their agreement proves only temporary. During the eras of the flood and the tower of Babel, the human proclivity toward evil again raises its ugly head and the angels take this opportunity to raise anew their question about the advisability of creating humankind. God replies in a terse and somewhat mysterious way, "*Until old age I am he, even until I am gray I will bear with them.*" The point of this reply is to underscore the deep and abiding love God feels for the persons he has created. The principle of mercy, a trait that defines the Godhead, shall hold sway over that of justice. The angels appear as unidimensional beings; they understand justice but are ignorant of mercy.

Some readers of this story have been bothered by God's response to the angels' complaint. The angels are concerned with the *moral* nature of humankind, and when God tells them human beings will commit evil as well as good, the angels argue, with good reason, that the creation of such wayward individuals will be an affront to divine justice. The silencing of these angels seems both unexpected and a bit harsh.

Some have suggested the tale would read better if we assumed that the original focus of the story was on the exaltation of Adam rather than the mere fact of his creation. Of course, the story we just read in the *Life of Adam and Eve* comes immediately to mind. Perhaps the Rabbis knew this tale and took an active role in undermining its primary point.

One can see evidence of this subversive energy in the numerous rabbinic stories that polemicize against any venerating of Adam. In one tale, the angels mistake Adam for God and almost shout "Holy" before him (*Genesis Rabbah* 8:10). God averts this error by casting a deep sleep on Adam so that his mortal nature would be evident. Rabbi Hoshaya compares this story to a parable in which a king and his governor go forth in a chariot together. The subjects of the king wish to acclaim the king as *Dominus*. But the king, worried that his citizens might mistake the governor for him, quickly pushes the governor from the chariot. There was to be no confusion about just who was to be proclaimed lord. One should venerate God alone, never man.

The Torah Does Not Belong to the Angels

I do not think that the matter can be framed so simply. As is customary in rabbinic literature, one cannot fully understand the treatment of Adam and Eve without comparing it to the treatment of Israel at Sinai. To understand the angelic reaction to the creation of man, and the sharp rabbinic polemic against any elevation of Adam, it is necessary to compare the rabbinic traditions about the giving of the Torah to Israel. There are many rabbinic texts we could use to illustrate this point, but a particularly good representative comes from a collection of homilies dating from the ninth century:

When [God] came to give the Torah [to Israel], the ministering angels began to register their protest before the Lord and
said: "What is man that you mention him, the son of man that
you are mindful of him. . . . O Lord, our lord, how mighty is your
name in all the earth. Give your glory over the heavens" [Ps. 8:4,
9]. Rabbi Aha said that the angels said, "It would be to your praise
if you gave your glory to those of the heavenly realm. Give us
your Torah!" And the Holy One, Blessed be He, said to them,
"My Torah cannot be among you, 'It cannot be found among the
[eternally] living'" [Job 28:13]. . . .

For what reason does the Torah say, "I am the Lord your God
[you shall have no other gods . . .]" [Exod. 20:2–3]. Could you
deny my kingdom? Are you not beside me and do you not see the
image of my Glory every day? For what reason does the Torah
say, "this you may eat . . . but that you may not" [Lev. 11:9,14].
Since you cannot eat and drink, why would you request that I give
my Torah to you? . . .

But Israel, forty days later, violated the command, "you shall
have no other gods before me" [Exod. 20:3] [by venerating the
golden calf (Exodus 32)]. The angels began to say before the
Holy One, Blessed be He, "Lord of the Universe, did we not tell
you not to give your Torah to them?" Then, when the Holy One,
Blessed be He, sought to write the Torah a second time for them,
the angels would not let him. The Holy One, Blessed be He, said
to them, "Are you the ones who would keep the Torah? A weaned
child among the Israelites could keep it better than you. If he
came out of school and was able to eat meat and milk, he would
allow himself to consume the milk once his hands were clean
from the meat. But you, when you were sent to Abraham, he
brought before you meat and milk together and you ate them"
[Gen. 18:8]. (*Pesikta Rabbati* 25:4)

This text opens with the statement that God has come to deliver the
Torah to Israel. Though Moses is the one who will receive the Torah
in the name of Israel, his mediatory role is ignored. Instead, the dispute concerns the *competing claim of the angels for the heavenly Torah*.
When God is about to give the Torah to Israel they protest: "What is
man that you mention him? . . . Give your [Torah] to those who reside
in the heavens." The angels do not take umbrage at some vague, unde-
termined "mention" of man; rather they are enraged because God has
specifically given the Torah to Israel.

God's reaction to this protest by the angels is short and swift: "My Torah cannot be among you [for as scripture says] '*It cannot be found among the [eternally] living*'" (Job 28:13). God then proceeds to outline several commandments within the Torah that can only pertain to mortal human beings and hence fall outside the purview of angelic existence. This fact silences the angels long enough for God to give the Torah to Israel. But just forty days later, when Israel commits the apostasy of venerating the golden calf—a deed known in certain rabbinic sources as simply "that deed ['*oto ma'aseh*]"—the angels protest again, now claiming the correctness of their original position over that of God. God responds by declaring them out of order. In the era of Abraham the angels had already violated the heavenly Torah by eating meat and milk together. Their quibble about the moral status of Israel proves to be hypocritical.

Consultation or Elevation?

Both stories of angelic rivalry—over the creation of man and the giving of the Torah—preserve a tension from a founding moment of rebellion to its recurrence in a later generation. In the story of man's creation the tension concerns the issue of theodicy; how can the world last under the weight of human sin? The angels renew their cry against the creation of man when they see the heinous sins of the generation of the flood. With the evidence of human sin now clear to all, God can no longer destroy the angels for their insubordination. Instead he must answer their question, and he does so by responding with mercy ("Until old age I am he, even until I am gray I will bear with them").

In the story of the giving of the Torah, the matter is different. The angels are not concerned with the moral nature of humankind. What bothers them is the *elevation* of the Israelites. Unlike the creation story, the angels are not *consulted*. God does not ask, "Shall we give the Torah to Israel?" Instead the angels are presented with a fait accompli: God simply gives the Israelites the Torah. The angels show no interest in the moral impact of this event, but they show great umbrage at the loss of stature they have suffered ("Give your [Torah] to those who reside in heaven!"). As a result, when God responds to the angels' complaint after the veneration of the golden calf, he does not respond with mercy but rather retorts, "Are you the ones who would keep the Torah?"

In both traditions about creation and Torah giving we see a decided emphasis on God's prerogative to do as he wills. But in the Sinai materials this prerogative concerns the question of election. "The presentation of man's superiority over the angels," writes the scholar of rabbinic Judaism Peter Shäfer,

> finds its sharpest point in the discussion about Israel. The people Israel are the chosen people of God and this is true not only in reference to the other peoples but also in view of the relationship between angels and Israel.

We are left with a surprising outcome. The rabbinic material that most closely parallels the story from the *Life of Adam and Eve* about the elevation or election of Adam finds its nearest equivalent in rabbinic traditions about the giving of the Torah to Israel. Adam's story is principally one about God's *consultation* with the angels. In the tradition of Torah giving a very different situation is imagined: the giving of a heavenly boon to Israel *elevates* Israel but diminishes the angels' status. Here the angelic cry "What is man" lacks all moral purpose; it is instead the cry of those who feel their position in the heavenly hierarchy has been usurped.

Of Whom is Satan Jealous?

If Jewish sources were loath to shower praise on Adam in Eden for fear that he would overshadow Israel at Sinai, then we would expect to find the same view in Christian sources regarding the relation of Adam to Christ. Christ is the *eschatos* or "last" Adam according to the idiom of Paul (1 Corinthians 15), but the term "last" in Greek means not only the end of a sequential order but the fullest and most robust expression of a given category. *The last Adam is the most complete Adam.*

According to the well-known hymn that Paul cites in his Epistle to the Philippians, Christ must empty himself (*kenosis*) of his divine glory and take on the form of a lowly servant before God can exult him and grace him with a name higher than any name. When the Father has so elevated the Son, *only then* shall "every knee bow in heaven and on earth." If Adam has already been accorded the universal acclaim of those in heaven, then what honor is left for the second Adam?

Not surprisingly, certain Christian writers attacked the story of Satan's fall as we have it in the *Life of Adam and Eve*. Ironically, after the rise of Islam the whole tradition could be denigrated as a Muslim invention. This was because Muhammad had included this tradition in the Koran. But despite this polemical reaction, the reservation of Christian thinkers about this tradition was not any different from that of the Rabbis. The elevation of the first Adam could not be allowed to overshadow the second. For this reason Christian writers preferred to speak of the incarnate Son as he who was elevated over the angels.

This argument is made at greatest length in the Epistle to the Hebrews. For this writer, Christ is

> the reflection of God's glory and the exact imprint of God's very being. . . . When he had made purification for sins, he sat down at the right hand of the Majesty on high, having become as much superior to the angels as the name he has inherited is more excellent than theirs. (Heb. 1:3–4)

But as the Jewish tradition simply stated Moses' superiority to the angels as a mere fact—it dramatized the matter through a story about who deserved the Torah—so the declaration of Christ's superiority also required some concrete, narrative display. The angels must bow before him.

The proof text for this is the very same one used by the Rabbis: Psalm 8:4–6. The author of the epistle begins by citing the verses of the psalm in question:

> What is man that you are mindful of him. . . . You made him for a little while just lower than the angels, but then you crowned him with glory and honor, subjecting all things under his feet. (Psalm 8, as quoted in Heb. 2:6b–8)

The writer then interprets the psalm against the pattern of the incarnation:

> Now in *subjecting all things* to him, God left nothing outside his control. As it is we do not yet see *all things in subjection* to him, but we do see Jesus, who *for a little while was made lower than the angels*, now *crowned with glory and honor* because of the sufferings and death, so that by the grace of God he might taste death for everyone. (Heb. 2:8b–9, italics added)

This remarkable interpretation of the psalm has put a decidedly Christological spin on the nature of man's royal glory and honor. *This power is dependent on a prior act of humiliation.* As Milton's heroic angel Abdiel knew, embracing the ignominies of suffering and death would be rewarded by God with the highest of honors.

In addition, what is striking about this New Testament writer is the freedom to shift the generic referent of this psalm from the figure of mankind more generally ("what is man") to Son of Man alone. The psalmist certainly intended his poem to sing the praises of man more generally. This is clear at the end of the psalm when those elements of creation that will fall under man's feet are itemized. They include the sheep, oxen, birds and fish, exactly those parts of creation that mankind has jurisdiction over. But the Rabbis and the author of Hebrews extended this paean of praise to include the subjection of the angelic host as well, so that truly *"all* things were put under his feet."

When the angels are included, the Rabbis and the author of Hebrews understand the figure of man as either the elected nation of Israel or the elected Son, God's Christ. But man as a generic figure is not left out of the equation all together. In Judaism and Christianity the status of the universal (all humanity) is always dependent on the particular (Israel or Christ). All humanity will be elevated through the favor shown Israel or Christ. This is the mystery of election: all nations shall find blessing through the promise given Abraham.

Reprise: What is Man that You Mention Him?

The move from the particular to the universal is evident in *Paradise Lost,* and, not coincidentally, the prism through which the particular moves is that of Psalm 8. As readers of *Paradise Lost* are aware, the poem does not proceed chronologically. The epic opens with Satan and his confreres in hell after their expulsion from heaven. The earliest moment in time narrated in the poem is the moment of Christ's elevation (5:582–615); the arrival of Satan and his horde in Hades (1:50–83) takes place some ten days later after a furious pitched battle in heaven (Book 6).

What is striking is that Milton does not use Psalm 8 to fill out the picture of Christ's exaltation in heaven, even though the New Testament provides clear justification for this. Instead, Milton understands

Psalm 8 in terms of Adam and Eve themselves. At two points in Books 1 and 2, while Satan is mulling over his future in Hades, he mentions a rumor about the making of man. In the first instance he mentions that

> there went a fame in heaven, that he ere long
> Intended to create, and therein plant
> A generation, whom his choice regard
> Should favour equal to the sons of heaven.
> *(PL* 1:651–654)

The reference to a "favour equal to the sons of heaven" certainly echoes the lines of our psalm (*"a little less than the angels"*), and the implication of divine election ("his choice regard") more than accounts for Satan's ill ease over the rumor being circulated.

Later, when Satan and Beelzebub are thinking about how to avenge themselves on their usurpers, they despair of launching a frontal assault on heaven itself. Satan seeks "some easier enterprise" and claims to have found one in the plan of God to fashion man:

> There is a place
> (If ancient and prophetic fame in heaven
> Err not) another world, the happy seat
> Of some new race called Man, about this time
> To be created like to us, though less
> In power and excellence, but favoured more
> Of him who rules above; so was his will
> Pronounced among the gods, and by an oath,
> That shook heaven's whole circumference, confirmed.
> *(PL* 2:345–353)

The echo of Psalm 8 is patent; man "though less in power . . . but favoured more" recalls almost exactly the words of the psalm, *"a little less than the angels but crowned with glory and honor."* But what is intriguing here is the question of chronology. Satan must have heard this "ancient and prophetic fame" about the creation of man prior to the exaltation of Christ. Yet Milton and his readers certainly recognized that Psalm 8 was normally understood in terms of Christ. Why has Milton chosen to subvert the Christological import of this psalm?

The First Adam in Light of the Second

The answer lies in the story of Satan's fall in the *Life of Adam and Eve*. If Adam emerges with too much glory and honor, the character of the second Adam will be seriously compromised. On the other hand, theologians have always claimed that the categories of Christology and anthropology are deeply interwoven. How one defines Christ has profound implications for how one defines man.

In order to get the picture right, one must define the first Adam in terms of the ideal character of the second. We should recall that Milton made the story of Satan's fall "kosher" in exactly the same way Jewish writers did: he made it refer to the true focal point of election. But Milton was not satisfied to put the spotlight solely on Christ; the glory of the elected Son must redound to the men and women God so highly favored.

Milton achieves this by a brilliant literary move. Satan has heard of the honor to be showered on humankind, yet before he can react to this figure, God elevates his Christ. On one level we can view this as a sober precaution taken by God the Father. By elevating the Son first, Christ must bear the fearsome and brutal hatred of Satan while Satan is still possessed of full angelic power. In a very real sense the elevation of the Son fleshes out the ire that is already brewing in Satan's mind about the fashioning of man.

Because Christ is elevated first, Satan is compelled to exhaust his most precious resources in attacking the Son in heaven. Once he has fallen and considers his miserable lot in hell, he must reckon with the impossibility of ever storming heaven again. Now his designs must be of a more muted variety. Rather than a frontal assault on those whom God has "so lately favoured" he is limited to a furtive ambush in Eden. Rather then attack, he must tempt.

The sudden elevation of Christ in heaven has always been a problem for those who wished to defend the orthodoxy of Milton's theology. If Christ's status as the exalted Son is dependent on this elevation, one could claim that Milton is on the verge of theological heresy: He seems to claim there was a time when Christ was not publicly known as Messiah. Or, to reverse the language of the creed, Christ was not *eternally begotten* of the Father but *made* the Son *at a particular point* in time.

But another way to view the matter is to see this sudden elevation of Christ in heaven not as a change in his status but as a provoking moment.

The correlation of Satan's prior fears about Adam and Eve with his subsequent refusal to bow the knee to Christ is necessary for Milton to make an important argument about the relation of Christ to humankind in general. The elevation of Christ is not so much a moment according him a new status, but a tactical strategy in the economy of salvation. God sought an opportunity for provocation, *a moment wherein he could smoke out the insidious designs of Satan toward the human creature.*

O *Necessary* Sin, O Happy Fault!

Of course, the irony of the entire episode is that Satan does not understand that his desires to humiliate man will lead to man's exaltation. His efforts will produce what he fears most. Because God foresaw that man would fall, he asked the host of heaven who would act as a ransom for this creature so deeply favored. When the Son volunteers to empty himself of his divine glory and go into exile on earth to retrieve this fallen being, he is immediately subject to the grandest of honors. The angels laud and praise him without cessation. Such is the mystery of the *felix culpa* or "happy fault."

But this doctrine brings in its wake a thorny problem. One might imagine that the exaltation of the Son, and by extension the glory intended for man, *depended* on the Fall. Could the self-emptying of God—the high point in the revelation of God's essential being—have occurred without the entry of sin into the world?

In theory yes; on this all theologians are agreed. Yet at the same time there is a paradox. As Origen, a third-century theologian from Alexandria, put the matter,

> One must dare to say that the goodness of Christ appears greater, more divine, and truly in the image of the Father, when he humbles himself in obedience unto death—the death of the Cross—than had he clung onto his equality with the Father as an unalienable gift, and refused to become a slave for the world's salvation. (*On the Gospel of John*, 1.32)

This is the heart of the Christian story and the very soul of the doctrine of original sin. Satan cannot understand that "becoming a slave" would make one's "goodness . . . appear even greater." Yet his rebellion puts in motion a model of salvation that will exalt every man and woman to a status superior not only to him but also to all the angels.

Do Jews and Christians Think the Same?

It is a striking fact that for all their differences both Judaism and Christianity chart rather similar courses in depicting why the angelic host resists the exaltation of humankind. Both define what it means to be created in the image of God along the lines marked out by Psalm 8: "What is man that you mention him. . . . You made him a little lower than the angels yet you crowned him with glory and honor."

In rabbinic tradition, these words were spoken by the rebel angels, both at creation and when God was ready to bequeath his Torah to Israel. "What is man" became a taunt, even a broadside against the providence of God. "What is it about man," these angels want to know, "that makes him worthy of being your most precious possession?" Israel at Mt. Sinai both recapitulates creation and goes beyond it. For at Mt. Sinai God reveals his most precious possession, what he has reserved for Israel since the time before creation. The perfection of humanity rests in Torah. At this, the angels take umbrage, and God must dismiss them from his presence.

In Christian tradition, the same psalm was deployed to speak of a different climax in the order of creation: the incarnation of the divine Son. In his act of self-emptying, he plumbed the true depths of the divine being, and so God's deepest nature was made manifest in creation. Though some apocryphal traditions—such as the *Life of Adam and Eve*—would tie Satan's rebellion to the story of Adam at creation, Milton and others were not so sanguine about this association. The true image of God was Christ, and it was he who must play the role of Satan's archnemesis.

In both traditions, there is a concern for the *universal* figures of Adam and Eve as the image of God. But these generic figures need to be filled out with richer content in order to bear this title fully. Hence stories that once spoke about Adam wound their way toward Mt. Sinai or Bethlehem before finding their way back to Eden. Indeed, with some motifs it is hard to know where they originate, so interchangeable do they become. In the end, it is the vehicle of creation's *end* or *goal*—be it Torah or incarnation—that is the key to unlocking our common human destiny.

Chapter 2

Where Did Adam Know Eve?

"This time, at last! Bone of my bones and flesh of my flesh." This Biblical verse teaches that Adam attempted to have sex with all the beasts and animals but his sexual desire was not cooled off by them.
—Babylonian Talmud, *Yebamot*, 63a

Nothing seems more unusual than celibacy for those raised in our highly eroticized culture. If sexuality is a divine gift—the Bible commands us to "be fruitful and multiply"—then to renounce it would be odd. Yet for numerous Christian and Jewish interpreters of Genesis, Adam and Eve were chaste in Eden and only "knew" one another after their sin and eviction. Should we conclude that sex is tainted? Not at all. The goodness of sexuality, we shall see, depends on where *Adam knew Eve.*

Scripture's Double Message

The story of Adam and Eve's sexual relationship is not a simple one to interpret. First of all, the Bible declares that Eve was made to fill a void in the created order. When this first woman is presented to Adam he cries, "At last! Bone of my bones and flesh of my flesh" (Gen. 2:23). It is as though she was the answer to prayer. Secondly, the Bible shows no bashfulness about telling us just what void Eve was meant to fill. As soon as Eve is presented to Adam, our narrator turns aside to inform us that from now on a man will "leave his father and mother and cling to his wife in order to become one flesh" (2:24). Coital union between man and woman: this is the end toward which our story is heading.

Yet something is amiss. As soon as we learn of this end we are told that Adam and Eve were both naked in the Garden but unashamed. This would imply that they had not yet reached the age of sexual maturity.

Here is where things begin to turn ugly. For in the very next scene Eve consumes the fruit and offers some to Adam. He eats and their eyes are opened to their sexual difference. They are ashamed and attempt to cover up what appears to be a blot on their character.

And so our paradox: *Adam and Eve were created for the purpose of becoming "one flesh," yet the actualization of that purpose seems to be occasioned by human sin.* No doubt this peculiar story about how the world's first couple awoke to their sexual desires reflects the fact that our amorous nature is profoundly ambiguous.

The question early Jewish and Christian readers put to our text is as simple as it is timely. How is sex related to sin? One way to frame the matter is that of a simple either/or alternative. If Adam and Eve were celibate in Eden and only after their expulsion knew one another, then sexual knowledge was caused by sin. It made possible the feeling of shame and embarrassment. Part of the task of retrieving our ideal human form would be to renounce sexual desire. On the other hand, if Adam wedded Eve upon meeting her, then marriage is rooted in the very fabric of creation. To renounce marriage would be to reject the very goodness of God's creation.

This One at Long Last

I would like to consider Adam's physical passion for Eve as it is described in two different streams of Jewish interpretation, that of the book of *Jubilees* and that of the Rabbis. Why the book of *Jubilees?* Because it gives an important perspective on the *variety* of Jewish interpretations of Genesis. There were many forms of Judaism in the ancient world. In the literature of the Rabbis, we find one very important strand that eventually gave birth to the predominant form of Jewish belief and practice in our own time.

Jubilees represents a different Jewish circle of considerable antiquity that did not survive beyond the first century of the Common Era. The text itself dates to the second century B.C.E. A copy was found in the caves that housed the Dead Sea Scrolls. Some historians believe that the sectarians who retreated to the Dead Sea to await the end of the world had close contacts with the circle responsible for *Jubilees.*

Both *Jubilees* and the Rabbis are agreed on one point: Adam discovers his need for a sexual partner while naming the animals. This particular biblical scene poses a couple of problems for the careful reader. The tale in Genesis begins with God observing that "it is not good that man should be alone." God will make a partner for Adam. Yet contrary to all expectation, we do not read of the formation of Eve but the creation of the animals: "so out of the ground the Lord God formed every animal of the field and every bird of the air and brought them to the man to see what he would call them" (2:19). This is curious; there seems to have been a hiatus in the formation of Eve. God's purposes seem to be subject to some delay.

Our worries about the ineptness of the Creator seem to be confirmed at the close of this episode when our narrator informs us that "no helper was found for Adam" (2:20). This peculiar use of the passive voice ("was found") is troubling. The agent of the verb could be either God or Adam. One might first conclude that it must be God, because he is the one who has taken the initiative in the tale; Adam has been entirely passive. But this hunch is dashed by Adam's own words when Eve is presented to him: "At last, bone of my bones and flesh of my flesh" (2:23). These words would indicate that all along Adam has been documenting his loneliness. Only the creation of Eve has managed to assuage him.

This is the interpretive solution of the Rabbis and the book of *Jubilees*. As Adam watches the animals proceed before him two by two, he notices his own singleness and longs for a mate who will make him whole. Indeed, some Jewish traditions, sensitive to what a farmhand knows so well, declare that as Adam looked on, some of the animals engaged in sexual intercourse. Adam envied their pleasure and longed for a mate. In response to this need, God is more than ready to respond. He removes one of Adam's ribs, fashions Eve from it, and presents her to a just-awakened Adam. At this point, Adam *knows* Eve; their marriage is consummated. *Jubilees* puts the matter thus:

> And [God] brought her to him and he knew her and said to her, "This is now bone of my bones and flesh of my flesh. This one will be called my wife because she was taken from her husband." (*Jubilees* 3:6)

Because *Jubilees* has described Adam as learning of his need for a mate while naming the animals, we find it reasonable that he cried, "This time, *at long last*" when he first saw Eve. While watching the animals, Adam had grown restless for a partner. Marriage has been consummated in Eden.

Eden Was Like a Temple

Was Eden like a temple? A closer examination of *Jubilees* reveals a subtle but quite significant distinction. Eve has been presented to Adam *before* they enter the Garden.

> And God brought her to him and he knew her and said to her, "This is now bone of my bones and flesh of my flesh.". . . And after forty days were completed for Adam in the land where he was created *we brought him into the garden of Eden* so that he might work it and guard it." (*Jubilees* 3:6,9)

According to this text, Adam and Eve were created *outside* of Eden. It was outside of Eden that they met and initiated sexual relations.

This interpretive move involves some juggling of the narrative order of our tale as presented in Genesis. For, according to a strict reading of the Bible, Adam was first placed in Eden (Gen. 2:9) and afterwards given a mate (2:21–23). Evidently, much like a novelist or a screenwriter, our interpreter has understood the story of Eve's creation as a flashback to an earlier moment in the tale. The Genesis story does not unfold in simple chronological order. Adam, Eve, and the animals exist together outside of Eden. After the naming of the animals and the presentation of Eve, this first couple underwent a period of purification ("after forty days were completed") and only then could they enter Eden. *In this sacred temple-like garden, they refrained from sexual contact* (fig. 4).

This is a dramatic move, and I would like to pause a moment to consider it. For the writer of *Jubilees*, Eden was not just a horticultural marvel. It was regarded as the pinnacle of holiness itself. Eden was like a temple and the function of Adam and Eve was similar to that of the priesthood. They must be chaste before their maker.

Pure of Hands, Clean of Heart

In the eyes of many, it is only Christians who have placed a high value on celibacy. But this is patently untrue. Christians are unique insofar as they have commended life-long celibacy as one model of discipleship. Judaism, however, also holds sexual renunciation in high esteem, albeit for shorter durations of time. And for both traditions the reasons for renouncing sexuality are nearly the same: *to mold oneself as closely as possible to the image of the divine.*

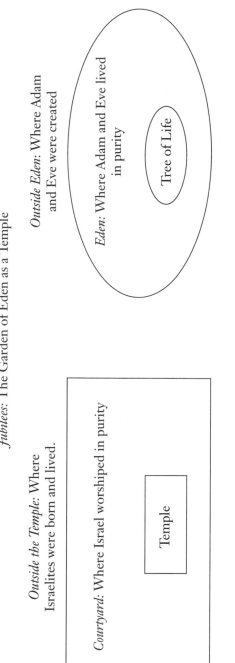

Jubilees: The Garden of Eden as a Temple

Outside Eden: Where Adam and Eve were created

Eden: Where Adam and Eve lived in purity

Tree of Life

Garden of Eden

Outside the Temple: Where Israelites were born and lived.

Courtyard: Where Israel worshiped in purity

Temple

Tabernacle

Figure 4

According to *Jubilees*, Adam and Eve were created in the vicinity of Eden but not in Eden itself. They can only enter the Garden once they have completed a period of purification. The book of *Jubilees* derives this period of purification from the purity legislation that pertained to the Temple (Leviticus 12). The analogy is patent: Just as an average Israelite would have to undergo purificatory rites after childbirth or a sexual emission in order to enter the Temple compound, so Adam and Eve had to do likewise in order to enter Eden. And, most significantly for our interests, just as sex was *hallowed outside* the confines of the Temple but *unimaginable within*, so for the region of Eden itself. Adam could "know" Eve outside Eden ("Adam knew his wife Eve and she conceived . . .") but was altogether forbidden to do the same within Eden.

Our human condition can be defined, in part, by the various bodily effluvia we emit: feces, urine, spittle, menstrual blood, and semen. In biblical culture, these various bodily fluids were considered unclean and were the markers of a body susceptible to disease and death (Leviticus 15). Such bodily wastes are not found among the angels or God. Those who would dare to enter the sacred confines of the Temple must conform to a heavenly pattern of life.

Here we stand face to face before a theological paradox that is at the very heart of the Bible's teaching about sexuality—a paradox that is very difficult to place within our more secular categories of reflection. We are both *anthropos* and *theos*, part human, part divine.

On the one hand, sexuality is at the very center of what it means to be a human. And to be truly human is a very good thing. Falling in love, marrying, and raising children is part of the divine plan for human life. On the other hand, our vocation as persons often follows a quite different trajectory. As persons created in God's own image, we are commanded from time to time to draw near to him. As God is a being beyond sexuality, so we must renounce our sexual nature in order to enter his sacred space.

Israel had to abstain from sex when she stood at the base of Mount Sinai to hear the Ten Commandments: "Moses said to the people, 'Prepare for the third day; *do not go near a woman*'" (Exod. 19:15). And Moses was under even more severe restrictions when he ascended to the top of the mountain to stand before God. He had to put away his wife altogether. Even the apostle Paul in the New Testament commends abstention from sex in order to devote oneself, for a short duration, to earnest prayer (1 Corinthians 7).

A Little Less than the Angels

According to Jewish tradition, the holiest day of the year is Yom Kippur, the Day of Atonement. During this day all Jews must fast and be chaste. When the Temple still stood in Jerusalem, the high priest was required to enter the Holy of Holies, the very throne room of God. So dangerous was this moment that every precaution was taken to safeguard the priest's purity. The day before his entry, he was kept awake all night in order that he not have a nocturnal emission and be disqualified from performing his sacred duty (Mishnah, *Yoma* 1).

According to the Bible, we are of a composite nature. To the degree that we participate in the divine life, we must periodically renounce our sexual nature. But from this renunciation we cannot and must not conclude that this nature is bad in and of itself. As persons, created with a nature distinct from God, we must embody these sexual passions to their fullest. *Emphasizing one side to the exclusion of the other is where error creeps in.*

This composite character of the human person—part animal, part god—is brought out well in a rabbinic tradition about humanity's creation. On this view there were two acts of creation involved in the making of man. One part of his nature was drawn from heaven, the other from earth.

> God created Adam with four attributes of the angels and four attributes of the animals. Like the animals, he eats, procreates, excretes, and dies. Like the angels, he stands upright, speaks, understands, and sees with both eyes in the front of his head. (*Genesis Rabbah* 8:11)

As this midrashic tradition nicely teaches, the Bible presents us with two seemingly contradictory paradigms for understanding our human nature. As animals we are bidden by our biology to seek a mate, but as gods we can soar beyond the confines of bodily desire.

The temptation has always been to elide one side of this equation in favor of the other. Our era, in particular, has been witness to an ever-increasing celebration of our erotic side. Devoid of any sense of purity or semblance to God, the very concept of abstinence has become unintelligible.

But the profundity of the biblical tradition has been to seek some deeper level of integration. We are both sexual beings and beings who can transcend our sexual selves. Or, to paraphrase the words of Jesus, we must live in this world but not be defined entirely by it. Our sexual nature is integral to our humanity, but it must not be allowed to define us.

The question, then, is not whether Adam and Eve had sex in Eden but how to orchestrate the rhythm between abstinence and our bodily passions. Here *Jubilees* is silent, and the Bible is not much more vocal. We must await our consideration of several Christian writers to pursue this question at greater depth. But for now let me be clear about one thing: the book of *Jubilees* has opened up a new way of considering the sexuality of Adam and Eve. Renouncing sexuality need not be construed as declaring sexuality intrinsically bad or evil. Quite the contrary. Sex was a good of the highest order, but its enjoyment was restricted to the household. For certain forms of ancient Judaism, Eden was a sacred place. Sexuality, though good and created by God, was to be renounced upon entrance to this holy space.

Let the Bridegroom Rejoice with His Bride

Geography is not the only variable I would like to consider. Alongside the concern for the sacred, one must also ponder how Eden is related to the theme of *Israel's destiny*. Sexuality in the Bible is not a private affair among two consenting individuals. Marriage is a defining moment for the people as a whole. *To enter into the rites of matrimonial love is to embody the destiny of the chosen people itself.*

As is well known, Judaism is a religion shaped by exile. The rise of modern Zionism has been powerful for modern Jewry because of its ability to address, however obliquely and imperfectly, this very problem. Twice in Israel's past, invading armies razed the Temple in Jerusalem (587 B.C.E. and 70 C.E.). According to biblical custom, such moments of national calamity were occasions for formal mourning. Because a mourner was forbidden to engage in sexual relations, prophets frequently described these moments of national calamity as ones in which the joys of marriage came to a close. "I will bring to an end the sound of mirth and gladness," Jeremiah prophesied just prior to the destruction of 587 B.C.E., "the voice of bride and bridegroom in the cities of Judah and in the streets of Jerusalem; for the land shall become a waste" (7:34).

The destruction of Solomon's Temple was felt so profoundly that Jeremiah himself was forbidden from taking a wife at all. The prophet Ezekiel, a near contemporary of Jeremiah, bore an even greater grief. His wife was taken from him. Compounding the pain, he was told by God not to mourn her death. Ezekiel explained this unusual circumstance in the starkest of terms:

> Say to the house of Israel, Thus says the Lord GOD: I will profane my sanctuary, the pride of your power, the delight of your eyes, and your heart's desire; and your sons and your daughters whom you left behind shall fall by the sword. (24:21)

But the mourning was not to last forever. Israel awaits the day when her redeemer will gather her dispersed children into the restored city of Jerusalem. The awaited New Age will be one of marital bliss, putting an end to mourning. These images of joy at the end of time were predicated on images of primordial time. No one makes this clearer than the prophet of the postexilic period who wrote under the name of Isaiah:

> For the LORD will comfort Zion;
>   he will comfort all her waste places,
> and will make her wilderness like Eden,
>   her desert like the garden of the LORD;
> joy and gladness will be found in her,
>   thanksgiving and the voice of song.
>   (Isa. 51:3)

The Second Temple, built in the late sixth century after the return of the exiles from Babylon, did not abide forever. Judaism still lived under the shadow of its desolation at the hand of the Roman Emperor Titus in 70 C.E. The destruction of that building was regarded as a calamity of the profoundest order by Jews. For some, the blow was so catastrophic that a return to the normal rhythms of daily existence seemed beyond recovery. Some extremists counseled against marriage altogether. Yet calmer minds prevailed, and the period of mourning was brought to closure. The joys of Eden were not to be altogether absent from the everyday, quotidian life of the religious Jew.

Even today, the importance of Eden is emphatically evident in the Jewish ceremony of marriage. During this ritual, six blessings are spoken over the bride and groom. The Talmud, a collection of Jewish law and custom from roughly the fourth to sixth centuries, requires that the blessings be said before ten people during the seven days of the marriage celebration. The last of these blessings reads,

> Blessed art thou O Lord Our God, King of the Universe, who created mirth and joy, bridegroom and bride, gladness, jubilation, dancing and delight, love and brotherhood, peace and fellowship. Quickly, O Lord Our God, may the sound of mirth and joy be heard in the streets of Judah and Jerusalem, the voice of bridegroom and bride, jubilant voices of bridegrooms from their canopies and youths from the feasts of song. Blessed are you O Lord who makes the bridegroom rejoice with the bride. (Babylonian Talmud, *Ketubot* 8a)

This blessing has borrowed the words of Jeremiah to characterize the period between the destruction of the Temple and the end of time as an era of mourning. After this destruction the sounds of mirth and joy, of bridegroom and bride, ceased from the cities of Judah and the streets of Jerusalem. By contrast, the era of restoration is to be characterized by the return of these joyful sounds.

Each and every married couple provides a link between the unsullied beginnings of human life in Eden and the restoration of that manner of living at the end of time. It is human love that binds our temporal existence together.

Eve was joined to Adam that they might become one. This powerful—and oftentimes nearly uncontrollable—urge to unite the sexes became a rich and productive metaphor for Israel herself. At Mt. Sinai, Israel pledged herself to God as an adoring young wife, eager to respond to her husband's gracious bidding. In ruins as a result of Babylonian and Roman destruction, Israel awaits full reconciliation with her divine bridegroom. And so every Jewish marriage is both a retrieval of the marriage that crowned creation in Eden and a testament to the nuptial joy that will characterize the end of time when God restores his chosen people.

Even Marital Joy
is Part of God's Torah

As is the custom for almost all habits of the body in Judaism, those of a sexual nature were not left simply to human choice or ingenuity. Jewish law invests the sexual life of married persons with the highest significance. To make love properly and passionately is a matter worthy of attention in God's own Torah.

In our modern age, talk of eroticism is almost invariably linked to the pursuit of individual pleasures. In considering the moral goodness of any particular sexual practice, the most significant moral concepts are those of consent and privacy. What two persons mutually agree to in the privacy of their own homes is their own business. End of question. There is little room for talk about the intrinsic goodness of a particular form of sexual practice or the power of the claims of a community over the behavior of any given individual. In Judaism the reverse is the case. Because the relation of God to Israel is imagined in erotic terms, it is incumbent on the people of God to be faithful stewards of this precious gift. Sexual passion is a matter of divine command.

There is a famous story in the Talmud about an aspiring student of Torah who follows his Rav or "teacher" home and hides underneath his bed. When evening comes the Rav begins to make amorous advances on his wife, only to discover the student in hiding. "What are you doing here?" he demands. The student responds, without missing a beat, "The Torah God gave Israel encompasses all of human life; even this is God's Torah." The Rabbis were not content to leave the matter as just a general exhortation. One must learn how to make love just as one learns how to pray.

Marital satisfaction is defined by its mutuality. The sanctity of the marriage bed would be irreparably harmed, for example, if the sexual act were reduced to fulfilling the interests of the male animal. Jewish law, which assumed a basic difference between the sexes, sought to humanize the more predatory characteristics of men. It is a religious obligation for the husband to delight his wife. Her pleasure became his responsibility.

In the Middle Ages, many of the teachings on sexual pleasure found in rabbinic writings were gathered together. In one famous text, "The Epistle of Holiness," husbands were exhorted to "engage your spouse in conversation that puts her heart and mind at ease and gladdens her. Thus your mind and intent will be in harmony with hers." In addition, one must resist overpowering a woman as an animal would, for "so a boorish man strikes and copulates and has no shame" (Babylonian Talmud, *Pesahim* 49b). Finally, "Do not hurry to arouse her passion until her mood is right. Begin in love, and let her pleasure be realized first."

Texts like this are bound to surprise those who view religious traditions as uptight about sex. I must confess that it is nearly inconceivable to imagine such material in the works of early Christian writers. (Though almost the exact same sentiments show up in medieval Catholic writers [among the canon lawyers] due to direct borrowing from Jewish sources!) It is not that they abhorred sexuality—as we will see, quite the opposite is true—but they had no place for a vigorous defense and encouragement of its sensual pleasure. Judaism, on the other hand, has no problem with erotic expression.

To be sure, sex must be set aside when approaching the Almighty Himself. But in the confines of one's home, in the bed hallowed by the rite of matrimony, sexual passions were to be displayed without reserve. Yet this ardor was not to be the private domain of any given married couple. Sexual passion was *the* root metaphor for the relation of God to Israel. For in that passion and commitment shown toward one another was mirrored the very love God had bestowed on the people Israel. Sex in our day, the Rabbis urge, draws its power from that bond fashioned in Eden.

The (Sexual) Imitation of Christ

The Christian church prior to the Reformation charted a course that had no exact parallel in Judaism. For the Latin West (Catholicism) and the Greek East (Orthodoxy), the supreme virtue was sexual renunciation. St. Paul, first among the apostles, counseled sexual continence for those who were capable of it. "The appointed time has grown short;" Paul observed, "from now on, let even those who have wives be as though they had none" (1 Cor. 7:29).

And Jesus himself gave impressive support for the chaste life when he said, "Those who belong to this age marry and are given in marriage. But those who are considered worthy of a place in that age and in the resurrection from the dead neither marry nor are given in marriage" (Luke 20:34–35). Jesus exemplified this teaching in his own chastity.

The highest vocation the early Christian community could imagine was the imitation of Christ (*imitatio Christi*). It is hardly accidental that the first Christian martyr, Stephen, prayed, "O Lord, do not hold this sin against them" (Acts 7:60), as he was stoned to death. Like Christ on the cross, his was an ethic of love towards one's enemies. Time and again in the various apocryphal *Acts of the Apostles* that circulated in the early church, the apostles and virtuous women, such as Thecla, emulated Christ's every deed. They preached the gospel, healed the sick, and distributed their wealth to the poor. Thecla was honored in the early church for renouncing wealth and marriage and being saved from death by lions in an amphitheater in Antioch.

Renunciation of sexual relations became so prized that some early Christians took matters to a considerable extreme: they put off baptism until old age, when the lusty desires of their youth had cooled. But in the main, the church fought these extremist tendencies. As appealing as the model of *imitatio Christi* was, it could not apply literally to everyone. The book of Genesis understood marriage as part of God's plan for creation. Only heretics could denounce it as an institution to be avoided at all costs.

The scriptural admonition "to be fruitful and multiply" (Gen. 1:28) therefore kept the orthodox tethered to the institution of marriage.

But the value of marriage went beyond the good of procreation. One will badly err if Christian esteem for the celibate state is understood too woodenly. Both marriage *and* its renunciation were established by God as worthy vocations of the Christian. The paradox of our sexual nature was not to be resolved in some simplistic manner toward one of its poles. Sexual renunciation is just as delicate and difficult a state to understand as sexual knowledge.

A test case for this thesis can be found in two brilliant and influential thinkers from the fourth century. One was Gregory of Nyssa, a speaker of Greek trained in the belles-lettres of Greco-Roman culture. The other, St. Ephrem, is not as well known in the West. He was a speaker of Syriac, a dialect of Aramaic, the language spoken by Jesus and most of the Jewish world. Ephrem was nicknamed the "Harp of the Holy Spirit" in praise of his many hymns that were a treasure trove of rich theological symbolism and profound observations on the human spirit. It has been claimed that Ephrem was a theologian-poet of the early church who could rank beside Dante.

Adam Brashly Drew Too Near

Ephrem's cultural milieu would not seem to bode well for marriage. Ancient Syria was a center of excessive asceticism. In its most extreme form, certain individuals renounced all worldly ties, distributed their material possessions to the poor, and took to the wilderness of the steppe or the harsh climes of the mountains to wander like animals. Eating roots and tubers, drinking from streams, and growing hair like the beasts of the field, these spiritual gymnasts attempted to wean their bodies of all worldly pleasures. Simon the Stylite ascended an enormous pillar to pray to the Creator on behalf of the wretched masses below. The impact these men and women made in the ancient world was so profound that travelers from hundreds of miles away came to observe the spectacle and derive some spiritual succor.

What we see in these individuals is the audacious act of fashioning the human person anew. By letting go of those bodily desires that define human nature—the desires for honor, wealth, and sexual pleasure—they were anticipating the transformed life that would define the next. Yet for all the rigors of this brand of Christianity, its chief theologian, St. Ephrem, took a more balanced view. Part of Ephrem's brilliance was his ability to mediate between the extremes of the various contesting parties of his own day. In particular, he was able to honor the rigors of ascetic discipline but at the same time affirm the goodness of the coital bond.

Like the writer of the book of *Jubilees*, Ephrem conceived of Eden as a mountain sanctuary. His interpretation was grounded in the second half of the command given to Adam and Eve: Don't draw too close to the tree of knowledge. This warning, Ephrem reasoned, was modeled on the warnings given to priests.

If Eden was similar to a holy place, then the sin of Adam must have been a violation of law pertaining to its sacredness. The tree of knowledge was understood by Ephrem as a veil that separated the outer court from the Holy of Holies, wherein resided the tree of life (fig. 5). In this relatively impure state, Adam was not allowed full access to the inner reaches of Eden.

> For God did not give permission
> For Adam to enter
> The inner realm of the Tabernacle,
> For this was kept under guard
> That he might do well in his service
> Within the outer realm of the Tabernacle.
> *(Hymns on Paradise* 3:16)

Adam was like the high priest described in the Old Testament. Had he obeyed the commandment, he could have entered the inner sanctum of the Temple, the very throne room of God.

The laws of Eden were just like those of the Temple. "For the mystery of Paradise," Ephrem declared, "was depicted by Moses, when he made two holies." To the outer realm of the Temple, ordinary priests were granted continual entry. But only the high priest, on a single day of the year, could enter the inner throne room.

Adam's transgression was understood to be a wanton act of disregard for this restriction.

> In his state of pollution,
> Adam had desired to enter
> the very holy of holies,
> which desires only those similar to it.
> But he who brashly enters
> the inner sanctum of the Tabernacle,
> even to the outer court
> He cannot permit him to enter again.

Ephrem: Eden as a Tabernacle

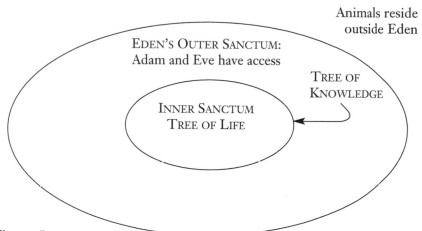

Figure 5

The TREE OF KNOWLEDGE guards the entry-point to the Holy of Holies wherein the TREE OF LIFE was found. Adam and Eve were not sufficiently holy at creation to enter this room, but had they not disobeyed the command, access to this INNER-SANCTUM would have been given. Since they prematurely tried to enter, they were driven out of Eden altogether.

The story of King Uzziah in 2 Chronicles 26 was a type of "Fall narrative" for Ephrem. Uzziah was a king who brashly entered the Temple to offer incense. For this act of hubris, he was smitten with leprosy and hence was "unclean" for the rest of his life. So Adam and Eve were smitten with a similar skin-disease, "mortal-flesh," and prevented by virtue of this state of uncleanness from ever entering Eden during their lifetime.

> Just as the sea of life,
>   when it sees a corpse within,
> it cannot permit it to remain
>   but casts it out.
>   (*Hymns on Paradise* 4:2)

Because of his violation of Eden's strictures of purity, Adam was cast out just as an encroacher would be cast from the Temple. He could never be permitted entry again.

Ephrem's picture is hardly different from that of *Jubilees*. He imagined the life of Adam and Eve in Eden to have been a celibate one. Sexual knowledge began after transgression, but it was not defined by that transgression. The goodness of sex was dependent on the proper location. Only when Adam was outside the Garden could he "know" Eve.

Sexual Renunciation Is Good; Marriage Is Better

Gregory of Nyssa was part of a circle of theologians from Cappadocia, a region in the mideastern reaches of modern Turkey. Though he lived just a few hundred miles from Ephrem, the cultural ambience of these two men could not have been more different. Gregory's intellectual compass took its bearings from the high culture of classical Athens. Ephrem's world was rooted in the culture and language of ancient Mesopotamia, with some affinities to even more exotic lands to the east, including Persia and the Indian subcontinent.

Gregory was part of a circle of theologians from the region of Cappadocia. This was a group of considerable intellectual prowess. It consisted of Gregory of Nazianzus, Basil, Gregory of Nyssa, and Macrina, whom Nyssa called both his sister and his teacher. "Theirs was a stern, ceremonious Christianity," writes Peter Brown, the noted historian of early Christianity, "firmly rooted in the continued life of great households. In these households, the women were crucial. They were the guarantors of physical and moral continuity."

Some have thought that Gregory, in spite of his respect for feminine virtue, cast a pall over the marital bond. Indeed, in his well-known treatise *On Virginity*, he appears to justify this conclusion. "Since marriage is the last stage of our separation from the life that was led in Paradise," he reasons, "marriage is the first thing to be left; it is the first station as it were for our departure to Christ" (*On Virginity*, 12). To undo the legacy of the Fall one must begin by renouncing marriage.

Yet Gregory was married. Clearly, his writings require further unpacking.

For Gregory, marriage is a good alongside the good of celibacy. It is the first thing to be abandoned by those who desire the beatific vision (*visio Dei*). The root metaphor is as Jewish as it is biblical; only the pure shall see God. To do so they must put on the very form of God. Sex is dispensed with, but it is not intrinsically evil. Gregory turns to the Old Testament to make this clear.

> How can you offer [yourself as a sacrifice] to God, when you do not listen to the law forbidding the unclean to offer sacrifices? If

you long for God to manifest Himself to you, why do you not hear Moses, when he commands the people [of Israel at Mt. Sinai] to be pure from the stains of marriage [Exod. 19:15], that they may take in the vision of God? (*On Virginity*, 24)

Sex, per se, is not evil, and sexual continence does not automatically confer sainthood.

For Gregory, the heart of the problem lies in our inability to understand the paradoxical status of the human person as a "rational animal." There is a strong tendency among ancients and moderns to resolve this paradox in one of two ways. Some emphasize our affinity with the animals and give free reign to bodily impulses. This is a tendency we know very well from our own age. The passions exist in order to be indulged. Seize the moment. Enjoy the present. You can't take it with you. These are the catchphrases that define our culture.

There are others, however, of a more straitlaced and often unforgiving character that put undue confidence in our rational capabilities. In their view, sexual passions are no more difficult to control than any other bodily habit. Celibacy is not so much a charism or gift from God as a potential attribute of any person, provided the individual exercises his or her will. These despisers of the coital act pretend that we possess no "animal" or bodily nature at all.

Neither of these two extremes is true for humans as God created them. For Gregory, there is a middle position. Both celibate *and* married persons are necessary parts of "the image of God." Indeed, just as Gregory compares the vowed monastic to an angelic being already well on the way toward reentering paradise, so the married couple, living the life of virtuous citizens, can be compared to God Himself. Just as God took on human flesh to redeem humans, so the married couple can channel their corporeal nature to a greater public good. Here, Gregory is dependent on an ancient Greek moral convention that the richer citizens must finance the public needs of the city. True marriage is rooted in public service (*leitourgia*).

Whereas the monastic has a unique opportunity to manifest detachment in daily life, a married couple can reflect the power of incarnate love through the tender care they show their children and the community. Both the monk and the married person are necessary parts of a larger theological whole. Neither should be sacrificed in favor of the other.

Gregory readily concedes that living the married life is no easy task. A good marriage requires more than merely eschewing adultery. The pleasures of body, wealth, career, and fame are so great that they can easily metastasize into ends in themselves.

For persons prone to infatuation with the body, Gregory counseled celibacy as a form of medicine. In a surprising rhetorical turn, celibacy becomes a second-order good to that of the married life! "He who is of so weak a character that he cannot make a manful stand against nature's impulse," Gregory declared, "had better keep himself very far away from such temptations, rather than descend into a combat which is above his strength" (*On Virginity*, 8). Such a person is likely to be fooled by his animal nature into thinking "that there exists no other good but that which is enjoyed along with some sensual emotion, and turning altogether from the love of immaterial delights" (*On Virginity*, 8). Once he is committed to finding pleasure only within the flesh, his character will be that of "a Pleasure-lover, not a God-lover."

Everything in moderation, Gregory counseled. He was not alone. Clement, a citizen of the bustling third-century city of Alexandria, also saw the married man or woman as a person of the highest moral order:

> True manhood is not shown in the choice of a celibate life; on the contrary, the prize in the contest of men is won by him who has trained himself by the discharge of the duties of husband and father and by the supervision of a household, regardless of pleasure and pain—by him, I say, who in the midst of his solicitude for his family shows himself inseparable from the love of God and rises superior to every temptation which assails him through children and wife and servants and possessions. On the other hand, he who has no family is in most respects untried. (*Stromateis* 7.12.70)

Married life is not some cheap concession to our lower animal nature; *it is the ultimate testing ground for human virtue.*

Between Priest and Layperson

In the culture of the early church, celibacy and marriage belong together. If we are to do justice to the complexity of Christian thought, we must realize that the renunciation of marriage and the enjoyment thereof were both highly esteemed. The complex nature of Adam and Eve's marriage in scripture gave rise to an equally varied embodiment in the church. Man was created for the very purpose of being joined to woman. Yet he must renounce this very tie to be at one with his creator.

In a deeply biblical and Jewish manner, Gregory and Ephrem argue that those who wish to gaze upon God directly (*visio Dei*) must be pure of the stains of marriage. Yet this was no broadside against sexuality. When our bodies ache to return to Eden, the sexual life must be renounced, either temporarily as St. Paul advised for moments of prayer, or for good in order to live the monastic life.

But not all Christians were called to take their place among the angels in perpetual adoration of God Almighty. For those Christians located outside the monastic conventicles, the life of marriage and creation of children was a good and hallowed thing. By mapping Eden on the model of the Temple, Ephrem established the celibate life on a primordial foundation but at the same time made sufficient allowance for the good of marriage. *Adam could know Eve as long as they were outside Eden.* This was a distinctly Jewish move.

The difference between Judaism and Christianity on this issue was that Judaism limited the state of abstinence to periodic moments in the life of the faithful, moments when a priest or layperson drew near to God's very presence. The Christian position simply extended these periodic moments to a lifetime.

Our own age has not shown much respect for even temporary moments of abstinence. Purity itself, as the anthropologist Mary Douglas reminds us, is a category without meaning to most modern persons. Yet the category has been with the human species for thousands of years and across several continents. It certainly is not a surprise that the life of vowed celibacy has become well nigh unintelligible, even to many Catholics and Orthodox. Modernity, through its ever-present media, encourages us to pursue the passions of our bodies with utter, even reckless, abandon.

As Gregory indicated, one need not practice celibacy in order to derive its benefits. The celibate stands as a beacon reminding us that the goods of this world do not possess infinite value. Loving husbands and wives offer examples of how true virtue is won: in the midst of negotiating the hardest of temptations. We are as pilgrims on this planet, always in service to a higher order. A culture that honors the chaste life recognizes the need to subordinate and transform the personal to the public and the sacred.

What we have seen over the course of this chapter is a careful weaving together of two interpretive poles. The first is rooted in the interpretation of Genesis 2–3. In this arena, the crucial point to be determined is whether Eden constitutes a sacred space. If so, then Adam and Eve cannot enjoy sexual relations therein. This is true for both Jewish and Christian readers.

The second pole is that of the place of marriage in the larger theological horizon of the tradition in question. A favored image for the present age in rabbinic thought is that of exile. Since exile is equated with mourning, the onset of the kingdom of God will be marked not by mourning but by renewed marital vigor. The dour words of the prophet Jeremiah ("I will bring to an end the sound of mirth and gladness, the voice of bride and bridegroom in the cities of Judah and in the streets of Jerusalem; for the land shall become a waste") will no longer apply in the projected era of marital bliss ("Quickly, O Lord Our God, may the sound of mirth and joy be heard in the streets of Judah and Jerusalem, the voice of bridegroom and bride, . . . Blessed are you O Lord, who makes the bridegroom rejoice with the bride"). And if this is how the end of time is to look, then such joy must have also characterized the beginning of time. For the Rabbis, the picture of Eden was clear—it was not a temple, and Adam knew Eve while he was in Eden.

Christians followed a path marked out by a different Jewish tradition, that of *Jubilees*. Eden was like a temple, and sex was not possible within its precincts. Their opting for this perspective was certainly conditioned by their chief theological metaphor: the imitation of the life of Christ. As Christ was celibate in his preparation to enter the kingdom of God, so must those be who would follow him most closely.

Certain Christians carried the logic of this to a *reductio ad absurdum*, the denigration of human sexuality altogether. But the church itself never adopted this extreme posture. The text of Genesis assured that the goods of marriage could not be left behind in the advance toward the kingdom. God commanded Adam and Eve to "be fruitful and multiply" at their very creation. They were chaste in Eden, not simply because they were without sin, but because they were located in a temple-like environment.

Chapter 3

How Did Adam Know Eve?

*I do not understand my own actions. For I do not do what I want,
but I do the very thing I hate. . . . Wretched man that I am! Who
will rescue me from this body of death?*

—Romans 7:15, 24

*St. Augustine, the late fourth-century African bishop, is probably
the most influential and radical Christian thinker on love and marriage. According to Augustine, Eden was no chaste sanctuary;
Adam and Eve should have consummated their union in the Garden. All they lacked was sufficient time. Sexuality has become a
problem for us, Augustine argues, because we have lost the tal-
ent for making love as God had intended. A return to Eden through
Christ will restore us to the type of erotic attachments for which
we were created.*

Augustine and Sexual Desire

Enter the figure of St. Augustine, and the tenor of our conversation about sexuality changes completely. No single person is more important for understanding Christian sexual ethics than he. Yet no man is more misunderstood. However uncomfortable he may make us feel, there can be no doubt that this North African theologian and bishop had a deep grasp of what it means to be a *sexual* being.

To understand the human person as a sexual being, we must put away all talk of purity and turn to the biological roots of the sexual drive itself. For it was the heated passions of sweaty, fleshy bodies that interested St. Augustine. *Where* lovemaking takes place is no longer the issue, but *how* and under what conditions. How the desires of the amorous couple are to be correlated with the love of God toward his people is Augustine's question. His is a voice that would resonate well in our own public square.

O Lord Make Me Chaste, but Not Yet

Augustine did not grow up a pious Christian boy. He led a somewhat dissolute life as a young man. For some time he had lived out of wedlock with a woman and fathered a child. Though he renounced such actions on being baptized, he remained resolutely honest about the ever-present attraction of the carnal life. Becoming Christian did not erase his libido.

His sexual realism was certainly influenced by his social location. He did not write from the rarified atmosphere of the academy or the monastery. He lived his life among common, ordinary folk who traversed the streets of North Africa and Italy. Contrary to Gregory of Nyssa or Ephrem, he did not believe that the stirrings of the human heart were so easy to repair. The waves of passion that swept over soul and body were so overwhelming that none could escape their terrifying power.

Why are human motivations so tortured by and riddled with conflicting desires? The answer was clear for Augustine: the sin of Adam and Eve. We all bear the scars of that single, unfortunate choice.

Peccatum Originale, or "On Original Sin"

In her book, *Adam, Eve, and the Serpent,* Elaine Pagels offers a very critical reading of Augustine. According to her, Augustine departed from the tried and true path marked out by the first several centuries of Christian thought. No doubt she is correct. Prior to Augustine, Christian writers had put a higher value on the power of free choice. We can both know the good and do it. This optimism about human potential was conveyed most vividly in a myriad of stories about the saints and martyrs. These men and women had freely chosen to renounce all personal gain in order to advance the kingdom of God.

The most powerful symbol of free will was a life lived in perfect chastity. It showed that even the most powerful of human urges could be overcome by sheer force of choice. But to renounce marriage in the ancient world was to deny oneself not only bodily pleasures but also the many and varied obligations of Roman civic life. This had profound social consequences, Pagels argues, even for those who did not take this extreme measure.

> The majority of Christians married but continued nonetheless to assert the primacy of renunciation. In their resistance to con-

ventional definitions of human worth based upon social contribution, I suggest, we can see the source of the later Western idea
of the absolute value of the individual—the value of every human
being, including the destitute, the sick, and the newborn—quite
apart from any contribution, real or potential, to the "common
good."

Enter the figure of Augustine, and Christian thought cuts a more dour
and tragic figure. For him, the results of Adam's sin were catastrophic:
the onset of uncontrollable lustful desires for sexual satisfaction.

The case against Augustine seems weighty indeed. But before we
accept Pagel's view, let's consider the broader ramifications of the optimistic perspective.

"I Cannot Do the Good That I Wish"

To be fair to Augustine, we must be fair to his historical context. His
views on human sin were framed in the context of a vigorous debate
with Pelagius, a bright young monk from England. Having been
raised on a diet of stories about the virtuous saints and martyrs, Pelagius vigorously affirmed the power of the gospel to transform human
nature. Sainthood was not for the few; it was within the grasp of anyone who willed it.

And how natural this position seemed to the young Pelagius. Like
any Christian living in the early fifth century, he was intimately familiar with the lives of the saints. Men and women of highest standing
had left behind family wealth, spouses, and all concern for worldly
honor in order to retreat to the desert or monastery. Biographers of
these monks and ascetics spelled out in great detail how these persons
had attained a life like that in Eden. The life of virginity itself, Gregory of Nyssa liked to say, "seems to be an actual representation of the
blessedness of the world to come, showing as it does in itself so many
signs of the presence of those expected blessings which are reserved
for us there" (*On Virginity*, 13). These religious virtuosi, whom Gregory knew, were no longer bound to the sentence imposed on Adam.

Pelagius went even further. For him, the sin of Adam was not some
indelible stain, never to be removed from our mortal garments. On
the contrary, we learned this habit through the power of imitation or
example. Like other bad habits, what Adam had learned could be
unlearned.

But these cool and refreshing words of optimism and human potential for Pelagius—which remain so for modern defenders of his position, such as Pagels—became a scorching fire and a searing iron to Augustine. Such a remedy would not cauterize our wounds, but make them fester and bleed all the more. The simplicity of this message was also its terror: "If perfection was possible for man, then it [could become] *obligatory*." [Italics added.]

The cultural consequences of remaining a Pelagian are formidable. If we view our sexual nature as completely under the control of the will, then we can legislate the harshest of penalties for those who do not conform. Adulterers, fornicators, homosexuals, and others who deviate from cultural norms could be put to death. Pelagius believed that everyone had it within him- or herself to conform to the moral law. It was, after all, simply a matter of choice. As Peter Brown puts the matter, Pelagius imposed "the terrifying weight of complete freedom on the individual: he was responsible for his every action."

Because Augustine held that our wills were corrupt from birth, he could argue for a greater tolerance toward those who failed. This did not mean a lowering of moral standards—sin was still sin in his view. But his pessimistic view of our control over the passions brought about a far more tolerant stance toward those who err. Augustine singled out sexuality for such special attention, the historian Paula Fredriksen has persuasively argued, because "[sexuality] was the most extreme instance of the disjuncture between will and affect; [it] marked man's every erotic attachment. For this reason in Romans Paul had lamented, 'Wretched man that I am! Who will deliver me from this body of death?' Even though the Apostle delighted in the law of God in his inmost self, he nonetheless saw another law in his members, 'making me captive to the law of sin'" (7:22–24).

Adam Should Have Known Eve in Eden

What is the bearing of this Pauline theologian on our understanding of Adam? If our will is corrupt from origin, then that corruption must have begun in Eden. Augustine broke dramatic new ground when he defined the chief effect of the Fall as the fracture of the human will. In one fell swoop, the value put on Adam and Eve's angelic bodies and the holiness of Eden was diminished considerably. Eden was not a sanctuary.

The implications of this interpretive move were enormous. The *sanctity* of Eden had been the principal objection to sexual intercourse in paradise. Because of his focus on the *will* of Adam and Eve, Augustine passed over the theme of sanctity in silence. The objection to sex in Eden disappeared. Augustine knew the revolutionary consequences of his position: Adam and Eve were not chaste in Eden by design but by *accident*. They sinned too quickly; they had no time to consummate their marriage. God had appointed the marriage bed for Eden, but Adam and Eve were late for their wedding. The angels were left holding the flowers.

Augustine's suggestion that marriage had been arranged for Eden was shocking and without adequate parallel in the Christian world. So novel was his thought that it requires more unpacking. Augustine did not think about human sexuality in terms of simple binary opposition: sex outside the Garden is good, sex within is bad; sexual renunciation good, married life less so. For Augustine, the *quality* of the sexual experience was what defined its moral value.

Sexual Organs Run Amok

If Adam and Eve had had sex in paradise, their bodies would have behaved in perfect concord with their will. Just as we can move our hands and our feet to perform varied functions whenever we will them, so we could have done with our sexual organs had Adam not sinned. C. S. Lewis, the well-known Christian apologist and scholar of English literature, summarized this point nicely in his *A Preface to Paradise Lost:*

> He means that the sexual organs [after the Fall] are not under direct control from the will at all. You can clench your fist without being angry and you can be angry without clenching your fist; the modification of the hand preparatory to fighting is controlled directly by the will and only indirectly, when at all, by the passions. But the corresponding modification of the sexual organs can neither be produced nor dismissed by mere volition.

The reasons for implicating the sexual organs in the tale of the Fall were two. The first was biblical. Before Adam and Eve sinned they felt no shame and did not recognize their nakedness; afterward they felt shame and covered their pudenda. Something untoward had happened to those organs. The second reason was part biblical and part psychological. Augustine read the text of Genesis through the eyes of Paul. That famous apostle had confessed that knowing the good and being able to do it were two very different things. "I do not understand my own actions," Paul lamented. "For I do not do what I want, but I do the very thing I hate" (Rom. 7:15). The onset of this division within the personality was marked out in the lives of Adam and Eve. Prior to their sin (Gen. 2:25) they knew no shame. But as soon as they sinned, shame took center stage.

Why this shame? Because the harmonious relation between erotic desire and bodily obedience was broken. This was evident from the arrival of two forms of sexual dysfunction: lust and impotence—lust because the body's desire frequently overrode the freedom of the will; impotence because the overheated body would frequently grow cold in those circumstances when sexual desire was altogether healthy and good. Lust and impotence are the fruits of post-Eden life; Adam and Eve would not have known them had they stayed in Eden. This, Augustine claimed, was because prior to their sin their bodies acted in concert with their desires. Omit that harmonious cooperation, and in comes the penalty of shame. Why was the shame focused on the genital organs? Because they illustrated, better than any other part of our body, how the passions could trump the best efforts of our reason.

No matter how long and hard one may argue for the freedom of the will, it is impossible to deny the power of sexual desire. This was Augustine's strongest argument against Pelagius. Augustine not only put sex back in Eden but restored the struggle against it to monastic life as well. Monastic virtuosi were not as clean of Adam's "habit" as they had claimed. Augustine could not have praised the virginal life in the same terms as Gregory of Nyssa. This unmasking of monastic pretension did not sit well with its defenders, such as Pelagius. The raw power of sexual desire, Augustine argued, continued unabated throughout human life, irregardless of religious vocation.

We are left, again, with a paradox. Human concupiscence is so deeply woven into the fabric of our being that even those who renounce it continue to suffer its pains. Augustine's opponents reduced the body, and by extension sex, to a set of anatomical properties that could be freely chosen or renounced. Speech about our sexual nature was reduced to the mechanics of reproductive biology. But sex to Augustine, as Fredriksen so aptly reminds us, is not reproductive biology [but] eroticism. This is a more complex (not to mention more interesting) phenomenon. And for Augustine it is the measure of a theological problem more complex, and a human situation more desperate, than the Pelagians with all their healthy-minded talk of medical science and philosophical freedom could or would acknowledge.

Marital relations, when directed to their proper end, need not take a back seat to celibacy. Both, in Augustine's view, were flawed, but both were amenable to the power of divine grace. It is precisely this subtle complexion of Augustine's teachings on human sexuality that renders it supple enough to guide Roman Catholic thinking even in our own day. And Protestant thinking as well.

"Hail Wedded Love!"

That Augustine's ideas also influenced Protestant thought may surprise. How could Augustine serve as the font of both Catholic and Protestant thinking about human marriage? Surely the two must part company. Augustine's proposal that Adam and Eve could have had sex in Eden was groundbreaking. Human sexuality, properly enjoyed, was part of God's intention for humanity at its very inception. The mere declaration of such an assertion severely qualifies the intrinsic value of sexual renunciation. If sexual renunciation is not identified with life in Eden, then what does it represent? What was the value in seeking this difficult charism if such rewards were denied it?

For John Milton, the logical extension of Augustine's thinking was clear. The celibate life, robbed of its distinctive reward and goal, was without defense.

> Whatever hypocrites austerely talk
> Of purity and place and innocence,
> Defaming as impure what God declares
> Pure, and commands to some, leaves free to all.
> (*PL* 4:744–747)

Celibacy is not even an equivalent to marriage in the eyes of this Puritan and Reformer. It is the talk of hypocrites. Or worse. Milton casts a dark shadow on monastic virtue, darker than ever imagined by Augustine:

> Our maker bids increase, who bids abstain
> But our destroyer, foe to God and man?
> Hail wedded love.
>
> (*PL* 4:748–750)

Milton goes beyond Augustine. But he goes beyond Augustine solely because he goes through him. Milton's depiction of human sexuality in *Paradise Lost* could be described as simply a narration of what Augustine had suggested in his more learned commentaries. Milton has elegantly played and ornamented the musical score Augustine had bequeathed him.

The dependence of Milton on Augustine can be seen from how he maps out Adam and Eve's sexual life across his epic poem. Two scenes are dedicated to their amorous moments, one before the Fall and another after. Before the Fall, all matters are in good order. Eve is presented to Adam, and their desire for one another is quickened. Having taken these desires into his providential arrangements, God prepared a special chamber or bower within the wooded recesses of Eden wherein this happy couple may retreat to fulfill their pleasures. Within that divinely appointed bower, Eve prepares the marriage bed:

> Here in close recess
> With flowers, garlands, and sweet-smelling herbs
> Espoused Eve decked first her nuptial bed.
>
> (*PL* 4:708–710)

Jewish guidebooks of the Middle Ages counseled that nighttime was the ideal period for carnal pleasure. Milton proves a good student of such advice.

As Adam and Eve enter this nuptial chamber, they offer a prayer of praise to their maker, extolling him for his promise to multiply their number. The prayer completed, they enter their bower. Adam "turned not from his fair spouse," Milton informs us,

> nor Eve the rites
> Mysterious of connubial love refused.
>
> (*PL* 4:741–743)

Their lovemaking finished, Adam and Eve, like any other ravished but satisfied couple, fall fast asleep.

Adam Cast a Lascivious Eye on Eve

So were sexual relations before the Fall. Afterward, the story is quite different. After Milton completes his retelling of the transgression, we might expect him to tell us how Adam and Eve's eyes were opened to their shame. That was how the Bible, in its own terse way, had told the story:

> Eve took of [the tree's] fruit and ate; and she also gave some to her husband, who was with her, and he ate. Then their eyes were opened and they knew that they were naked. (Gen. 3:6–7)

But Milton takes the liberty of prying apart these two sentences and introducing a dramatic new narrative into the story. Is this simply the license warranted by Milton's justly famous poetic skill? Perhaps. But it is just as much the result of Milton's careful study of St. Augustine. For Milton's treatment shows every sign of his indebtedness to the Bishop of Hippo. Having committed their trespass, but not yet having taken notice of its penalty—"their eyes were [not yet] opened"— Adam and Eve anticipate its effects:

> [Adam] on Eve
> Began to cast lascivious eyes, she him
> As wantonly repaid; in lust they burn:
> Till Adam thus gan Eve to dalliance move.
> (*PL* 9:1013–1015)

The ovens of their carnal passion were heated full; they were pained at the thought of even a moment's delay. There was no time to consider their elegantly appointed bower. In this condition, *any* place would do. Nor was there need for prayer to sanctify this embrace. In wonderful Miltonic irony, Adam and Eve thought this embrace would be different from their former embraces. As their eagerness reached a boiling point they wondered aloud whether this moment of coupling might outdo all others:

> if such pleasure be
> In things to us forbidden, it might be wished,
> For this one tree had been forbidden ten.
> (*PL* 9:1024–26)

But their ardent hopes and heightened fantasies of how good it was to be did not come to pass. They awaken from their slumber as would any self-deceived victim of a casual, one-night stand. The embrace of their burning bodies had more in common with adultery than a sacramental bond. To be sure, they had not violated the letter of the law—how could they? On the level of mere externals they were innocent of any adulterous charge. But the *quality* of their carnal knowledge was not what it should have been. It admitted no thought of person or sacramental bond. The sexual organs no longer acted in harmony with Adam and Eve's good wishes. Now their organs were set free to display their impudence and independence. The nuptial bower appointed by God and arranged by Eve was altogether lost.

Augustine had considered sex before the Fall a realistic possibility. Milton simply raised the ante and made it a reality. For both, sex after the Fall was the single most vivid sign that the desires of the body could tragically steer the person toward unseemly ends.

In the figure of Milton, we also see how important the theological legacy of Augustine was. If we imagine the words of Genesis 1–3 as similar to the bare conventions of a written musical score, then Augustine's earlier performance of this text was of such virtuosity that Milton simply could not hear it apart from that influence. What an irony this simple truth is: Milton, the quintessential child of the Protestant Reformation, thought of himself as returning to the pure biblical roots of his tradition. Yet at the very heart of his construal of the marriage of Adam and Eve we do not hear a pure and simple voice from scripture itself. Instead we hear, in the poetry of this seventeenth-century Englishman, the "still small voice" of that venerable Bishop of Hippo echoing across time and space. We never hear the biblical voice in stark and unpackaged purity. It is always refracted by those who have gone before us.

The Goods of Marriage

Jew and Christians have different views about the "goods" of human marriage, and they are reflected in how writers in both traditions treat the "problem" of sex in the Garden. But their treatments of this theme follow from a careful examination of the Genesis story. They do not stand over the text but before it. They do not dictate its meaning; they listen reverently.

The bogeyman of all discussions on sexuality within the Garden—

St. Augustine—winds up being a man of considerable influence. He recast the Christian focus from a concern with the "when and where" of sexual relations to a concern with "how and why." Augustine puzzled over why the biblical author had characterized the Fall through the discovery of nakedness. Only one answer seemed apparent: within the sexual organs we see most prominently displayed the divided loyalties that rule our passions. These powerful desires can lead us to sexual dalliances that do not uplift; they can also disappear precisely in moments when their presence is most precious, most needed, even most appropriate. "I do not understand my own actions, " St. Paul had confessed, "for I do not do what I want, but I do the very thing I hate" (Rom. 7:15).

This verse from Paul shed immeasurable light for Augustine on the shadows of the terse texts in Genesis. By placing his focus on the nature of the human will, Augustine brought a far more profound layer of meaning to the question of sex within the Garden. No longer is the question one of "Did they or didn't they?" Now we must ask *how* they experienced the joys of unitive love. The *quality* of the human marital bond was put front and center. Augustine's figure cast a long shadow. Practically no one, at least in the Western world, has gone untouched.

Chapter 4

Mary As Second Eve

Adam, however, did not wish to speak to Eve the way the Holy One, blessed be He, had spoken to him. Rather he said this to her: "Of the tree that is in the midst of the Garden God said, 'You shall not eat or touch it lest you die!'"
—*The Fathers according to Rabbi Nathan*

Then Adam knew that his wife Eve had conceived by Sammael, the [wicked] angel of the Lord.
—*Targum Pseudo-Jonathan, ad loc.* Gen. 4:1

Perhaps no other cultural issue has defined our era as that of the dignity of women. And so, nothing has appeared more suspicious—if not simply wrong-headed—than the attempt to pin the blame for the Fall solely on the figure of Eve. Jewish and Christian interpreters present a complex picture on this subject, one that is not reducible to any simple truism. Culpability for the Fall revolved around two sets of issues: who knew what and when? And toward whom do these figures point? With these questions answered, the question of blame is bathed in new light.

The portrait of Eve in Genesis has not always been a flattering one in the history of Judaism and Christianity. Eve, it seems, is at the very root of the human predicament. Had she only acted differently, the saying goes, the entire course of human history would have been changed.

No writer better represents this lamentable perspective than Tertullian, a leading Christian thinker of the second century who hailed from North Africa. "You are the one who opened the door to the Devil," he declares in words that barely disguise his feelings toward women. "You are the one who first plucked the fruit of the forbidden

75

tree, you are the first who deserted the divine law; you are the one who persuaded him whom the Devil was not strong enough to attack. All too easily you destroyed the image of God, namely, man" (*On the Apparel of Women* 1.1).

And one need not consult only the learned theologians to find this sort of demeaning commentary on the first woman. In Geoffrey Chaucer's *Canterbury Tales*, the Wife of Bath complained bitterly of Eve's baneful deed, or at least, her husband's assessment of its results,

> But now to purpos, why I tolde thee
> That I was beten for a book, pardee!
> Upon a nyght jankyn, that was oure sire,
> Redde on his book, as he sat by the fire,
> Of eva first, that for hir wikkednesse
> Was al mankynde broght to wrecchednesse,
> For which that jhesu crist hymself was slayn,
> That boghte us with his herte blood agayn.
> Lo, heere expres of womman may ye fynde,
> That womman was the los of al mankynde.*
>   (*Canterbury Tales*, "Wife of
>   Bath's Prologue," 711–720)

I could provide an extensive litany of such citations. Western literature abounds with them. But doing so would only tell half the story. For what one would find is that many of the worst assessments about Eve are to be found in moralizing literature, occasional letters, and novellas such as *Canterbury Tales*.

Curiously, when one turns to the central theological documents and artistic renderings about the Fall, one finds a different story. Here Eve is not so much the villain but the necessary counterpoint to a "Second Eve," the source of salvation. Eve, through the agency of her double, is not vilified but nearly deified. But I am again running ahead of my story. Before turning to these more positive portrayals, it will do us well to pause for a moment and ask whether Eve is the more guilty party.

---

*But now to the point of what I told thee / I was beaten for a book, pardieu! / Upon a night, Jenkin, who was our sire, / read in his book, as he sat by the fire, / of the first Eve who by her wickedness, / was all mankind brought to wretchedness, / for which Jesus Christ himself was slain, / that bought us with his heart's blood again. / Lo, here expressly of woman you may find, / that woman was the loss of all mankind.

"You Shall Not Eat or Touch the Fruit"

The complications with our biblical story begin with the very giving of the command. According to the Bible, only Adam hears it directly:

> The LORD God took the man and put him in the garden of Eden to till it and keep it. And the LORD God commanded the man, "You may freely eat of every tree of the garden; but of the tree of the knowledge of good and evil you shall not eat, for in the day that you eat of it you shall die." (Gen. 2:15–17)

Eve had not yet been created and therefore was not present to hear these words. Yet we know that Eve was familiar with the command, for she divulges its contents when she converses with the snake:

> The woman said to the serpent, "We may eat of the fruit of the trees in the garden; but God said, 'You shall not eat of the fruit of the tree that is in the middle of the garden, nor shall you touch it, or you shall die.'" (Gen. 3:2–3)

How did Eve know this? Presumably Adam taught it to her. The biblical text for some reason has chosen not to disclose this detail.

But our problems do not end here. When Eve repeats the command in the presence of the snake she does not repeat it word for word. She makes a slight addition: "We may eat of the fruit of the trees in the garden," Eve declares, but regarding the tree in the middle " 'you shall not eat . . . nor shall you *touch* it.' " Nowhere in the original formulation given to Adam do we see any prohibition against touching.

The Rabbis, as we have seen, were very careful readers of scripture. For them, no word in this sacred text was superfluous. If Eve added a word to the command, there must have been a reason. In their opinion, the cause of this innovation rested in faulty communication. Adam, they surmised, was suspicious of Eve's moral scruples. In order to protect her from any inkling of temptation, he decided "to hedge in" the original command with a protective fence. It wasn't enough that she be forbidden to eat; even drawing near to that tree must be off limits. "What was the hedge that Adam made about his words?" the Rabbis asked.

> Scripture says that Lord God commanded the man saying, "Of every tree of the garden you may freely eat; but of the tree of the knowledge of good and evil, you shall not eat; for in the day that you eat thereof, you shall surely die" [Gen. 2:16–18]." Adam, however did not wish to speak to Eve the way the Holy One, blessed be He, had spoken to him. Rather this is what he said to her: "But of the fruit of the tree which is in the midst of the garden, God said: you shall not eat of it, *neither shall you touch it*, lest you die" [Gen. 3:3]. (*The Fathers according to Rabbi Nathan*, 1)

One may be tempted to reason that this interpretation adds insult to injury. This postbiblical Eve is in an even worse position than her biblical counterpart. Even fencing in the original commandment ("don't eat") with a protective codicil ("don't even touch!") proved an insufficient defense.

Yet the Rabbis confound this expectation. Eve's sin was the result of Adam's *condescending attitude* toward her. And for this attitude, Adam would pay a price. Our midrash continues,

> At that time, the wicked serpent thought in his heart as follows: Since I cannot trip up Adam, I shall go and trip up Eve. So he went and sat down beside her, and entered into a long conversation with her. He said to her, "If it is against touching the tree you say the Holy One, blessed be He, commanded us—behold I shall touch it and not die. You, too, if you touch it, shall not die!" What did the wicked serpent do? He then arose and touched the tree with his hands and feet, and shook it violently until its fruits fell to the ground. (*The Fathers according to Rabbi Nathan*, 1)

What did Eve make of this demonstration by the serpent? She made of it just what her tempter had hoped. If touching it proves to be no danger, then eating it certainly would bring no harm. And so she concluded, with good reason, that "everything which my master admonished me at first are false." With that, she took of the fruit and ate.

Adam, it turns out, had built too big of a hedge around his words. Rabbi Yose concluded, "Better a [standing fence] of just ten handbreaths than one of a hundred cubits which has broken down." Had Adam not patronized Eve with his beefed-up version of the command, history might have taken a different course. Surprisingly, Eve is not the one to blame. Adam is.

A Two-Fold Command

Christian interpreters saw the same problem in the biblical text, but traversed a different terrain in search of an answer. For them, the command God gave to Adam and Eve had two parts: don't eat and don't touch. When Eve speaks to the serpent we don't learn a corrupted form of the command, but rather its original formulation. According to many Christian interpreters Adam heard an abbreviated version. The different formulations are simply a literary accident. We are to draw no larger conclusions about the faulty communication of the command from Adam to Eve.

The twofold nature of the original command is illustrated by Ephrem's poetic retelling:

> In the very center God planted
>   the Tree of Knowledge
> endowing it with awe
>   hedging it with dread,
> so that it might straightway serve
>   as a boundary to the inner region of Paradise.
> *Two things did Adam hear*
>   *in that single decree:*
> that they should not eat of it
>   and that by shrinking from it,
> They should perceive that it was not lawful
>   to penetrate further, beyond the Tree.
>   (*Hymns on Paradise* 3:3)

Eve's version of the command not only revealed that God had forbidden two different actions (eating and coming too close to the tree); it also revealed the geography of the Garden. For the only parts of the Bible that take great care about improper touching or encroachment are those texts that deal with the sacred. Adam and Eve were prevented from drawing near to the tree, Ephrem reasoned, because the tree was holy. The tree of knowledge guarded the most sacred enclosure, the inner sanctum that housed the tree of life (fig. 6). God had "hedged that tree with dread," the dread of the supremely holy. As befits such holiness, Adam was neither to eat from that tree nor "to penetrate further" and violate its sanctity. Adam knew the command as a bipartite interdiction.

A good number of Christian interpreters went another step beyond

Ephrem: Eden as a Tabernacle

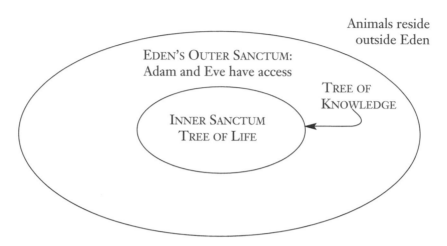

Figure 6
According to Ephrem, Adam and Eve have access to most of Eden. The animals live just outside the sacred confines, and Adam and Eve have to go to the edge of Eden to tend them. It is here, at Eden's border, that Eve converses with the snake. The TREE OF KNOWLEDGE guards the entry point to the Inner Sanctum, the Holy of Holies, wherein the TREE OF LIFE is found. Adam and Eve were not sufficiently holy at creation to enter this room, and if they hadn't disobeyed God's command, they would have been given access to the INNER SANCTUM. But since they tried to enter prematurely, they were driven out of Eden altogether. (See the story of King Uzziah in 2 Chronicles 26 for a parallel. Uzziah's story was a type of "Fall narrative" for Ephrem.)

Ephrem's map of Eden almost matches the maps of Eden in *Jubilees* and *Life of Adam and Eve*, but whereas Ephrem imagines a separate room enshrining the TREE OF LIFE, the latter two texts do not.

Ephrem. Not only did Adam and Eve hear the same command, but they heard it at the same time, from God himself. This is a surprising innovation because it would seem that the Bible is perfectly clear that Adam heard the command prior to the creation of Eve. To understand this detail we have to take into consideration the form of the early Christian Bible.

Christian interpreters were dependent on a Greek translation of the Hebrew original, the Septuagint as it is commonly known. This translation was the product of the Jewish community and probably had its origins in Alexandria. Yet the Greek Bible, by the time of the expansion of Christianity in the second and third centuries, assumed a Christian identity.

The Greek translation of our text is somewhat odd. Where the Hebrew original read,

> "But of the tree of the knowledge of good and evil, you [singular, like old English "thou"] shall not eat of it: for on the day that you [sing.] eat thereof, you [sing.] shall surely die."

the Septuagint translated,

> "But of the tree of knowledge of good and evil you [plural] shall not eat of it: for on the day that you [pl.] eat thereof, you [pl.] shall die."

Whereas the Hebrew original implies that there was only one person who heard the command ("thou"), the Greek requires at least two. By framing the command this way our translator left no room for ambiguity about those who are addressed: Eve was present along with Adam.

But now the narrative order of Genesis is problematic. How can Eve be present when she has not yet been created? Perhaps God was dropping a hint to Adam about the woman who was to come. Or maybe the narrative order of the story in Genesis did not coincide with the actual progression of events. In this case, God issued the command about the tree *after* the creation of Eve. This juggling of the biblical order was not uncommon in early Jewish and Christian exegesis. Indeed, we can find evidence of just this interpretation in certain Jewish circles. Consider this midrash, which retells the events of the first twelve hours of creation:

> How was Adam created? In the first hour the dust of which he was made was collected [Gen. 2:7]; in the second the model after which he was formed was created [1:26]), (. . .) in the sixth a soul was added to him [2:7]; in the seventh he stood upright on his feet; in the eighth Eve was joined to him [2:22]; in the ninth he was brought into the Garden of Eden [2:15]; in the tenth he was commanded [2:16–17]; in the eleventh he sinned [3:6–7]; in the twelfth he was banished and left the Garden [3:22–24]. (*The Fathers according to Rabbi Nathan*, 1)

The perspective on the first half-day in Eden is told from the view-point of Adam alone. But it is very striking that the command is given in the tenth hour, whereas Eve was joined to Adam in the eighth and they entered the Garden *together* in the ninth.

This ordering of events coincides precisely with the common understanding of early Christian interpretation. Compare this Armenian retelling of the story:

> And the Lord God brought a deep sleep upon Adam and he took one of his ribs, and he filled in flesh in place of it. And when Adam awoke from sleep, he saw the woman and approved [Gen. 2:22]. And Adam said, "Behold this is bone of my bones and flesh of my flesh. She shall be called woman" [Gen. 2:23]. And the Lord God brought them and put them in the midst of the Garden of Eden, which is very splendid and the Lord God commanded them and said, "You may eat from all the fruits of these trees, but you may not eat from the tree of life, nor may you touch it. For when you eat of it you shall die" [Gen. 2:15–17].

This retelling of the story has reordered the events in the way we would have expected from either the Septuagint or the Jewish midrash about Adam's first twelve hours. It has also included both parts of the command as part of God's own direction to the first couple. Let there be no mistake; Eve's version of the command was learned *directly* from God.

When we turn to early Christian iconography we find exactly the same thing. Nearly every depiction of the giving of the command shows Adam and Eve hearing it together. The upper half of an illustration from one medieval manuscript shows Adam, as he is molded by his creator and then, animated with the divine breath (upper register). The lower half of the same illustration (fig. 7) shows Eve, first, as she is being created, and then, united with Adam, while God is instructing them about the Tree of Knowledge. This reordering of scriptural events was not the result of artistic license, nor merely a matter of convention; it was a result of a dominant stream of biblical interpretation.

We have followed two different lines of interpretation, each involving a certain leap beyond the minimal confines of the biblical original. According to one view, Adam altered the command he heard from God when he spoke to Eve. This conversation is understood as implied by our text and sets the stage for Eve's succumbing to the serpent, who happens to know the true form of the command. Accord-

Figure 7
Creation of Eve, Giving of the Command
Hortus Deliciarum, Late twelfth century. (Warburg Institute, London)

The remarkable Abbess of Hohenbourg oversaw the production of an enormous encyclopedia which depicted the human drama from the moment of creation, through the events of the Old Testament and New Testament, until the end of historical time.

In this scene, the narrative order of Genesis is subverted. Whereas Genesis 2 recounts that Adam was created first (2:4–7), given a commandment (2:16–17), and only then received a spouse (2:19–24), the *hortus deliciarum* has it that Adam was created, then Eve was drawn from his rib, and finally *both* were given a commandment. In this artistic representation, a long-lived interpretive tradition has trumped the biblical text itself.

ing to a second view, Eve got the command right. This is because she heard the command along with Adam when God first delivered it. This perspective does not require us to add any implied conversation, but it does require a juggling of the narrative order. The moment of commanding (Gen. 2:16–18) must take place after the creation of Eve (Gen. 2:20–23). And for early Christians who read the Greek Bible, there was ample textual reason to suggest precisely this sort of juggling, for the command given Adam in 2:16–18 was given in the plural.

Both strategies have significant consequences for how we play out the matter of legal culpability for the Fall. If Adam misrepresents the command to Eve, then he bears the consequences for her disobedience. On the other hand, if Eve has heard the command directly from God, she stands without excuse when she chooses to follow the advice of the serpent.

Eve in Light of Mary

The almost unanimous decision by early Christian interpreters to understand the command as twofold left no room for an exoneration of Eve. When Eve sins, she follows her own lead, not that of Adam. Indeed, when one turns to Christian commentators on the role of Eve in the Fall, the rhetoric can be quite caustic, far more caustic and detailed than that of any known Jewish source. Eve is understood as gullible, dumb, beholden to the desires of her senses, and desirous of taking Adam with her when she falls. The picture drawn of her, and by extension the rest of the female gender, is not a flattering one. Why might this be? Was Eve, and hence the gender she represents, more negatively weighted in the early church than in Judaism?

There are some that would answer, "Yes." But I believe this fails to do justice to the problem at hand. For, as the church historian Jaroslav Pelikan has noted, one can *only* grasp the significance of Eve if one has some notion of how she points toward Mary. Conversely, one will not understand the figure of Mary unless she is seen against the backdrop of Eve. "The elaborations upon the disobedience of Eve," Pelikan writes,

> and the obedience of Mary [have] produced extensive psychological comparisons between the two women. In those comparisons the negative interpretation of woman as embodied in Eve—vulnerable, irrational, emotional, erotic, living by the experience of the sense rather than by the mind and reason, and thus an easy prey for the wily tempter—propagated the all-too-familiar stereotypes of misogynous slander that have so embedded themselves in the thought and language of so many nations, also but not only in the West.

Modern polemical writers, Pelikan further observes, have scoured the writings of Christendom to produce a massive catalogue of all these stereotypes. This massive catalogue is passed on from book to book, creating the impression that Christian writers had very little to say about Eve that was positive in nature. Those who seek to verify a charge that Christianity is hostile to women parade these proof texts about Eve as exemplary witnesses. Yet, Pelikan counters,

> those same works of patristic and Medieval thinkers presented a counterpoise to the stereotypes, in their even more extensive interpretations of woman as embodied in Mary, the "Woman of Valor (*mulier fortis*)" who as the descendant and vindicator of the First Eve crushed the head of the serpent and vanquished the devil.

If my thesis holds, that first things can only be understood by virtue of last things, then interpreting the figure of the "first woman," Eve, without recourse to the "last woman," Mary, will be a grave error.

Mary, Mother of God

In the fifth century C.E., an ecumenical church council met at Ephesus and declared that Mary should be addressed as *Theotokos*, or the "Mother of God." This title has been vastly misunderstood in the modern world. Popular opinion would have it that much of the reverence shown toward Mary in early Christendom was simply derived from Greco-Roman goddess worship. A Christian veneer was hastily and somewhat clumsily fastened to a widespread pagan practice. On this view, the veneration of Mary caused a dramatic setback in the advance of the gospel. It has no scriptural warrant. Rather it represents a capitulation to the vagaries of popular culture in the ancient world.

But this prejudicial evaluation of the status of Mary is overdrawn. To be sure, the development of Mary's character goes beyond scripture. But going beyond scripture need not mean eclipsing scripture. For the early Catholic world, the veneration of Mary was an *amplification* of scripture. The title *Theotokos* was given to Mary in order to safeguard the Bible's teaching about the incarnation.

In short, the sanctity of Mary depended on the fully divine status of her Son. If Christ really was *God* (a scandal to the ancient world even as it is to ours), and Mary bore him in her womb, then she could not have been unaffected by him. As the primal locus of the incarnation, Mary's womb had to be holy enough to contain God. It was out of reflection on the mystery of God's decision to take human form and inhabit a womb that the adoration of Mary as the "Mother of God" took root. Mary's womb became a veritable temple in which Mary wove the "garment of human flesh." And on these images of womb and garment I would like to pause.

Weaving the Body

At the close of Genesis 3, just when one expects God to cast Adam and Eve out of the Garden, our biblical writer pulls back the reins and allows the narrative line to take a brief respite. Two tangential but important matters need to be clarified: the name of Adam's wife and the apparel they would wear outside Eden.

> The man called the name of his wife Eve [*Havvah*], because she was the mother of all living [*hay*]. And the Lord God made for Adam and Eve garments of skin and clothed them. (Gen. 3:20–21)

In these verses Eve's role as progenetrix, or mother, of all who would come after her (thus the word play on Eve's name, *Havvah*, and the Hebrew word for life, *hay*) is linked to a curious description of God adorning Adam and Eve with garments of skin.

These vestments are a curious and difficult matter. As we shall see in a subsequent chapter, one line of interpretation among Jews and Christians understands these garments of skin as nothing other than mortal human flesh. Prior to their transgression, Adam and Eve were adorned with god-like bodies; now that they have sinned, they are forced to put on different dress. Because our fleshly bodies are prone to corruption, the claim that Eve is the mother of all living has a certain tragic tone. Through Eve's womb, the penalty of original sin will be passed on to all humanity. Eve and every subsequent mother shall "weave" garments of flesh for their offspring.

One might conclude that this image of the womb as a loom and Eve as a weaver is wholly negative. Through our mothers, we all bear the stain of original sin. But this is only one side of the equation. For it was through a woman's womb that the body of Christ was also woven—a body no different from the bodies we inherit as sons and daughters of Eve. As the one who helped "weave" the incarnate flesh, Mary was a guarantor of the essential humanity of Christ.

A formidable heretic group of the second and third centuries, known as the Gnostics, held the human body in utter disdain. In their view, Mary was but a tube through which divinity had passed. The Godhead was untouched and so unaffected by the body. But for the orthodox, Mary's *active* participation in the incarnation was an essential part of the gospel message. Christ was truly "born *of* [Greek: *ek*] the Virgin Mary." As the Nicene Creed explains, he did not simply "pass through [Greek: *dia*] her."

By choosing to be born of a woman, God sanctified the womb profaned in Eden. The first Eve is the mother of all mortals, but Mary, the "last Eve" or summation of all women, is the mother of all immortals. And those women touched by the gospel bear the imprint of both.

This double portrayal of "Eve as Mary" and "Mary as Eve" is well documented on the ceiling of the Sistine Chapel. There, as I have already shown, Eve's middle finger points to a womb that was the source of both sin and salvation.

Let us examine another example of such a double-faced Eve as found in the cupola of the Church of San Marco in Venice. The image in question is that of the expulsion (fig. 8). The mosaic itself was constructed in the Middle Ages as part of the church, but it harks back to an artistic model dating to the early patristic period, perhaps as early as the fourth or fifth century.

In this scene we see Adam and Eve after their expulsion from Eden. The image is puzzling. According to the Bible, life outside of Eden is supposed to be hard, if not downright cruel. Adam is doomed to till the earth by the sweat of his brow and Eve is to suffer mightily in childbirth. Yet in this visual depiction only Adam seems to bear the visible signs of any punishment. It is he who toils on the soil, while Eve sits on a throne, gazing on Adam and holding a distaff and spindle. Though Eve is clearly pregnant, there is no sign of impending pain.

This can be explained by means of a comparison. As has long been noted, this portrait of Eve is remarkably similar to the image of Mary at the annunciation found in the fifth-century church Santa Maria Maggiore in Rome (fig. 9). There, Mary, portrayed as the Mother of God, sits enthroned with distaff and spindle. The royal imagery is apt: she is the one who will weave the body of the incarnate Christ. Eve, as she is represented at San Marco, foreshadows this aspect of Mary. Indeed, we can legitimately ask whether we are looking at Eve or Mary. Surely, I want to argue, we are seeing both.

Figure 8
The Expulsion and Labor of Adam and Eve
Detail from the Creation cupola, San Marco, Venice.
(National Gallery of Art, Washington, D.C.)

Figure 9
Annunciation
Mosaic on triumphal arch, Santa Maria Maggiore, Rome.
(Alinari/Art Resource, New York)

It is striking to consider that Venice was founded on March 25, 421 C.E., the same date as the Feast of the Annunciation, when Gabriel appeared to Mary. It is certainly no accident that Mary is the patron saint of the city. But Mary was not merely that *unique* Mother of God who bore the Christ child. Mary was also a type of the *church at large*, and her obedient reception of Gabriel's proposal about the incarnation has always been a model for all Christian piety.

In thirteenth-century Venice this model of *imitatio Mariae* went even further. According to matrimonial custom, on the eighth day of marriage—which corresponded to the day Eve was evicted from Eden and became "the mother of all living"—women were given their own distaffs and spindles. The eighth day corresponds to the eviction from Eden but also to the day of the Lord's resurrection and new creation.

Eve's eviction was at one and the same time fit punishment for the Fall and the very means of its undoing. These newly married women, bearers of distaffs and spindles, have their wombs compared to that of the ever-virgin Mother of God. The children they were to bear were none other than the "image and likeness" God had intended at the very inception of the world. It would be hard to give a higher valuation of connubial love.

The Serpent Deflowered Eve

In spite of the rich associations of childbearing and salvation, one might argue that the image of women is still not salutary. After all, it could be argued, the author of 1 Timothy grounded the subordination of women in this very context:

> Let a woman learn in silence with full submission. I permit no woman to teach or to have authority over man; she is to keep silent. For Adam was formed first, then Eve; and Adam was not deceived, but the woman was deceived and became a transgressor. Yet she will be saved through childbearing, provided they continue in faith and love and holiness with modesty. (2:11–15)

For this writer, Eve's error has had the gravest of consequences. Not only is Eve to bear the punishments meted out in Genesis, but in addition she is forbidden any position of authority over men. Her only saving grace is her ability to bear children, a matter of importance, to be sure, but hardly just compensation for the other ills she must suffer.

I will begin my consideration of these verses from 1 Timothy with a very important apocryphal text from the second century, the *Protevangelium of James*. This book tells the story of the miraculous birth of Mary, daughter of the wealthy Joachim and Anna, her upbringing within the Temple, her selection by lot as the one to sew a veil for the Temple (the same veil that would be ripped in two when her son was crucified), and the virginal conception of the Son of God and his wondrous birth in Bethlehem.

Those raised in Catholic households will have no problem recognizing many of these details about Mary's life, nor will they appear unusual to anyone who is familiar with the rendering of Mary in Christian art. But it should be noted that, with the exception of the virgin birth, none of these well-known details about the biography of Mary can be found in the Bible. They owe their beginnings to the rich tradition of apocryphal narrative.

Of the large literature that grew up in wake of the interest and veneration of Mary, the *Protevangelium* takes pride of place as the earliest and most influential. Indeed it is striking how this text, composed already in the second century C.E., contains *in nuce* nearly all the details of Mary's life that would be the subject of further elaboration in the church.

As we have already seen, the treatment of Eve was nearly always correlated to that of Mary. The *Protevangelium* does not disappoint on this score. Indeed, it provides us with one of the more important, if not shocking, points of comparison. Mary was but a young maiden of just sixteen years when she was betrothed to Joseph, a much older man. Joseph did not seek out Mary, he was designated as her husband by lot and, against his will, was compelled to take the young woman under his wing.

Before their wedding, Mary resided in the Temple. Joseph had no need to attend to her and left her on her own. During this time, Gabriel appeared to Mary and she conceived. This angelic visit was unknown to Joseph but not the result. He was immediately shaken with fright:

> He smote his face, threw himself down on sackcloth, and wept bitterly, saying: "With what countenance shall I look towards the Lord my God? What prayer shall I offer for her? For I received her as a virgin out of the Temple of the Lord my God and have not protected her. Who has deceived me? Who has done this evil

in my house and defiled her? Has the story [of Adam] been repeated in me? for as Adam was [absent] in the hour of his prayer and *the serpent came and found Eve alone and deceived her and defiled her*, so also has it happened to me." (*Protevangelium of James* 13:1)

Joseph's retelling of Genesis is striking. While Adam was absent, the serpent found his way to Eve. No such story can be found explicitly in scripture, but it could be implied from the context. Eve, after all, speaks to the serpent on her own; Adam appears to have no role whatsoever in their conversation. Our author presumes that Adam was separated from Eve at the hour of the temptation.

According to another apocryphal text, the *Life of Adam and Eve*, Adam was busy in a different part of the Garden from where Eve was, and when it came time for prayer, even the angels who normally attended Eve left Eden to go worship God in the heavens. In this brief moment, while Eve was unattended, the snake saw the occasion for his approach and temptation. According to this text, Eve ate the fruit on her own and later gave it to Adam. But the *Life of Adam and Eve* does not seem to know a tradition that the snake had *deceived and defiled* Eve.

Where could this idea have originated? No doubt the prime suspect for this understanding was Eve's own attempt to exonerate herself. According to Genesis, Eve explained to God that "the serpent deceived me and I ate." This verse had a large impact on early Christian thought about original sin because of what happened to the word "deceive" when it made that short but treacherous journey from its original home in the Hebrew text to its exile within the Greek and Latin Bibles.

In Hebrew, the word for "deception" is somewhat rare but hardly ambiguous. It refers to an act of representing something as what it is not. When it was translated into Greek, however, the sense of deception remained but far more dangerous semantic cargo was taken on board. The Greek and Latin Bibles allow us to construe the verse as *an act of sexual seduction*. This fateful accident of overlapping semantic fields allowed for the creation of a far more pernicious picture of the deed Eve had wrought. Not only did she consume the forbidden fruit, but she was seduced by the evil serpent and engendered the demonic figure of Cain.

One could argue that the theme of Eve's demonic conception of Cain is an older Jewish tradition that was picked up by Christian writers who were looking for a suitable antitype to Mary's virginal conception of the Son of God. Indeed a tradition like this can be found in two Jewish sources: the *Targum Pseudo-Jonathan*, an Aramaic translation of the Hebrew Bible, and *Pirke de Rabbi Eliezer.* But both of these sources are very late, having been written nearly five hundred years after the *Protevangelium.* It is altogether possible that this tradition of a demonic conception by Eve came into Jewish materials from a Christian source.

She Conceived a Son through Her Ear

But the question of origins is not my interest here. What is striking, first of all, is *how* these two traditions of conception travel together in Christian materials. For whatever the origin of the idea that Eve had sex with the serpent, Christians preserved it because of its contrast to the conception of Mary. In fact, few Christian sources repeated the lewdest form of this tradition, that Eve actually had sexual relations with the serpent. Christian writers preferred to speak of Eve's conception of *death* (not Cain) through her obedience to the snake's *word,* or verbal suggestion. Through her ear, the organ of hearing, Eve conceived disease, decay, and death. Mary, on the other hand, knew an obedience of a different order. Her receptive ear to the word of the angel Gabriel resulted in the conception of the Son of God. This tradition of "conceiving through (obedient) hearing," *conceptio per aurem,* transformed the point of emphasis from carnal knowledge to an act of reasoned understanding and willed obedience.

This emphasis on a *reasoned* obedience originated in the story of the annunciation. In the Gospel of Luke, the angel appears before Mary and greets her with the words "Hail, O favored one! The Lord is with you" (Luke 1:28). But Mary does not respond to this friendly greeting with the customary hospitality of the Middle East. Instead she is troubled by the words and ponders what they might mean. The angel, evidently aware of Mary's perplexity, attempts to reassure her:

> Do not be afraid, Mary, for you have found favor with God. And now, you will conceive in your womb and bear a son and you will name him Jesus. He will be great, and will be called the Son of the Most High, and the Lord God will give to him the throne of his ancestor David. He will reign over the house of Jacob forever, and of his kingdom there will be no end. (Luke 1:30–33)

Unfortunately this explanation does not assuage Mary. She remains in doubt about the whole matter. She presses the angel with a question: "How can this be, since I am a virgin?" (1:34). The angel, in turn, declares that the Holy Spirit will come upon her and effect the birth of the child: "For nothing," he asserts, "will be impossible with God." Only at this point does Mary finally relent: "Here I am, the servant of the Lord; let it be with me according to your word" (1:38).

This text is striking in that Mary evidences such reluctance in view of the task appointed for her. Only after a long explanation will she say, "Here I am . . . let it be with me according to your word." This is a striking contrast to the example of Abraham. When God calls him by name, he immediately responds, "Here I am," (Gen 22:2), a biblical idiom that conveys a sense of complete availability for whatever mission might be commanded. Further, when Abraham is told that he must offer his first-born son as a holocaust sacrifice, he again responds with great haste, a point not lost on later interpreters. Abraham's obedience was total; he offered no hesitation to the Lord's desires. Mary, on the other hand, offers us a very different picture. Her obedience must be won. But Mary was never criticized for her reluctance; rather she was valorized. It was her mission to undo the docile gullibility of Eve. Indeed, for readers of the Latin Bible, the undoing of Eve's original error seemed indelibly inscribed in scripture itself, for the greeting extended to Mary by the angel Gabriel in Latin was *Ave* [*Maria*], a perfect reversal of *Eva*.

Mary as Archetypal Christian

This theme of Mary arguing with Gabriel reaches its highest pitch in a homily attributed (inaccurately) to Chrysostom in honor of the Feast of the Annunciation. This homily takes the form of an apocryphal elaboration on the meeting of Gabriel and Mary. Our homilist takes the bare story of Luke and amplifies its content so as to render clearly just why Mary is so hesitant in her response to the angel's proposal. When Gabriel greets her, Mary stands back in fright. "She stood aloof," our homilist records, "looking at the speaker through the corner of her eye."

She was astonished at the sight, but she weighed his words in her mind. "What was this greeting? . . . Either you are ignorant of common convention or you are testing whether I [like Eve] can be easily snared." Pondering the matter briefly in her mind, she resolves to dismiss her visitor. "Go away, go away Sir, from before me. . . . Do you wish to take me captive like Eve, the mother of our race?" Failing with her impassioned plea, Mary decides to threaten this stranger: "Before [my poor suitor] returns, be gone from my home, leave! He will not ask you for a reason; he is a jealous man. It is best that you go. Should he see you talking to me and about such improper matters you will be at risk of bodily harm."

The angel is undeterred by Mary's blunt rebuttal and not worried about the threat of Joseph's return. He continues to speak his message. When Mary hears of the wondrous son she is to bear she wavers for a moment, teetering ever so slightly toward consent. But quickly she reverses herself and takes the offensive. Like a skilled lawyer, she proceeds to take apart the case made by the angel. "You have stumbled unwillingly in your own words," Mary asserts. "Your own mouth accuses you; your own lips rebuke. A little earlier you said, 'The one to be born shall be called the Son of the Most High.' Now you say, 'Son of David.'" Mary is puzzled as to the identity of this child. How could he have both divine and human parentage? After a long discourse on the mystery of the incarnation, Mary comes to an understanding of the mystery before her. In the end, she consents to the mystery and the angel takes his leave. Christ will be born of Mary, but only when Mary is fully cognizant of the implications and yields to her task with prudent and wise resolve.

Nicholas Constas has written elegantly on the theme of *conceptio per aurem* and correctly observes that "the notion of Mary's conception through hearing was a theological shorthand, a signature flourish in whose arabesques were entangled a complex range of narrative, exegetical, and doctrinal traditions organized by the figures of Eve and Mary." Not only do literary texts evidence this correlation but so does early Christian art. In a tenth-century Coptic illuminated manuscript, the angel Gabriel and Mary point to her ear as if it were worthy of special emphasis (fig. 10). In addition, an Ethiopic depiction of the transgression shows the snake in a rigidly upright position with his mouth directly opposite Eve's ear (fig. 11).

Along these lines, I should mention the Egyptian necropolis of El-Bagawat. In the so-called "Peace Chapel," one finds a cycle of images that utilize the theme of hearing as an organizing principle. In the depiction of the flood, a large dove—itself a symbol of the Holy Spirit—emerges from Noah's ark, and instead of finding dry land on which to rest, it literally enters the ear of Mary. In the depiction of

Figure 10

Annunciation, from Egyptian synaxarium.

(The Pierpont Morgan Library, New York, Ms. M. 597, f. 1v.)

Mary and the angel Gabriel point to her ear as the location of obedient hearing and conception. Mary is seated on a large throne with a gold nimbus adorning her head. She holds a spindle in her left hand. The inscription between the two figures is the text of the annunciation from the Gospel of Luke. This is a book illustration taken from an early tenth century Coptic synaxarium found in Egypt. For a discussion of this image, see Urbaniak, *"Conceptio,"* pp. 167–68.

Figure 11
Eve Beguiled by the Serpent, from Ethiopia.
Sixteenth-seventeenth century. (Photo Researchers, Inc., New York)
In this image, the snake stands upright and speaks directly into the ear of Eve.
The upright posture is as one might expect, given that the serpent's punishment is to crawl along the ground eating dust as its food. The placement of
the snake's mouth adjacent to Eve's ear, however, cannot be explained on the
basis of the snake's pre-Fall condition. Its purpose is to inform us about Eve's
disobedient hearing. Many parallels to this motif exist, including numerous
examples where the snake is not standing upright. For a few of them, see
Baggatti "L'iconografia della tentazione," figures 3, 7, 12. Compare, also, the
fourth/fifth century wall painting found at El-Bagawat, Egypt, where the
snake speaks into Eve's ear and directly to the right, in the same image,
the dove enters the ear of Mary (Urbaniak, *Die "Conceptio,"* figures 1 and 2).

Adam and Eve both are shown flanking the tree around which a large
serpent has coiled himself. As Constas notes, "Not only is the figure
of Eve visually assimilated to that of Mary as her naked twin, but the
serpent is shown winding its way toward the ear of Eve, while Eve herself is depicted as gesturing prominently toward that same fateful
organ of sense."

The Angels Stood in Silence

The comparison of Mary to Eve gives us a much larger tableau against which we can view the matter of gender and sexual identity in Late Antiquity. If all we had was Genesis, we might conclude that early Christian writers were interested solely in condemning women on the grounds of their gullibility. But in Mary, we encounter an example of feminine obedience that rubs against the grain of these misogynistic stereotypes. Mary's obedience to the angel's charge was neither craven nor easily won.

In perhaps the most extravagant paean of praise to Mary, the late Byzantine writer Nicholas Cabasilas asserted that the Word could not take up residence within Mary *until* she had given her consent: "Let it be done according to your word." The angels stood in hushed silence awaiting the verdict from Mary. The very balance of human history and God's providential plan for that history hung on how she would respond. The hold of the human over the divine was never so powerful as on that fateful day of the annunciation. There, Mary redrew the course of all creation. "By the word (*logos*) of the mother," Cabasilas wrote, "the Word of the Father is fashioned, and the Creator is created by the voice of a creature. Just as when God said, 'Let there be light,' and immediately there was light, so too as soon as the Virgin uttered her voice, the true light began to dawn."

It is against this rich tableau of devotion to Mary that one must read the character of Eve. Eve is a Janus-faced figure for early Christian writers. On the one hand, she is the exact opposite of Mary. Her disobedience and conception of a demonic son, Cain, contrast with Mary's obedience and virginal conception of a divine son. But at the same time Eve anticipates Mary. And so, in the cupola of San Marco in Venice, Eve sits, with distaff and spindle, on her throne. Adam toils, she spins; they sinned, but *she* prepares the way of the Lord.

Chapter 5

Is Eve the Problem?

Adam was not deceived, but Eve, having been deceived, came into transgression

—1 Timothy 2:14

This text does not mean that Adam was less guilty, [indeed just the reverse] . . . for the Apostle Paul does not say "Adam did not sin" but, "Adam was not deceived."

—St. Augustine, *City of God* 14:11

There is a no more embarrassing remark about gender in the New Testament than the phrase that lies buried in the second chapter of 1 Timothy. Adam did not sin, this text declares, only Eve did. Can anything positive be extracted from this? The plain sense of scripture, modern readers would argue, puts the entire burden for sin upon the shoulders of the woman. But for early Christian readers the plain sense conveyed exactly the opposite: Adam was the one at fault, and Eve's guilt was of a far lesser variety.

Eve was Deceived

The rehabilitation of Eve in light of her virtuous counterpart, Mary, is one way of redressing what many have thought to be the worst effect of the story of the Fall: the preponderance of blame was pinned on a woman. Yet having followed in some detail how eager early Christian writers were to do exactly that, we have ignored the most difficult text in the entire Christian Bible about the person of Eve. In 1 Timothy 2:14–15 we find those fateful lines that have proved such a problem in our modern age: "*Adam was not deceived, but Eve, having been deceived, came into transgression. So Eve will be saved through childbirth, if she remains in faith, love, and sober chastity."* The message is about as clear as it could be: Adam was absolutely innocent; Eve was entirely guilty.

It would be hard to overstate the difficulty these verses have provided modern readers. The noted New Testament scholar, Richard Hays, has elegantly summarized the problem:

> The assertion that women will be saved through bearing children clashes flagrantly with Paul's profound conviction that all human beings are saved only by virtue of the death of Christ. The lame exoneration of Adam (2:13–14) also sits oddly in conjunction with Paul's portrayal in Romans 5:12–21 of Adam as the source of sin and typological representative of sinful humanity. The peculiarity of the passage has given rise to various imaginative exegetical attempts at damage control, but the overall sense of the text is finally inescapable: women (or perhaps wives) are to be silent and submissive and to bear children.

For Hays, the danger of 1 Timothy can be cordoned off by noting its peculiarity within the larger set of writings we call the New Testament. Hays believes that in order for a text to carry a strong moral voice it must resonate across a broad spectrum of New Testament writings. Because 1 Timothy is at variance to other voices in the New Testament, Hays is able to isolate and defuse its potentially combustive results.

But his methods are, of course, peculiarly modern in that they involve setting the biblical text against itself. He contrasts the historical Paul of the Epistle to the Romans with the author of 1 Timothy, an unknown person who wrote in Paul's name. And he then contrasts this anonymous imitator of Paul with the rest of the New Testament.

This is not an answer that would have resonated with early Christian readers. Yet for many of these readers—and here I am anticipating my conclusions—this text from Timothy was equally difficult and troubling. I urge some caution here, for I use the phrase "many of these readers" advisedly: the tradition of reading we are about to examine was not shared by all early Christians. As expected, many did use 1 Timothy as a point of inspiration for a more generally misogynistic evaluation. This can hardly be gainsaid.

Curiously, many of the texts that I will discuss are ignored in modern surveys of the problem. And these texts hardly constitute a minor voice. Quite the contrary. I shall consider three of the most important early Christian commentators on the Bible: Origen, St. Ephrem, and St. Augustine. And just as important, the reading of Augustine will have an illustrious "afterlife." It will live on in the work of Milton and Michelangelo. What we are to witness is not some blind alley in the history of Christian thought.

Origen: Eve as Bride of Christ

I would like to begin with Origen. Origen lived in the third century and was the most influential of all the early Christian commentators on the Bible. He was a rigorous philologian who also had a deep and abiding interest in the arcane matter of variant biblical readings. When he was living in Alexandria, he collected all the principal versions of the Bible that were known in his day and set them up in parallel columns. But his interests in scripture were not merely technical and scholarly. The vast tradition of mystical interpretation also has its beginnings in the interpretive methods of Origen. He was a profound theologian and a man of serious and earnest prayer. Over the course of his life he commented on nearly every book of the Bible and guided the church's interpretation of scripture for some centuries to come.

Though much of his work on the Bible has been tragically lost, we are fortunate to have Origen's exegesis of 1 Timothy 2:14. It is embedded in a commentary on the Song of Songs. The text that concerns us follows a citation of 1:6:

> "The Sons of my mother have fought in me, they have made me
> the keeper in the vineyards; my vineyard I have not kept."

For Origen, the central topic of this verse is the church ("Sons of my mother"), otherwise known as the bride of Christ. This identification of the church as the bride of Christ puts the individual members of the church in the role of a woman; it constrains the believer to think of himself as a woman. "The vineyards" refers to the divine inheritance or patrimony of the church, defined by Origen as sacred scripture. On the other hand, the claim that "my vineyard I have not kept" is understood as those poisonous doctrines that both Jews and Gentiles must jettison prior to joining the church.

This prods Origen to embark on a rather lengthy digression as to what we must be ready to cast overboard when preparing for membership in God's Holy Church.

But you should not be surprised that she who is gathered out of the dispersion of the nations and prepared to be the Bride of Christ, has sometimes been guilty of these faults. Remember how the first woman *was seduced and was in the transgression,* [1 Tim. 2:14] and could find her salvation, so the Scripture says, only in bearing children; which for our present purpose means those who *continue in faith and love with sanctity* [1 Tim. 2:15]. The Apostle, therefore, declares what is written about Adam and Eve thus: *This is a great mystery in Christ and in the Church* [Eph. 5:32]; He so loved her that He gave Himself for her, while she was yet undutiful, even as he says: *When as yet we were ungodly according to the time, Christ died for us* [Rom. 5:6]; and again: *When as yet we were sinners, Christ died for us* [Rom. 5:8].

Here we see a curious interpretation of 1 Timothy 2:14. Understanding this verse spiritually, Origen has extended the metaphor of the church as bride back to the beginning of time. The church takes its point of origin in Eve, the *"mother of all living"* (Gen. 3:20). It is Eve-as-church who *"was seduced and was in the transgression."* For Origen, Eve is not a representative of the female gender but a symbol of the entire body of believers. And this interpretation provides Origen with a perfect typology: *Just as the church must be understood as female in order to be understood as espoused to Christ, so we (both men and women) must imagine ourselves as Eve in order to understand the story of primal transgression.*

But this should give pause. Didn't Adam sin as well? Unfortunately we do not have the entire view of Origen on this complicated question. Much to our misfortune, due to the vagaries of text transmission and the unfortunate postmortem usage of a few of Origen's more speculative ideas, we no longer have his full commentary on Genesis 1–3. We do, however, possess the commentary of a near disciple, Didymus the Blind. And it is possible to use the evidence of Didymus to fill in what Origen has not left us.

Didymus also understood this text from Timothy allegorically. Adam was not deceived, he observes, because like Christ, he innocently went into exile to rescue God's espoused bride, Israel. Adam's venturing forth from Eden to Earth was typologically suggestive of the incarnation wherein God the Son left Heaven to come to earth to redeem humanity.

What is striking here is the fact that in this retelling, Eve is no more feminine than Christ is masculine. The sexual attributes of both are demanded not by the nature of the deity but by the needs of the erotic metaphor, bride and bridegroom. Consider the words of Gregory of Nyssa on this question:

> The divine power, though it is exalted far above our nature and inaccessible to all approach, like a tender mother who joins in the inarticulate utterances of her babe, gives to our human nature what it is capable of receiving; and thus in the various manifestations of God to humanity, God both adapts to humanity and speaks in human language. (*Against Eunomium* 2.419)

If we presume that Origen followed a line of thinking similar to Didymus's, then we can understand how easily and naturally he could take the more problematic part of our Timothy text—that women are saved by childbirth—in a completely nongendered way. For Origen the means of salvation was a life of virtue: to be saved by childbirth was nothing other than to be saved by abiding in faith, love, and sanctity. In this case, the gendered aspect of the biblical verse is deconstructed by Origen and then writ large over all humankind.

That Adam is for Origen not so much the progenitor of all males but the typological pointer to our redeemer is indicated by his very next comment: "The Apostle, therefore, declares what is written about Adam and Eve thus: This is a great mystery in Christ and in the Church; [Eph. 5:32] He so loved her that He gave Himself for her, while she was yet undutiful."

In sum, we find in Origen's interpretation of 1 Timothy a real paradox: It was Origen's allegorical approach to scripture that allowed him to understand 1 Timothy in a literal manner. Because Adam represents Christ and Eve the church, Origen can affirm, without the slightest blush, the text's simple sense: "Adam was not deceived, but Eve, having been deceived, came into transgression." But amid this affirmation of the simple sense of the text is an allegorical deconstruction of what it implies for gender roles. Adam is no cipher for all men nor Eve for all women. Adam points solely to God's Christ, a person who stands over and above all gender, whereas Eve is representative of all God's church, both male *and* female.

St. Ephrem: Citing Adam against Himself

The second patristic writer I would like to examine is the fourth-century Syriac theologian, St. Ephrem. Though less well known in the West, he was a prominent figure in the East. Besides being the intellectual giant of Syrian Christianity, he also loomed very large in Armenian and Russian Christianity. Indeed, the writings of Ephrem were so popular in the medieval Russian Church that Ephrem himself became one of the most important patristic thinkers in that tradition.

The first thing worth noting is that Ephrem does not introduce 1 Timothy when he reaches that portion of Genesis that talks of the transgression (3:6–7). He tells the story of the transgression without any reference to this New Testament text. For Ephrem, and he is quite emphatic on this point, the transgression is shared equally by Adam and Eve.

St. Ephrem's concern to treat both Adam and Eve as equally culpable is obvious from the way he puzzles over the chronological order of the transgression and its effects (Gen. 3:6–7). Ephrem believed, as did nearly all other patristic writers, that Adam and Eve were *clothed* in glory prior to their sin. This meant that the moment of transgression was marked by an *observable physical transformation*. The discovery of nakedness was no metaphoric allusion to an internal transformation; it marked the loss of something physically real.

If transgression led to visible change, a real problem would result if Eve sinned first and was thus de-formed. For if Eve transgresses first, and so loses her garment of glory, Adam will see this visible change and know what the results of eating the fruit are. In order to forestall any such advantage given to Adam, Ephrem observes,

> Having once eaten, Eve did not die as God had said, nor did she find divinity, as the serpent had said. For had she been exposed, Adam would have been afraid and would not have eaten, in which case, even though he would not have been guilty in that he did not eat, yet he would not have been victorious either, seeing that he would not have been tempted. It would have been the exposing of his wife that would have restrained him from eating rather than love for, or fear of, Him who gave the commandment. It was so that Adam might for a moment be tempted by Eve's blandishments—just as she had been by the counsel of the serpent—that she had approached and eaten, but had not been exposed. (*Commentary on Genesis, ad loc.* Gen. 3:6–7)

Adam's act of transgression was every bit the act of disobedience Eve's was.

Matters turn worse when Adam must account for his actions before the Deity. Adam, at this point, casts the blame on Eve: "The woman with whom you provided me gave of the tree and I ate." The self-righteous tone of Adam is emphasized in Ephrem's paraphrase of these lines:

> "I *myself* did not approach the tree, nor was it *my* hand which presumed to stretch out for the fruit."

Then Ephrem adds,

> This is why the Apostle too says, "Adam himself did not sin, but Eve [did sin and so] transgressed the commandment" [1 Tim 2:14].

By the very way Ephrem cites 1 Timothy, we can see he understands Paul's assertion, "Adam himself did not sin," in an ironic manner. First Timothy is not telling us anything new about the *nature* of the transgression; Ephrem presumes we all know that Adam most definitely did sin. Instead, Ephrem understands 1 Timothy as an allusion to Adam's cowardly act of dissembling before the Deity! It is as though the fact that Adam did not, himself, take from the tree somehow lessens the consequences of the act. Ephrem, in order to forestall any such foolishness, interrupts the third-person voice of his commentary and addresses Adam directly in the second person:

> But if He gave you a wife, Adam, He gave her as a *helper* and not as a harmer, as someone who receives instructions, rather than as one who gives orders. (*Commentary on Genesis, ad loc.* Gen. 3:10)

Ephrem's rare use of a direct address connotes an emphatic act of chastisement. Though Adam did not, in a technical sense, violate the commandment by taking from the tree himself, he is nonetheless just as culpable for what has transpired.

St. Augustine: Taking Scripture Literally

The most radical—and, by far, the most influential—approach to Timothy is found in the writings of St. Augustine. At first, this may strike one as all the more curious, for St. Augustine, in general, strives to be faithful to the literal sense of scripture. As we will see, part of the problem lies in the fact that moderns are heirs to a much different idea of the "literal sense" than was prevalent among the ancients. Augustine's interpretation will appear far more sensible if we bear in mind his approach to the Bible's compositional history.

Augustine's interpretation is of even greater moment than that of Origen or Ephrem because of his influence over later Christian thought in the West. His treatment of 1 Timothy has been quoted approvingly by most after him.

The problem that concerns St. Augustine is the relation of 1 Timothy to Romans 5:12–21 or, to be brief, the relation of a text that focuses blame on Eve to a text that pins all blame on Adam.

> We cannot believe that the man was led astray to transgress God's law because he believed that the woman spoke the truth, but that he fell in with her suggestions because they were so closely bound in partnership. In fact, the Apostle was not off the mark when he said, "It was not Adam, but Eve, who was seduced" [1 Tim. 2:14] for what he meant was that Eve accepted the serpent's statement as the truth, while Adam refused to be separated from his only companion, even if it involved sharing her sin. That does not mean that he was less guilty, if he sinned knowingly and deliberately. Hence the Apostle does not say, "He did not sin," but "He was not seduced." For he certainly refers to the man when he says, "It was through one man that sin came into the world," and when he says more explicitly, a little later, "by reproducing the transgression of Adam" [Rom. 5:12ff]. (*City of God* 14.11)

In brief, Augustine will not allow 1 Timothy to usurp the picture drawn by Romans 5. For Augustine believes, not unlike Hays and other moderns, that the affirmations made in Romans 5, like those of 1 Corinthians 15, proceed from the very heart of Paul's theology. If we are forced to read Romans 5 and 1 Timothy as part of the same inspired Bible, then the meaning and force of Romans will trump 1 Timothy.

Moderns and St. Augustine are on equal footing: both decenter 1 Timothy in favor of Romans. But things become more difficult and delicate when we consider what Augustine must do with 1 Timothy once he has subordinated it to Romans 5. Unlike Hays and other moderns, Augustine cannot propose that 1 Timothy was not Paul's writing, or that the doctrine of original sin was still taking shape in the first century and therefore allowed for several overlapping if not contradictory positions. Just because Romans has trumped Timothy, this does not mean that Timothy has lost all value. Augustine is bound by his sense of the inspired nature of all scripture to take every recess and corner of the canon seriously, however obscure and out of the way it may seem.

The text of Timothy as it stands must be interpreted and not in a way that sets it in contradiction to Romans. So, Augustine must reason, if we learn from Romans that Adam sinned and in so doing introduced death into the world, then 1 Timothy must qualify the *nature* of that sin not the *fact* of sin itself. "Adam was not deceived" cannot mean Adam was innocent; this would contradict the fact of Adam's sin that was established in Romans 5. It can only mean that Adam's sin differed from Eve's in the *manner* by which it took place. Adam's sin, Augustine is forced to conclude, was more a result of Adam's free will.

Augustine does not ignore 1 Timothy; he re-conditions it. First Timothy, so retrofitted, now fits better within the larger corpus of the Pauline writings. In a profound yet ironic sense, a reading one might have dismissed as wholly contrived appears more and more to be "the plain sense." Augustine's reading appreciates and respects the unity of the biblical witness. And this witness was not without significant heirs.

Milton and *Paradise Lost*

Although my next source—Milton's *Paradise Lost*—and the patristic tradition are far apart in time, they are not so far apart in ideas. This influential epic not only became a classic of English literature in the West, but it also achieved, in a odd way, a limited degree of authoritative religious status. I am thinking here of the peculiar but significant abridgment and annotation of this text done by John Wesley so that his newly minted pastors could have quick and easy access to the basic tenets of the Fall and redemption of humans.

For our purposes what is striking is Milton's strong continuity with patristic tradition, in particular with the figure of St. Augustine. C. S. Lewis, in his book *A Preface to Paradise Lost*, has documented very succinctly, yet ably, Milton's contacts with Augustine. Jaroslav Pelikan has also noted, rather wryly, Milton's dependence on the very patristic (and quite Catholic) notion of Mary as a Second Eve, despite Milton's frequent protests against all things Roman.

Catholic influence is particularly evident at the very moment Satan ends his discourse on the virtues of the forbidden fruit. Eve, standing in rapt attention, drinking in every word and syllable, proves an easy target for Satan's guile.

> [H]is words replete with guile
> Into her heart too easy entrance won:
> Fixed on the fruit she gazed, which to behold
> Might tempt alone, and in her ears the sound
> Yet rung of his persuasive words, *impregned*
> *With reason*, to her seeming, and with truth.
> (*PL* 9:733–738)

The curious phrase that Satan's words were "impregned/With reason" can only suggest our earlier trope of *conceptio per aurem,* "conception through the ear." But more important than the survival of this Marian idea is Milton's notion of how the guilt for the Fall was shared. And to this let us now turn.

Milton's story of the transgression begins, as does the biblical story, with the snake approaching Eve alone and engaging her in conversation about the tree. Eve, at first fearful of all things concerning this tree, slowly comes around to seeing the matter from the snake's point of view. The snake has argued that prior to his consuming of the fruit he had been mute like all the other animals. Yet upon eating from this tree not only did he not die, but he was given voice as if by miracle. Convinced of the snake's honesty and moral probity, she proceeds to praise the tree:

> Whose taste, too long forborne, at first assay
> Gave elocution to the mute, and taught
> The tongue not made for speech to speak thy praise.
> (*PL* 9:747–749)

If this tree could bring the dumb to the point of God's own praise, Eve reasons, then how could it be removed from human experience? "In plain then," Eve asserts,

> what forbids he but to know,
> Forbids us good, forbids us to be wise?
> Such prohibitions bind not.
>   (*PL* 9:758–760)

Eve sounds a philosophical critique similar to that of Immanuel Kant (eighteenth century). She claims that the law has been arbitrarily posited and so can impose no sense of duty. Human freedom can only be bound by laws that respect human reason and autonomy.

Eve, now truly deceived and convicted of her own good motives, resolves to consume the fruit:

> So saying, her rash hand in evil hour
> Forth reaching to the fruit, she plucked, she ate:
> Earth felt the wound, and nature from her seat
> Sighing through all her works gave signs of woe,
> That all was lost.
>   (*PL* 9:780–784)

Having eaten of the fruit, she turns to seek Adam to tell him of the wondrous tree. Adam will have nothing of this story. Quite the contrary, Adam recognizes from the very start the wrong that has occurred.

> Adam, soon as he heard
> The fatal trespass done by Eve, amazed,
> Astonied stood and blank, while horror chill
> Ran through his veins, and all his joints relaxed;
> From his slack hand the garland wreathed for Eve
> Down dropped and all the faded roses shed:
> Speechless he stood and pale.
>   (*PL* 9:888–894)

Though dumbfounded, Adam turns to consider his desperate state. Eve has eaten of the fruit and so is doomed to die. Adam, if he perseveres in his innocence, will condemn himself to a life alone. Immediately Adam sets to reasoning how this tragic circumstance might be averted. In so doing, he anticipates the very logic that Moses uses when he surveys the damage wrought by the veneration of the golden calf and hears of God's intention to destroy Israel down to every last woman and child.

> Nor can I think that God, creator wise,
> Though threatening, will in earnest so destroy
> Us his prime creatures, dignified so high,
> Set over all his works, which in our fall,
> For us created, needs with us must fail,
> Dependent made; so God shall uncreate,
> Be frustrate, do, undo, and labour loose,
> Not well conceived of God, who though his power
> Creation could repeat, yet would be loth
> Us to abolish, lest the adversary
> Triumph and say; Fickle their state whom God
> Most favours, who can please him long; me first
> He ruined, now mankind; whom will he next?
> (*PL* 9:938–950)

Adam, having given vivid expression to the predicament in which God will find himself should he be forced to destroy both Adam and Eve, now turns to his real concern: His overflowing passion and ardent love for Eve. Milton nearly becomes maudlin:

> So forcible within my heart I feel
> The bond of nature draw me to my own,
> My own in thee, for what thou art is mine;
> Our state cannot be severed, we are one,
> One flesh; to lose thee were to lose my self.
> (*PL* 9:955–959)

Adam's resolve to eat the fruit, whatever its consequences, moves Eve to great joy. She delivers a rather longish hymn of praise to Adam and, having finished, our narrator observes,

> So saying, she embraced him, and for joy
> Tenderly wept, much won that he his love
> Had so ennobled, as of choice to incur
> Divine displeasure for her sake, or death.
> In recompense (for such compliance bad
> Such recompense best merits) from the bough
> She gave him of that fair enticing fruit
> With liberal hand: he scrupled not to eat
> Against his better knowledge, not deceived,
> but fondly overcome with female charm.

Earth trembled from her entrails, as again
In pangs, and nature gave a second groan,
Sky loured and muttering thunder, some sad drops
Wept at completing of the mortal sin
Original; while Adam took no thought,
Eating his fill, nor Eve to iterate
Her former trespass feared.

(*PL* 9:990–1006)

The most striking line is also the most indicting line concerning Adam: "*he scrupled not to eat / Against his better knowledge, not deceived.*" In this line, as many commentators have long noted, Milton directly quotes our text from 1 Timothy.

Yet, and this aspect has rarely if ever been properly grapsed, he understands this text not in its simple sense. Rather, his understanding is very dependent on St. Augustine's daring misconstrual of the passage. For as we have seen, the simple sense of 1 Timothy demands that we put the onus on Eve; she was the root of the transgression. Augustine, however, by his gloss, stood the text from 1 Timothy on its head. In Augustine's reformulation of the verse, Adam was the chief culprit: "Adam was not deceived [for he sinned deliberately] but Eve having been [merely fooled] came into transgression." It was this Augustinian gloss that was holy writ for Milton, not the text itself.

The Sistine Ceiling

Michelangelo received his commission to paint the ceiling of the Sistine Chapel in the early sixteenth century. Originally, Michelangelo was commissioned to provide a rendering of the twelve apostles. Feeling that this was too insignificant a proposition, Michelangelo requested broader reign for his artistic talents.

Michelangelo, unlike many of his contemporaries, was not a simple, uneducated artisan. Rather, he was a deeply religious man who frequently attended Mass, pored over scriptural texts and commentaries, and, in his early years, was deeply moved by the infamous religious reformer in Florence, Savonarola. Like many in pre-Reformation Rome, Michelangelo was also deeply impressed with how the beginnings of creation not only were a witness to the glory of the Creator but also pointed, however mysteriously, to our end or *telos* within the cosmos.

It is worth mentioning that Rome, during this time period, was undergoing a massive revival of the study of the church fathers and a return to the scriptural texts in their original languages. Augustine loomed large in this era, for in his work *City of God* he, like his Renaissance counterparts, spent a good deal of time correlating the message of the Christian gospel to its near analogues in pagan culture. Augustine was also the favored thinker of one of the leading intellectuals present in the papal court, Egidio da Viterbo, who referred to Augustine as "my teacher" and did much to foster a renewed interest and appreciation for this seminal Christian thinker. There is little doubt that Michelangelo was dependent on some form of theological consultation regarding his subject, and it is possible that Egidio da Viterbo or someone like him provided that advice.

With these points in hand, we are ready to consider the sixth of the nine panels that make up the ceiling, the *Temptation and Fall of Adam and Eve* (fig. 12). This panel alters the more typical positioning where either Adam and Eve would flank the tree symmetrically, or Eve, alone beside the tree, would take the fruit and hand it to Adam. The striking features of Michelangelo's depiction are Adam and Eve together on one side of the tree, and Adam taking the fruit independent of any assistance from Eve. This stands in complete contrast to our biblical text, which explicitly states that Eve eats first and then gives some of the fruit to Adam.

In order to explain this, let us consider a few other compositional details. Consider the relationship of the snake to Adam and Eve. A first glance at this serpent reveals a similarity between the face of the snake and that of Eve. Their respective bodily postures also outline strikingly parallel contours, in particular, the lines that define both thigh and torso. One should add that the linkage of the snake to Eve is altogether common in early Christian art and commentary; Michelangelo seems to be following a conventional form.

This first reading of the image is something of a *trompe de l'oeil*, or optical illusion. Because one is so conditioned to expect these similarities, any hint of them conjures up this conventional reading. But we shall see that Michelangelo subjects this conventional image of Eve-as-serpent to a surprising reversal. Because they are so unexpected, the similarities between the snake and Adam are far more striking: The two figures share similar hair color, both are straining at the fruit— Adam to wrest it from the tree and the Serpent to give it to Eve— and most important, their muscles show the same tense constriction.

Figure 12
Temptation and Fall of Adam and Eve, by Michelangelo, Sistine Chapel Ceiling.
(Alinari/Art Resource, New York)

Indeed, both Adam and the snake are so intent on fulfilling their respective intentions that they must grasp and manipulate the tree for leverage as they lunge forward either with or at the fruit. The posture of Eve could hardly stand in bolder contrast. She sits in a reclined position as though a matron at a formal Roman dinner, and with little observable interest receives the fruit from the aggressive serpent. We might also add that a shadow casts a pall over the face of Adam. This is in strong contrast to the bright and vivifying light that adorns Eve.

This striking portrayal of Adam as an aggressive and active moral agent willfully, if not violently, straining to *seize* the fruit suggests an image of man that Christ decidedly avoided. As Paul so strikingly asserts in the famous lines from the Epistle to the Philippians (2:6), "though being in the form of God, he did not think that equality with God was something to be forcibly seized." In opposition to Adam, we have the serene and nearly angelic posture of Eve, who passively receives the fruit. This image, maybe better than any commentary, vividly portrays Eve's innocence relative to Adam's.

The accomplished art historian Creighton Gilbert has written quite elegantly on this subject, gender relations in the paintings on the Sistine ceiling, and has noted numerous other features there that serve to highlight the role of both biblical and pagan women. Most strikingly, he shows that such ideas were not out of the ordinary in Catholic Rome on the eve of the Reformation. Henricus Cornelius Agrippa, in 1509 at the University of Dôle, delivered a declamation on "The Nobility and Preeminence of Women" (*De Nobilitate et Praecellentia Foeminei Sexus*). This essay has been exceedingly popular among feminist scholars and has been hailed as an example of how the humanist movement within the early Renaissance period was able to subvert the misogynistic tendencies of earlier medieval Christian culture.

But Agrippa confounds such an evaluation. The intellectual pedigree of his text is not so much Renaissance humanism as it is 1 Timothy 2:14. But it is not 1 Timothy taken on its own but, rather, as it is refracted through St. Augustine.

> Man, had been forbidden to eat the fruit not woman, for she had not yet been created. God wanted her to be free from the start, so it was man, not woman, who committed the sin by eating, man not woman, who brought in death [*mortem dedit*], and we have all sinned in Adam [*et nos omnes peccavimus in Adam*], not Eve, and are charged with original sin not through the fault of our mother, a woman, but of our father, a man. . . . God did not punish the woman for eating, but having given man the occasion to eat, which she did from ignorance, tempted by the serpent. Man sinned in full knowledge [*ex certa scientia peccavit*], woman erred through ignorance and deception [*mulier erravit ignorans, et decepta*].

This declamation, which Gilbert rightly believes should be related to the *Temptation and Fall*, has drunk deeply from the history of exegesis we have documented. Yet Gilbert, as well as other feminist scholars working on this remarkable text, have missed the scriptural texts it depends on. The charge that Adam sinned and "brought in death" and that "we have all sinned in Adam" are clear allusions to Romans 5:12–14. Also, the claim that Eve "fell into error through ignorance *and deception*" while Adam violated the command with "full knowledge" is hardly intelligible apart from Augustine's reading of 1 Timothy 2:14.

Gilbert's selection of Agrippa's text as an apt parallel to the *Temptation and Fall* is brilliant. What is more, Agrippa represents not a stray and errant opinion in the sixteenth century, but an approach known to many; Gilbert errs in thinking that this insight was somehow privy to the Renaissance intellectuals of early sixteenth-century Rome. This text is not a salvo launched from the front lines of the Renaissance against an earlier, and now antiquated, Christian tradition. To the contrary, these ideas are as old as the patristic period. This particular Renaissance formulation is merely a more eloquent and systematic articulation of their logical tenor.

The Epistle to the Romans Trumps 1 Timothy

It is frequently stated that Eve, beginning with the first Epistle to Timothy, is subject to uninterrupted reproach from churchly elites. And there can be no doubt that this charge is often true. But clearly the evidence is not as uniform as might be expected. However we may wish to tell the story of Eve, if we wish to draw a complete picture, we must deal with all the data we have adduced here.

But more important is the question, How, in the end, are we to explain this sympathetic treatment of Eve? As a result of some unnoticed feminist undercurrent in patristic thought? I think not. The theological writers we have cited who picture Eve's guilt in a favorable light would not conform, in other aspects of their thought, to many other concerns of modern feminism. But then, how are we to explain this matter of culpability?

I would suggest that these ancient readers came to their position because they were skilled readers of *the full canonical form of their Bible*. They knew that Romans 5 presented a picture that cohered more naturally with the other voices of the New Testament. In the face of this strong headwind provided by Romans, the text of 1 Timothy 2:14 could do nothing but trim its sails and head for port.

But the premodern sources we have examined were also unique in one small but very important point. Having noted that 1 Timothy was a minority opinion, it could not be swept aside. Like rabbinic midrash, each verse of scripture pulsated with meaning; if its literal sense proved objectionable because it conflicted with another biblical text, then these two discordant voices would give birth to a third voice, frequently yielding a new narrative unintended by the biblical author(s).

And so it was for Romans 5:12 and 1 Timothy 2:14. One verse pins the blame on Adam, the other on Eve. But in the interpretive wrestling match that ensued, Romans pinned Timothy. The result: both are guilty, but Adam's guilt is greater than Eve's. This meaning is not found in either text on its own, but for most Christian readers of the premodern era, it was a meaning so obvious that it hardly needed argument.

Chapter 6

Garments of Skin

*Adam said to Moses: "I am greater than you because I have been cre-
ated [luminous] as the image of God" [Gen. 1:26]. Moses replied, "I
am far superior to you, for your glorious light was taken away but
as for me, the radiant countenance that God gave me [Exod. 34:
29–35] still abides."*

—*Deuteronomy Rabbah* 11:3

Among the saints none is naked, [Gen. 3:7a]
 for they have put on glory,
nor is any clad in those leaves, [3:7b]
 or standing in shame,
for they have found, through our Lord,
 the robe that belonged to Adam and Eve.

—*Hymns on Paradise* 6:9

*Even the most casual glance at artistic representations of Adam
and Eve will surprise. In contrast to the Bible, which says that this
couple was naked in Eden and clothed without, the artistic record
portrays Adam and Eve as clothed within and naked without. The
story of this dramatic reinterpretation is tied to a profound understanding of the importance of the human body. For both Jew and
Christian, the core of human identity does not reside in some
ethereal "soul" but in a very robust and full-bodied existence.*

A Rewritten Bible

The process of interpreting the Bible does not leave the sacred original unchanged. Just as last impressions can overtake and, not infre-
quently, completely expel the first, so the conclusion of an interpretive

117

argument can overwhelm its textual beginning. Such was the case in Augustine's reading of 1 Timothy. Milton cites it as though it were the plain sense itself.

Time after time in my research for this book I followed a tradition of interpretation only to see that in the end the biblical original had been completely transformed. In the case of Adam and Eve's culpability I saw that there was a fork in the interpretive path. Either Adam heard the command first from God and then taught Eve a new (and erroneous) form of that command, or Adam and Eve heard the command at one and the same time, but with two parts. No matter which option an interpreter chooses, the biblical story ends up in a different position from where it began.

These differences then became fully manifest in apocryphal retellings of Genesis and artistic representations of the same. I found that I could not understand what Milton or Michelangelo was doing if all I had in front of me was the bare biblical text. It was the shaping of that text through many centuries of interpretation that yielded the portraits they drew.

In this chapter I would like to examine what happened to Adam and Eve after they transgressed. According to what God had already said to Adam prior to the temptation, one would have expected to see Adam and Eve condemned to death. God clearly warned them: "On the day that you eat of it, you shall die." But this expectation immediately runs aground. God announces to Eve that she will bear children with difficulty and to Adam that he shall find the ground cursed and indifferent to his efforts (Gen. 3:14–19). No death.

To make matters more difficult, our author makes the most curious aside prior to expelling Adam and Eve from the Garden. In this brief interlude, Adam names his wife and then the Lord God steps forward, "and made for Adam and Eve garments of skin and clothed them" (Gen. 3:21). Adam and Eve don't die; instead they are given a change of clothes. They exchange their modest fig leaves for more substantial vestments—a truly extraordinary turn in our story. And things become even more peculiar when we turn to the iconographic representation of this scene. Almost no artist chooses to depict Adam and Eve as leaving the Garden clothed in such skins. This is clear in Michelangelo's *Temptation and Fall.* Adam and Eve leave the Garden naked. But doubly odd is the fact that many icons found in Greek and Russian Orthodox churches portray Adam and Eve as clothed in Eden (fig. 13).

Figure 13
Creation of the First Humans and Expulsion from Eden.
(Plate 14 from *Symbols of Glory: The Stroganov Icons*, La Casa di Matriona, 1992)

Though the Bible seems to be quite clear that Adam and Eve were "naked and without shame in Eden" (2:25) and only clothed at expulsion (3:21), the iconographic tradition reverses the matter. And this depiction is neither rare nor modern. Some of the earliest artistic depictions I have seen of this story show Adam clothed in regal glory in Eden.

Two problems, then, demand our attention: that of Adam and Eve's mortality and that of their apparel. In the minds of early Jewish and Christian readers, these two problems do not stand in isolation. If you figure out one, you solved the other. We have to start somewhere, so let me begin with the problem of mortality.

Did Adam and Eve Die?

A central problem of the story of the Fall is that Adam and Eve ate the forbidden fruit and did not suffer the threatened consequences. Indeed, Adam continued to live to the ripe old age of 930 years.

Before jumping straight into the problem, I must take a moment to establish the proper framework for interpretation. Adam and Eve, by virtue of the meaning of their very names, "man" and "life" respectively, represent the human condition as a whole. As has been noted, biblical writers believed that the human condition was best described through what happened to Israel. On the face of it then, we should expect some similarity between what happened to Adam and Eve and what happened to Israel.

And this expectation bears fruit. Just as Adam and Eve receive a commandment prior to their entrance into Eden, so Israel is given a set of commandments prior to her entrance into the Promised Land. Just as in the Garden Adam and Eve's well-being is predicated on their obedience, so for Israel. And, most important, just as the tree of life remains a tantalizing reward for Adam and Eve should they be found virtuous, so life itself is offered as a reward to Israel should they be faithful to the covenant.

Let's pause for a moment on this image of covenantal obedience as a path toward "life." In the Bible, there is a close relationship between life—understood as life lived before God in his holy land—and fidelity to God's commandments. The *locus classicus* is Moses' final speech to the people of Israel just before they enter the Promised Land:

> See, I have set before you today *life* and prosperity, *death* and adversity. If you obey the commandments of the LORD your God that I am commanding you today. . . . then you shall *live* and become numerous, and the LORD your God will bless you in the land that you are entering to possess. . . . I call heaven and earth to witness against you today that I have set before you *life and death*, blessings and curses. Choose *life* so that you and your descendants may *live*, loving the LORD your God, obeying him, and holding fast to him; for that means *life* to you and length of days, so that you may *live* in the land that the LORD swore to give to your ancestors, to Abraham, to Isaac, and to Jacob. (Deut. 30:15–16, 19–20)

The striking features of this text are the correlation of "life" with obedience to the commandments and the linkage of life to "blessing" and death to "curse." *"Life," in this text, does not refer to quantity of time but quality of experience*, that is, life lived in the presence of God, on his holy soil.

In the story of the Fall, I would suggest, we have a presentation of Israel's central story in miniature:

Eden	*Sinai*
God creates man	God elects Israel
Command is given	Torah is revealed
Violation	[Should] Israel violate the Torah
Expulsion from Eden	Exile from the Promised Land

If these parallel columns have any meaning, it is to underscore how the promise of life is related to the threat of death. In the sermonic language of Israel's covenantal charter, death was not defined simply as the termination of life. Death meant being deprived of God's blessing and bereft of life within his holy land.

It is not my point that Adam and Eve *already* enjoyed eternal life prior to their expulsion from the Garden. This would be to overread the story. But if Eden is conceived of as sacred space, it is hard to imagine just how they could have died had they been granted the opportunity to live out the rest of their days there. Eternal life was a possibility for Adam and Eve, but a possibility they never achieved. Transgression intervened; exile followed.

Who Shall Stand in this Holy Place?

This emphasis on eternal life as a quality of existence and not just duration in time is well reflected by early Jewish and Christian interpreters. For these readers, a life lived in the presence of God required a particular bodily form. They learned this from scripture itself. Temple-entrance liturgies, as found in the Psalms, frequently queried those reverent pilgrims who came to Jerusalem, to find out if they were fit to enter the City of God. "Who shall ascend the Mountain of the Lord?" the priests would ask. "Who shall stand in His holy place?" And the answer was as immediate as it was obvious: "Those who have clean hands and pure hearts" (Ps. 24:3–4).

These same requirements of bodily purity were imposed on Israel when she drew near to Mt. Sinai (Exod. 19:14). And for those individuals who were chosen to draw even closer to God and stand within his holy Temple, the requirements were stricter still. Besides bathing, they had to put on holy oils and special clothes. In fact, the vestments of the priest matched exactly those particular areas of the Temple to which he had access.

The Temple was divided into three gradients of holiness, each bearing a distinctive color and type of fabric for its wall tapestries and coverings (fig. 14).

1. The common priest wore garments that matched the tapestries and weavings of the outer court.
2. The high priest wore a more magnificent garment that reflected the holy room within the Temple.
3. And one day a year, on the Day of Atonement, the high priest put on a different set of garments altogether in order to enter the Holy of Holies.

Each time the high priest moved from one gradient of holiness to another, he had to remove one set of clothes and put on another to mark the change.

And now to the point: *If Eden was holy ground, then Adam's personal holiness must have approximated that of a priest.* And if Adam was like a priest, then one could presume that he was dressed like one. In the Old Testament, the closer a priestly figure gets to the Holy of Holies, the more elaborate his vestments. Each successive step toward God requires a different physical form. Origen, the most important Christian theologian of the third century, recognized this fact and realized the need to compare Adam to the high priest. Adam, Origen believed, had been wonderfully adorned in Eden. Like the high priest Aaron, his life before God was marked by glorious apparel. After his transgression, Adam was stripped of his glory and put on "garments of skin." These, Origen argued, were "a symbol of the mortality which Adam [fell prey to]" (*Homilies on Leviticus* 6:7).

At Sinai, God made his first concerted attempt to rectify this condition by ordaining that Israel wash and then put on new clothes. "When you have already been washed and purified through the Law of God," Origen declared, "then Moses will dress you with a garment of incorruptibility so that 'your shame may never appear' [Exod. 20:26] and 'this mortality may be absorbed by life' [2 Cor. 5:4]." And

Priestly Garments and the Garments of Glory

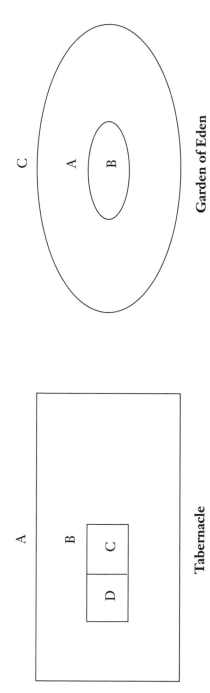

Tabernacle

Garden of Eden

Figure 14

Each zone of holiness in the TABERNACLE has a corresponding set of vestments associated with it. (a) Outside the Tabernacle priests wear ordinary clothes. (b) When on duty in the Tabernacle, they wear four pieces of clothing whose material and quality of workmanship match that of the fabrics found on the *outer walls* of the courtyard (Exodus 28). (c) The *High Priest* wears those four pieces plus four additional ones—these added garments match the fabric of the *Holy Chamber* where he must go daily to tend the incense altar. (d) A third set of clothes is required of the High Priest when he enters the *Holy of Holies* once a year on the Day of Atonement (Leviticus 16).

In EDEN a similar set of vestments is found, again each set suited to its particular space. (a) Adam and Eve were, at creation, vested like priests and granted access to most of Eden. (b) Had they been found worthy, an even more glorious set of garments would have been theirs (and according to St. Ephrem, they would have entered even holier ground). (c) But having failed in their test, they were stripped of their *angelic* garments and put on mortal flesh. Thus, when their feet met ordinary earth—the realm of the *animals*—their constitution had become "fleshly," or mortal.

what was done to Israel in this general way was done to the priesthood in a much more dramatic way. Priests' clothing anticipated the resurrection body that all would receive at the end of time.

There is a Jewish tradition that the high priest was exempted from the power of the angel of death while he wore those robes. Origen, who was aware of numerous rabbinic traditions, may have relied on this idea to draw his analogy. Regardless of source, it is striking to trace the course of Origen's exegetical reasoning. He begins at "the end" with the problem of Aaron's glorious vestments and then moves back to Eden to draw a picture of Adam as the antitype of Aaron. "Before we begin to say anything about these [magnificent priestly] garments," Origen wrote, "I want to compare [them] to those miserable garments, with which the first man [Adam] was clothed after he had sinned" (*Hom. Lev.* 6:7). Once again, the significance of Eden is only revealed when set against the backdrop of Sinai.

You Clothed Me with Skin

If Adam and Eve resided in Eden and enjoyed close communion with God, then it is logical to assume that they were "clean of hands and pure of heart." Like the people Israel at the foot of Mt. Sinai, this close proximity to God should have been marked by suitable vestments. But this puts us in a position of considerable narrative difficulty. The Bible seems to be quite clear that Adam and Eve were *naked* when they entered Eden and *clothed* when they left. Genesis 3:21 makes this, it would seem, crystal clear: "And God made garments of skin for Adam and Eve and clothed them." And then, in Genesis 3:22, God drives them from paradise.

But a closer inspection of this verse reveals a fissure or two in its simple foundation. Commentators of all eras have puzzled over two questions. First, just what were these garments—and where did they come from? Some have suggested the obvious: they were taken from animals. But this is problematic, for animals were not slaughtered until after the flood (Gen. 9:1–7).

A second question concerns the role of God. He is the one who clothes Adam and Eve. But why, we might ask, must *he* do it? They were fully capable of putting on their own fig leaves. Couldn't they put on their own tunics of skin?

Some Rabbis solved both of these difficulties with a single move. *They understood the phrase "garments of skin" not as a separate piece of clothing to be put on like a jacket but as human flesh itself.* In this view, Adam and Eve become fully human—meaning mortal flesh-bearing beings—just prior to their departure from Eden. This linguistic move does no violence to the Hebrew. Indeed, in the book of Job (10:11), one can find this exact idiom as a description of our human constitution: "You clothed me with skin and flesh." In his description of Israel's resurrection, the prophet Ezekiel (37:6, 8) describes the refashioning of the human form as an act of stretching skin over a frame made of bones.

But if this understanding makes sense of Genesis 3:21, it certainly wreaks havoc on the earlier narrative. If Adam and Eve put on human skin before leaving the Garden, what sort of "skin" do they discover after they eat of the fruit (Gen. 3:7)? To answer this problem, another wrinkle must be explored.

According to Rabbi Mcir, there was a copy of the Bible that had a different reading for Genesis 3:21 (*Genesis Rabbah* 20:12). Instead of saying that God dressed Adam and Eve in "garments of skin," it said that God had dressed them in "garments of light." This interpretation was derived from a wordplay in the Hebrew. The words for "skin" and "light" sounded exactly alike to a Hebrew speaker, so Rabbi Meir believed that God had vested Adam with a "garment of light." Adam and Eve, in this line of thinking, sinned, and only then put on mortal flesh (fig. 15).

For many Jewish interpreters, as with Origen, Adam's garments could not be separated from those of Israel or the priesthood at Sinai. According to a Samaritan tradition, Moses "was clothed with the image which Adam lost in the Garden of Eden" (*Memar Marqah* 5:4). In rabbinic sources a more common expression of this was the tradition that Israel put on crowns when they accepted the Torah. These crowns kept the angel of death at bay. When Israel venerated the golden calf, the crowns were stripped away and Israel returned to a mortal state. A classic proof text of this was Psalm 82:6:

> I say, "You are gods,
>   children of the Most High, all of you;
> nevertheless, you shall die like mortals,
>   and fall like any prince."

This verse was paraphrased "When you accepted the Torah you shined like the angels; but now, having worshipped the calf, you shall die like Adam." In both the rabbinic and patristic traditions a close relationship has been drawn between Adam's clothing in Eden and Israel at Sinai, a relationship that was not lost on Origen or other Christian readers.

Genesis 3:21 in Its Literary Context

The interpretation of Genesis 3:21 as the moment of Adam and Eve putting on human flesh creates some temporal problems for the events of Genesis 3. If, as this tradition presumes, the "garments of skin" signifies *mortal* flesh, then Adam and Eve should be clothed with them immediately upon their transgression. And if Eden is a place of supreme holiness, then expulsion from the Garden must follow the putting on of these "unclean" garments. The sequence of events in Genesis then proceeds as follows:

1. Gen. 2:25   Adam and Eve, being made in the image of God, were clothed in glory and hence naked of all signs of mortal flesh. As a result they knew no shame.
2. Gen. 3:1–6   The temptation of Adam and Eve.
3. Gen. 3:7   Upon transgression, three things occur:
   A. 3:21   Adam and Eve are *stripped* of their garments of glory.
   B. 3:21   They are *vested* with garments of skin.
   *In other words, 3:21 is both proof of their former glorious vestments and testimony to their present ignominious ones [so Rabbi Meir]. Also 3:21 and 3:7 refer to exactly the same moment in time.**
   C. 3:22–24   *Immediately* thereafter they are *cast from the Garden*.
   D. Events A, B, and C are instantaneous; they occur in a blink of an eye.
4. Gen. 3:14–19 The punishments are "discovered" *outside* of Eden. (See the next chapter.)

---

*See the commentary of the medieval Jewish interpreter Rabbi Shlomo ben Yitzhaq (Rashi) on 3:20–21, He is following the lead of *Genesis Rabbah* 18:6.

Figure 15

The Seventy Plagues of Adam

Like their Jewish counterparts, Christian commentators were very fond of the idea that Adam and Eve were clothed in glory in Eden and with perishable flesh on departure. The ubiquity of this tradition can be grasped by seeing how easily it worked its way into various early Christian narrative traditions. One of the most favored genres of early biblical interpretation was apocryphal narrative, or the retelling of the biblical story in contemporary idiom. By putting the Bible in their own words, early Christian writers could weave into their stories many treasured interpretive points.

One could compare this to the role of hymnody in eighteenth- and nineteenth-century evangelical Christianity. Hymns, under the guise of retelling the gospel story, worked into their lyrics many contemporary theological ideas. In this way hymns became very effective teaching tools for preachers and other church leaders. Similarly, early Christian apocryphal texts provided, in their compelling story lines, a marvelous opportunity to teach key biblical doctrines to the faithful.

Consider, for example, the remarkable picture of the Fall that is found in the *Life of Adam and Eve*, a text that probably dates to the first few centuries C.E. When Adam is on his death bed, he calls together all his progeny. When they have gathered, he retells the story of the Fall: One day while they were still in Eden, the angels ascended into heaven to worship their Creator. Satan saw that Eve was alone and took advantage of the opportunity to tempt her. First Eve, and then Adam, ate the fruit.

If our storyteller continued to follow biblical order, we would expect God to descend into the Garden, find Adam and Eve, and tell them of their punishments: for Eve, painful childbirth; for Adam, hard labor on the soil. But our writer takes what appears to be a completely unbiblical turn:

> When we had eaten, God became angry with us. He said, "You have scorned my commandment, I too will scorn you." And he sent seventy plagues upon us, to our eyes, and to our ears and as far as our feet, plagues and portents laid up in his treasuries.

The punishments found in the Bible have been ignored in favor of a quite different punishment, that of a mortal body ridden with disease. The reference to *seventy* afflictions is certainly a sign that the afflictions have *covered every inch of Adam's body*, seventy being a number of wholeness in the biblical tradition. In short, we have the exact same interpretive tradition in this Christian story that we found in Judaism: Adam has exchanged an angelic constitution for a mortal one. Chrysostom, a fourth-century theologian from the Syrian city of Antioch, summarized this line of thinking when he wrote,

> Let us both realize the degree and significance of the good things Adam and Eve had deprived themselves of through the trans-

gression of the commandment given them having been stripped
of an ineffable glory and life that was scarcely inferior to that of
the angels. (*Homilies on Genesis*, 18)

As soon as they put on mortal flesh, Adam and Eve became unclean
and were expelled from the Garden. The donning of ordinary flesh
and eviction from the Garden took place in the blink of an eye.
According to the fourth-century writer Gregory of Naziansus, a near-
contemporary of Gregory of Nyssa, "*at one and the same time* [Adam
and Eve] were both expelled from the Tree of Life and . . . put on garments of skin" (*Oration* 38.12). St. Ephrem was of a similar opinion:
"It seems likely to me that while their hands were on the fig leaves,
they found themselves dressed in garments of skin" (*Commentary on
Genesis, ad loc.* Gen. 3:21).

A basic assumption underlying all of these interpretive moves is that
of *bodily* holiness. If Adam and Eve resided in the very Garden of God,
then their physical form must have been of a commensurate status.
Because God was described in the Psalms as being "*clothed* with honor
and majesty, *wrapped in light* as though with a garment*" (Ps. 104:1–2),
then it follows that Adam and Eve, as God's very own image, approximated that form.

Construed this way, the loss of those glorious garments provides us
with the answer to our question. Adam and Eve *did die* when they ate
of the fruit. The loss of their angelic constitution entailed the onset
of decay and death.

But the emphasis of this understanding was larger than that of mere
mortality. Life and death, in the Bible, are not simply markers of a
physiological condition. The "life" Adam and Eve enjoyed in Eden
meant an "unencumbered access to the divine life," or *parrhesia* in the
language of the early church. Gregory of Nyssa writes,

> If, then, we should restore the divine image, from the foulness
> which the flesh wraps round it, to its primitive state, let us
> become that which the First Man was at the moment when he
> first breathed. And what was that? Destitute he was then of his
> covering of perishable skin, but he could gaze without shrinking
> upon God's countenance. (*On Virginity*, 12)

But such gazing directly on God's countenance is fraught with danger. Lest one be put at risk of death, rigorous purity is required, as it

was of the High Priest preparing to enter the Holy of Holies on the Day of Atonement. To preserve the creatures he had fashioned with his own hands and loved so dearly, God had to drive them from his presence. Exile was not simply punishment; it was a form of protection. For to remain before God in Eden, *while defiled by sin*, was to court unnecessary danger, perhaps even death.

Away from Eden, Adam and Eve could undergo the purification necessary for reentry. Men and women were created "to enjoy the Good in its purity," Gregory of Nyssa wrote,

> and to enjoy that is, in my judgment, nothing else than to be ever with God, and to feel ceaselessly and continually this delight, unalloyed by aught that could tear us away from it. (*On Virginity*, 12)

To behold and be ravished by the living God (*visio dei*), was not only the consummation of the mystic soul, it was the very pinnacle of all human aspiration.

Putting on the Garments of Christ

I could close here, for I have accomplished the primary goal of this chapter. Why didn't Adam and Eve die, many have asked? Well, they did, we have answered. They lost their original angelic bodies that allowed them to stand directly before God, and they put on perishable human flesh that allowed them to endure the earth.

But one detail remains. In Jewish sources, this theme of Adam's glorious garments is simply one Edenic trait among many. It receives no special emphasis in rabbinic literature. In early Christianity, on the other hand, it becomes *the dominant motif* that defines life prior to the Fall. What could explain this very different reception of a shared interpretive theme?

The answer lies in the liturgical life of early Christianity. The garments of glory assumed special prominence when they were absorbed into the rite of baptism.

The process begins in the epistles of St. Paul. In his Letter to the Galatians, Paul writes, "As many of you as were *baptized* into Christ have *clothed* yourselves with Christ" (3:27). The link between baptism and clothing is not hard to understand: after being stripped and immersed in water, the newly minted Christian was dressed in a white baptismal garment.

In his Letter to the Romans, Paul argued that a descent into the baptismal font was tantamount to descending with Christ into the realm of death,

> Do you not know that all of us who have been baptized into Christ Jesus were baptized into his death? Therefore we have been buried with him by baptism into death, so that, just as Christ was raised from the dead by the glory of the Father, so we too might walk in newness of life. (Rom. 6:3–4)

And in his Letter to the Corinthians, Paul described the resurrection as an act of "putting on immortality" (1 Cor. 15:53).

From these letters three sets of symbols emerge: first, baptism is marked by clothing; second, baptism is a participation in the death and resurrection of Jesus; third, resurrection is a putting on of immortality. All we need to do is add the theme of the stripping of Adam and the picture is complete: *At baptism the Christian is stripped of the garments inherited from Adam and vested with the token of those garments he or she shall enjoy at the resurrection.*

And, not by accident, the entire incarnate life of Jesus is read through the same lens: Prior to his incarnation, Christ resided in heaven clothed in glory. He descended to earth, assuming the garments of flesh bequeathed by Adam at his fall. There, he persevered all temptation and was obedient even to the point of death. As a result, God the Father raised him from the dead and reclothed him with a glorious body on Easter morning.

The best place to see how these themes were assembled into a single picture is in the actual liturgies of early Christian baptism. The catechumens, that is, those individuals who pledged to join the church, began their ordeal during the fast days of Lent. The process began with an act of "registration" wherein the catechumen and sponsor appeared before the gathered congregation. During this rite the name of the catechumen was registered and the power of Satan was renounced through a series of exorcisms. In one such rite, recorded by the fifth-century Syrian theologian Theodore of Mopsuestia, the catechumens were commanded,

> You stand, therefore, with outstretched arms in the posture of one who prays, and look downwards and remain in that state in order to move the judge to mercy. And you take off your outer

garment and stand barefooted in order to show in yourself the state of cruel servitude in which you served the Devil for a long time. . . . You stand also on garments of sackcloth so that from the fact that your feet are pricked and stung by the roughness of the cloth you may remember your old sins and show penitence and repentance of the sins of your fathers. (*On Baptism*, II, 32)

This act of stripping exposed the *shame* of the postulant. The process of redemption began by reenacting the sin of Adam.

At the close of Lent, at the great feast of Easter, another act of stripping takes place. While naked, the catechumen approaches the baptismal font in an entirely different state:

As when Adam was formerly naked and was in nothing ashamed of himself, but after having broken the commandment and become mortal, he found himself in need of an outer covering, so also you, who are ready to draw nigh unto the gift of holy baptism so that through it you may be born afresh, and become symbolically immortal, rightly remove your covering. (*On Baptism*, IV, 54)

This second state of nakedness was quite different from the first. The catechumens have now become like Adam and Eve before the Fall, knowing a nakedness *without* shame.

Let's stop for a moment and take note of the temporal sequence this rite imagines. The catechumens begin by stripping in order to reexperience Adam and Eve's shame after transgression. Now they have stripped again in order to lay claim on their state of innocence before transgression. In brief, time is unfolding in reverse direction from the Fall. They started outside of Eden in sin and now are on the verge of entrance into the glories of Eden itself. When they put on their baptismal garments the process will be complete: these robes are a sign of the glorious bodies they will inherit at the resurrection.

In a North African rite the catechumens not only stood on sackcloth at the beginning of Lent but they also trampled on a garment of animal skin. The allusion to the "skins" of Genesis 3:21 is clear, as is the promised punishment of Satan through the figure of the snake. According to Genesis 3:15 a descendant of Eve was promised the ability to trample upon the head of the serpent. By trampling on these skins, the cost of obeying that serpent, the catechumens enact their defeat of both Satan and the snake through whom he worked.

This typology is brought out also in the right of anointing or chrismation that immediately follows immersion in the baptismal waters. It was a standard feature of many early Christian oil ampoules to depict the cross of Christ as though it were the tree of life (fig. 16). In other words, the oil poured upon the catechumen was understood symbolically to derive from that extraordinary tree in Eden. Precisely this tree, that God denied Adam and Eve, is now available to the newly baptized.

The Last Become First

I have often participated in joint theological discussions between Western Roman Catholics and Eastern Orthodox. Frequently the discussion turns to variant understandings of the Fall. In the East, there is little affection for what those in the West call "original sin." The East would prefer to address the problem through the scriptural catchphrase "garment of skins." What we inherit from Adam and Eve is not so much the corruption of the will (so St. Augustine) but a perishable set of vestments (so St. Ephrem, Gregory of Nyssa, and many others).

To those brought up in the West, this sounds odd. How could one define the human condition on the basis of a stray verse at the conclusion of Genesis 3? The deeper I plunged into the literature of early Christianity and Judaism, the more clearly I saw the answer to this objection. This was no stray verse for these early readers of the Bible; it stood at the very heart of how Eden was imagined.

What struck me then, and still continues to do so, is how highly this stream of interpretation holds the figure of the human person. If I were to chart a graph of the hierarchy of creation I might start at the top with God the Father and work my way down through the archangels and angels until I reached the human realm. Yet the tradition of Adam and Eve's glorious vestments confounds such a configuration. Adam and Eve were *at least* the equal of the angels. And perhaps even more than that, as my discussion of the fall of Satan suggested. It is worth remembering that in the *Life of Adam and Eve*, when Satan complains about the honor due the human figure, he does not complain that Adam and Eve's (human) nature is lower than the angels. His only gripe is that he was born first. Evidently they are indistinguishable in nature. But with glory and honor, God has favored human persons over the angels.

With the tradition of Adam and Eve's garments of glory we have again witnessed the way scripture's *telos*, or "end," has configured its

Figure 16

Ampoule

From a fifth–sixth-century collection from Monza, Italy.

The Greek inscription reads: "Oil from the Tree of Life." Notice that Christ is crucified on a cross that looks like a tree—the actions of the first Adam are undone by the second. And those who benefit are the recently baptized, who enjoy the healing oils that were denied Adam once he was evicted from paradise.

beginning. There can be no doubt that for many of these early interpreters the priestly garments of Aaron were a crucial piece in the puzzle. What Adam lost in Eden was recovered, at least in part, at Sinai.
Or perhaps I could put the matter in the reverse: what God intended
to reveal fully at Sinai was given in part in Eden.

Christians took the matter one step further. For them, the moment
of salvation was realized when Christ descended from heaven to live
among those exiled from Eden on earth. This descent to earth was
described by many writers as the putting on of a garment of human
flesh. Mary, in the iconography and apocrypha of the early church,
was a weaver. At the annunciation she holds distaff and spindle, symbolizing the holy body she will weave within her immaculate womb
(fig. 17, see also figs. 8 and 9). Indeed in the language of St. Ephrem,
the term for incarnation meant precisely this: "to put on flesh as
though it were a garment" (Syriac: *lbesh pagrâ*).

The theological idiom of the incarnation, coupled with the fact that
Christians were joined to Christ by a liturgical act of clothing (baptism), drew a bold and indelible line between contemporary Christian
experience and the Garden of Eden. Adam's life was refashioned so as
to become the inverse of the Christian. Vested in glory in Eden, Adam
and Eve were stripped and driven out clothed in mortal flesh; Christian catechumens correspondingly were stripped of their prior clothing, instructed in the faith, and then clothed in glory at their baptism
on Easter morning. Last things have come full circle; they have
inscribed first things.

Figure 17
Annunciation
Mosaic on triumphal arch, Santa Maria Maggiore, Rome.
(Alinari/Art Resource, New York)

Chapter 7

Punishment or Penance for Adam and Eve?

*Scripture says: "You shall eat the grass of the field like an animal"
[Gen. 3:18]." How are we to interpret this? When Adam heard this,
his face shook in remorse and he said, "Am I to be bound to a trough
like an animal?" God replied, "Since your face has shook in remorse,
you shall eat bread."*

—Genesis Rabbah 20:10

*Adam ate, together with the beasts
   as a result of the curse, [Gen. 3:18]
grass and roots,
   and he died, becoming their peer.
Blessed is He who set him apart
   from the wild animals again.*

—Hymns on Paradise 13:5

Adam and Eve leave the Garden and are given their penance:
they are to eat grass and roots just like the animals of the field.
This curious punishment is meant to teach them how far they have
fallen from the angelic existence they once knew and enjoyed in
Eden. For those who follow in the footsteps of this first couple by
assuming similar penitential disciplines, Jewish and Christian
interpreters alike promise re-entry into Eden. What begins as an
object lesson in the difficulty of human life after the fall becomes
the very pattern of life required to secure salvation. What may
appear as a tool of humiliation becomes the necessary means for
glorification.

Context is Everything

For everything, to paraphrase a line from Ecclesiastes, there is a context. Even the most elementary student in a foreign language learns

how important linguistic context is for the determination of meaning. Verbs derive their meaning from prepositions that follow. Sentences, in turn, require larger paragraphs. And, frequently, a whole composition requires a particular setting in life in order to be understood.

For example, consider the sentence "I don't think Darwinian theory can bear the weight put upon it." This sentence may seem clear, but consider its placement in two different contexts. If the issue at hand is a vigorous discussion of creationism with some holding forth that the world was created in six days just a few millennia ago, then this sentence would indicate that the speaker agrees with the creationist position. In this situation, to side against Darwin would be to take a position contrary to the geological record.

On the other hand, if the discussion revolved around those who accept the general thrust of Darwin's proposal but do not believe that random mutation and natural selection are sufficient to explain the appearance of *Homo sapiens*, then such a sentence would be construed differently. A disagreement with Darwinian principles would simply leave the speaker on one side of an ongoing intellectual dispute among the scientific community.

Though I knew the significance of context at a theoretical level, at the practical level of my own research I had not given it serous enough consideration. But one afternoon, while reading Chrysostom's homilies on Genesis 2 and 3, I noted that they were given during the forty days of Lent. Lent is the time in the church year when members of the church take stock of their moral and religious life of the previous year and appeal to God's merciful and sustaining hand. Lent is also the occasion for preparing those who would like to join the church and undergo the rite of baptism on the Saturday evening just prior to Easter morning.

What this social context of Lent requires, then, is some deep familiarity with the rite of penance and forgiveness. This is a detail that is lost on many contemporary critics of the Christian doctrine of original sin. This teaching was never meant to stand as a contextless statement of fact: human beings at their core are selfish and out for their own gain. Instead, the knowledge of human sin grows deepest as one plumbs the vast depths of divine mercy.

A sort of inverse chemistry is at work here; it is as though one gets warmer and warmer the colder the air becomes. This ironic reversal was perhaps best captured by Pascal in his famous remark that humankind could be divided into two camps: the righteous who know that they are sinners, and the sinners who think that they are righteous. In some sense, the experience of Lent is that of moving from the latter category to the former. The true depths of human sin are only known to those most attuned to the power of mercy.

I will begin this chapter, as usual, with the text of Genesis and those points in Genesis where moments of penance and forgiveness might be found. But to sustain a full inquiry into this problem, I must make a rather significant detour. I will explore a contemporary Jewish short story about a Hasidic holy woman. Hasidism, as this movement is known in English, was a fervently pietistic strain of Jewish life that flourished in eighteenth- and nineteenth-century Eastern Europe. It produced a prodigious literature about various spiritual adepts and masters. This tale will reveal much about the religious life and help us situate the penance of Adam in its proper life setting.

Did God Forget the Snake?

After Adam and Eve sinned and covered themselves with fig leaves, God appears. According to our narrative, the Creator is taking a stroll through the Garden in the cool evening breeze when Adam and Eve hear his approach. Immediately, Adam and Eve seek refuge among the trees, being shamed by their naked state. God calls out to Adam, "Where are you?" To this question Adam lamely replies, "I was naked and I hid myself." "Did you disobey my command?" God inquires. "Well, yes," Adam answers, "but it was the woman you created for me who gave me the fruit!"

Next, God turns to Eve and questions her. A similar sort of dissembling occurs. Eve absolves herself by declaring that the serpent had fooled her.

The scene comes to a close with God turning to the serpent, Eve, and finally Adam in order to announce their punishment. The serpent is to go upon its belly and feel animosity toward the woman; Eve is to bear children with great effort and pain; Adam is to till the soil and eke a living through arduous labor.

The story is constructed in nearly perfect symmetry. God descends to the Garden and inquires about the motives of first Adam and then Eve. Having heard their stories, he proceeds to judge all three but this time reversing the order: first, the snake, then Eve, and finally Adam. The snake's place in this sequence is awkward. He is the first to be punished but not the last to be interrogated. In fact, *God never asks him about his motives in the whole sordid affair.*

The ancient Jewish author of *Jubilees* noted this odd detail about God's passing over the snake in silence. Although he faithfully followed scriptural text for most of this judgment scene, he adds one small detail to the punishment of the snake. Instead of inquiring about motives, *Jubilees* records that "the Lord cursed the serpent *and he was angry with it forever*" (3:23). This reference to everlasting anger is found nowhere in the Bible. It begs for some explanation.

And that explanation is grounded in the larger purpose of this entire narrative scene. God descended to Eden to question Adam and Eve about their misdeed. But what was the purpose of this interrogation? Certainly God Almighty knew what these two people had done. He didn't need to be informed.

The answer is as immediate as it was obvious to nearly every early Jewish and Christian interpreter: *in order to give Adam and Eve an opportunity to repent.* The serpent, for some unexplained reason, was afforded no such opportunity and so "God was angry with it forever."

St. Ephrem follows a train of thought very close to that of *Jubilees:*

> When [Adam and Eve] had been questioned and found to be lacking in contrition or valid excuse, God descended to the serpent, *not with a question*, but with a *punishment.* For where there was a possibility of repentance He made use of questions, but with a creature that is alien to repentance He employed a sentence of judgment. (*Commentary on Genesis, ad loc.* 3:14)

Because the serpent was often understood to be a cipher for Satan, this motif of punishment without repentance took on added importance. Christians held that Satan's fall was categorically different from that of Adam and Eve. Satan was not and never will be afforded any chance at repentance. Human beings, on the other hand, are offered the opportunity to mend their ways from the age of majority until the close of their lives. For men and women, God's mercy has no bounds.

God Had No Time for Punishment

There is yet another important wrinkle in this story of God's punishments for the Fall. To the naïve reader of Genesis, it appears that the punishment is painful childbirth for Eve and toiling on the soil for Adam. Yet, as we saw in our previous chapter, the donning of garments of skin had trumped these punishments. The onset of human decay and death became the fitting consequences of primordial sin.

Because Eden was the spot of supreme holiness, mortal flesh rendered Adam and Eve unfit to remain there. According to many interpreters, they sinned and then were *immediately* expelled. It happened in the blink of an eye.

Didymus the Blind, a fifth-century theologian from Egypt, offers a very striking picture of how this chronology affected the story line of Genesis. If Adam and Eve were immediately expelled, then God's question to Adam, "Where are you?" takes on an ironic tone. It can no longer be a innocent inquiry about Adam's hiding place in the Garden, for he had already been expelled. It is, rather, a searing indictment of Adam's ignominious state after the Fall. Didymus transformed God's question about Adam's whereabouts into a simple declaration: "Adam, you are now in an [earthly] place (*Sur la Genèse*, 253).

This dramatic alteration of chronology is also paralleled in a mid-third-century Jewish work, *Genesis Rabbah*. There, the question God poses to Adam, "Where are you?" (Hebrew: *ayyeka*) is reread as "O how [well] it was with you previously" (*êk hawah leka*). What had been a question about Adam has become an expression of lamentation over his fall:

> I brought the first man into the garden of Eden, commanded him, he transgressed, and I judged him with an act of sending forth and an act of expulsion, then I mourned over him. "O how well it was with you previously!" (*Genesis Rabbah* 19:9)

The order of events is remarkable. After the transgression (Gen. 3:7), God expels Adam and Eve (Gen. 3:22–24) and only then addresses them with this lament (Gen. 3:8). In other words, the interrogation and punishments occur *after* the expulsion of Adam and Eve (fig. 18).

Did God Punish them Twice?

An interpretive picture is slowly coming into focus. Adam and Eve sin, are clothed with human skin, and then driven from the Garden. Outside the Garden, God approaches them with yet more bad news. As if the loss of their angelic bodies is not sufficient punishment, God

---

Genesis in Its Literary Context

The Punishment of Adam and Eve (Gen. 3:14–19) *follows* their eviction
from the Garden (Gen. 3:22–24).

1. Gen. 3:1–6   Temptation of Adam and Eve.
2. Gen. 3:7   Upon transgression three things occur:
   A. Adam and Eve are stripped of their garments of glory (3:21).
   B. They are vested with garments of skin (3:21).
   C. *Immediately* thereafter they are cast from the Garden (3:22–24).
   D. Events A, B, and C are instantaneous; they occur within the blink
      of an eye.
3. The punishments are "discovered" *outside* of Eden (3:14–19).
   A. Because the loss of the angelic vestments is thought to be the true
      cost of the Fall, the biblical "punishments" must be re-cast.
   B. Punishments are no longer the cost of the Fall; they are the means
      of restoration.
   C. Adam and Eve become model penitents.

Figure 18

seems to declare that matters are even worse: Eve shall suffer birth
pains and Adam, endless labor on the land. The punishments are pil-
ing up, and God is on the verge of appearing vindictive.

In order to forestall such a conclusion about the divine nature, our
interpretive tradition must make one more turn. Perhaps this last set
of punishments is not what it appears. God is not getting even; he is
marking out the way of a return.

For modern readers this may seem peculiar. Punishment is not seen
as a form of rehabilitation. Our struggle with this point reflects a set
of profound changes over the past century or two. Modern persons
have found it increasingly difficult to understand, and so sustain, the
penitential disciplines of fasting, temporary sexual abstinence, and
other forms of bodily deprivation. Not even the Catholic tradition—
where these disciplines were at one time deeply entrenched—has been
immune. As testimony to this, simply witness the disappearance of
abstinence from meat on Fridays. Yet just a few centuries earlier, it
would have been inconceivable to think that reconciliation could be
achieved without some form of penance. Where moderns see painful
punishment of the body, early Jewish and Christians readers saw the
very enactment of redemption.

King Nebuchadnezzar's Reform

A striking illustration of this can be found in the narrative about the punishment of King Nebuchadnezzar in Daniel 4. This infamous king of Babylon became one of the most despised figures of the Bible. It was he who stormed the city of Jerusalem, razed its Temple to the ground, and carried its most precious vessels, along with a good portion of the city's population, back to Babylon. Though initially called by God to carry out this duty as punishment for Israel's apostasy, he fell into disfavor by taking too much delight and pride in his accomplishments.

Here our story turns grim. This presumptuous king does not simply lose his right to rulership. He descends even lower still. "You shall be driven away from human society," Daniel announced,

> and your dwelling shall be with the wild animals. You shall be made to eat grass like oxen, you shall be bathed with the dew of heaven, and seven times shall pass over you, until you have learned that the Most High has sovereignty over the kingdom of mortals and gives it to whom he will. (Dan. 4:25)

Outside of the gates of Babylon, Nebuchadnezzar became like a beast of the field. In a quick reversal of the evolutionary cycle, he went from human to animal form.

What is truly striking, however, is not the nature of the punishment but the goal toward which it leads. Though this architect of the first Jewish diaspora deserved terrible punishment, scripture speaks of a higher and more noble aim. "You shall be driven away from human society," Daniel writes, ". . . until you have learned that the Most High has sovereignty over the kingdom of mortals and gives it to whom he will." This is not simply measure-for-measure justice; God's intention is not to get even but to instruct and transform.

The earliest form of this biblical story was written in Aramaic. This version leaves open the question of whether Nebuchadnezzar took the lesson to heart and was transformed. Though he praises God in the end, we don't know if this praise was a begrudging acknowledgment of God's authority or a reflection of change in the person and piety of the king. What is striking, however, is that within just a generation or so from the penning of these lines in Aramaic, a Greek translator added several new features to the story, including Nebuchadnezzar's confession. In the Greek version, Nebuchadnezzar was restored because of his personal contrition and repentance.

The Prayer of Manasseh

This transformation of a sinner into a hero has ample biblical precedent. A model can be found in the person of King Manasseh. This apostate king of Judah was responsible for undoing all the religious reforms put in place by his father, King Hezekiah. As a result of Manasseh's wicked rule, the author of the book of Kings condemns him in the strongest terms possible; he is made the primary cause for the exile of Israel at the hands of Babylon some fifty years after his death. In short, it is the apostasy of Manasseh that occasions the rise of Nebuchadnezzar.

Yet for all this bad press, King Manasseh is rehabilitated by a latter Israelite historian, the author of the book of Chronicles. According to this book, written as a revision of the book of Kings, Manasseh was a man who had come to terms with his own apostasy. He turned to God in sorrow over the tragic nature of his rule. So moving was the Chronicler's achievement that an even later writer memorialized his words of contrition in a book entitled The Prayer of Manasseh. This prayer became a model of penitential prayer for much of the ancient and medieval world. To this day it remains a part of the Catholic Bible.

A similar theological transformation happened with respect to King Nebuchadnezzar. Though his deeds of wickedness were nearly unmeasurable, he emerged—at least in early Christian circles—as the quintessential penitent. Tertullian, a third-century Christian theologian from North Africa, had only the highest words for praise for this king of Babylon:

> Will the sinner knowingly spurn *exomologesis* [a technical expression meaning public confession of sin and bodily penance], which has been instituted by God for his restoration? That *exomologesis* which restored the king of Babylon to his royal throne? Long did he offer the Lord a sacrifice of penance, performing his *exomologesis* for seven squalid years, his nails growing wild like the talons of an eagle, his hair unkempt like the shaggy mane of a lion.
>
> *Oh the blessedness of this harsh treatment!* One whom men shunned with horror, God received! Pharoah in Egypt, on the contrary, pursuing the people of God . . . perished in the parted sea, passable to none but the chosen people, when the waters rolled back upon him. For he had rejected penitence and its instrument, *exomologesis. (On Penance,* 12)

From these words of Tertullian we can learn why the model of Nebuchadnezzar's penance was so appealing. *If even this king could be saved*—a king who had ransacked, profaned, and completely razed the very temple of the Lord—*then no one could possibly lie outside the boundaries of God's mercy.*

Adam and Eve in Dust and Ashes

Nearly all of the themes I have been tracing come together in a single, well-ordered apocryphal narrative, the *Life of Adam and Eve.* This tale, which had wide currency throughout the Christian world, from Ireland to Armenia, told the story of Adam and Eve's life after the Fall. It begins where the Bible leaves off: Adam and Eve are outside of the Garden attempting to make their way in a world they do not recognize.

They begin by making themselves a hut to live in and weeping over the life they have lost. After seven days, they embark on a search for edible food. In the Garden, they had feasted on the food of angels (*esca angelica*), but now, in exile, all they see is the provender of cattle.

When their first attempts fail, they decide to escalate the severity of their penitential discipline. Adam commands Eve to "go to the Tigris River and take a stone and place it under your feet and stand in the water up to your neck" (*Life* 6:1). Adam, for his part, will do the same thing in the Jordan River. Adam urges Eve to remain in the river for thirty-four days "until we learn that God has hearkened to us and will give us our food" (*Life* 6:2). Numerous calamities happen along the way but Adam perseveres. As a reward, the archangel Michael appears and bids Adam to leave the Jordan. He gives him seeds for the sowing and reaping of grain. The horrible punishment of being forced to eat food like the beasts has been averted; Adam's vocation as a sower of grain begins.

By the Sweat of Your
Brow You Shall Eat Bread

The penitential appeal for better food has no explicit counterpart in the Bible. Genesis simply records that Adam and Eve left Eden (Gen. 3:22–24), and shortly thereafter Eve gave birth to Cain and Abel (Gen. 4:1). The textual gap between Genesis 3:24 and 4:1 passes over their transition to life outside the Garden in silence.

But early Jewish readers found hints of this transition stage already tucked away in the corners of Genesis 3. These ancient readers were drawn to the curious diction of the curse upon Adam. According to the Bible, God issued this decree: "*[The earth] shall bring forth thorns and thistles for you; and you shall eat the grass of the field; but by the sweat of your brow you shall eat bread.*" But this struck a discordant tone among many early readers. In the first chapter of Genesis, creation ended with God granting human and animal life their distinctive forms of food. Man was to eat grain sown by seed (1:29) whereas the animals were to eat the green grasses of the field (1:30). If this fact was established as the norm at creation, then it could not serve as a punishment as well.

The answer to this problem, Jewish interpreters reasoned, was simple: Adam's initial punishment was that he should become like the animals. He would be given the *grass of the field* in place of the grain sown by seed. Like King Nebuchadnezzar, Adam was reduced to the state of an animal.

This ingenious solution, however, brings in its wake another problem. If Adam and Eve were condemned to eat the "grass of the field," allocated to the animals, then we should expect to hear something about it. Yet the biblical text is silent. Was this a punishment that was never carried out?

Some retellings of the Bible solve this problem by leaving out this particular punishment, evidently sensitive to the interpretive problems it created. But the rabbinic move was more striking:

> Scripture says: "*You shall eat the grass of the field [like an animal].*" How are we to interpret this? When Adam heard this, his face shook in remorse and he said, "Am I to be bound to a trough like an animal? God said to him, "Since your face has shook in remorse, *you shall eat bread.*" (*Genesis Rabbah* 20:10)

This interpretation has understood the Hebrew verb "to perspire" (by the *sweat* [of your brow]) as closely related to the verb, "to shake [with remorse]." This slight shift in the meaning of the verb resulted in a completely new story line: First, Adam is told he is to eat food fit for animals ("you shall eat *grass* . . ."). Second, in remorse over how far he has fallen, his face begins to shake uncontrollably ("because your *face shook* . . ."). Finally, when God has taken notice of Adam's display of regret, he rewards him with better food ("you shall eat *bread*").

This rabbinic interpretive tradition provides the backbone of our story in the *Life of Adam and Eve*. After the fall, Adam and Eve have only the food of animals to eat. They undergo arduous penance; God takes note of their remorse and gives them seeds to grow cereals. Although this interpretive tradition arose in a Jewish environment, it quickly assumed Christian dress. First of all, Adam makes amends for his sin by doing penance in the Jordan River, the same river Christ would be baptized in. But equally important is the observation that Adam spent forty days in the Jordan. This exactly matches the period Christian penitents spent in prayer and fasting during Lent, as they awaited full redemption from the Fall through the saving action of Christ.

Nebuchadnezzar as Second Adam

The story is not quite over. Our early interpreters draw one further analogy that transforms this piece of interpretive information into a template for the religious life.

By reducing Adam and Eve to the state of animals after the Fall, a clear analogy was drawn to the punishment of King Nebuchadnezzar. Indeed, no other person eats the grass of the field apart from this king. Surprisingly neither the Rabbis nor the author of the *Life of Adam and Eve* made any connection between these two events. But the significance was not lost on St. Ephrem.

In his *Hymns on Paradise*, Ephrem recounts the glorious kingdom that God had conferred upon Adam. Eden was a "glorious garden, a chaste wedding canopy" that God gave to Adam, "that king created from the dust." In order to signal the distinctive honor given this first "king," God "separated and sanctified him from the abode of the wild animals." Adam resides and is feted within the holiest portion of Eden; the animals make their way on abundant but far poorer fare on the outskirts of Eden. Adam was superior, Ephrem sings, with respect to his "home, food, radiance, and dominion." Having portrayed the glorious honors that accrued to Adam, Ephrem turns to consider the king of Babylon. Like Adam, Nebuchadnezzar had been a king graced with universal sovereignty, and like Adam he had "lifted [himself] up and was brought low."

Having drawn these general parallels, Ephrem turns to points of more specific interest. Adam sinned "by means of an animal" and so "God likened him to the animals. Thus he and they ate, by way of a curse, herbs and roots." This depiction of Adam consuming roots and tubers follows the exact contours of the interpretive map drawn by the rabbinic sages and the *Life of Adam and Eve*. Ephrem, however, does them one better by comparing the condition of Adam to that of Nebuchadnezzar:

> In that [Babylonian] king
>   did God depict Adam:
> since he provoked God by his exercise of kingship,
>   God stripped him of that kingship.
> The Just One was angry and cast him out
>   into the region of wild beasts;
> he dwelt there with them
>   in the wilderness
> and only when he repented did he return
>   to his former abode and kingship.
> Blessed is He who has thus taught us to repent
>   so that we too may return to Paradise.
>   (*Hymns on Paradise* 13:6)

As we know from Daniel 4, Nebuchadnezzar was also cast out of his royal palace and forced to roam the steppe like a wild animal, consuming whatever roots and herbs he might find. But Nebuchadnezzar, unlike our *biblical* figure of Adam, repented and so "returned to his former abode and kingship."

One could surmise that Ephrem knew our Jewish tradition about Adam's penance. But even if he did, Ephrem's interests are fundamentally different from those of his Jewish source. For the Rabbis had no interest in restoring Adam to the glory of Eden. Such a restoration would have to wait until Sinai. Ephrem was also reluctant to restore Adam; his restoration would have to await the incarnation.

Does this mean that the entire period between creation and Christ was bereft of hope? No. The Old Testament, in Ephrem's eyes, provided numerous glimpses of the era of ultimate salvation, and one of those glimpses came through the story of King Nebuchadnezzar.

Ephrem conceded that for those of us who live many millennia after the fall of Adam, it is not always easy "to see [the extent of] our fall; How and from where we fell at the beginning." We fool ourselves into thinking that things are not so bad. Why bother with penance? Knowing this tendency toward sloth, scripture engraved our human condition in the story of Nebuchadnezzar. "God depicted [through] his fall," Ephrem wrote, the "way of our fall; and our repentance, by way of his repentance."

In Nebuchadnezzar one can see the entire human condition in summary form. Graced with honors beyond numbering, the king grew proud. In punishment for this overweening pride, God transformed him into a beast so that he might rue his haughty state. But God did not stand by idly and watch this sinful man suffer. Nebuchadnezzar's prayer of contrition moved the Merciful One to pity. He restored the king to his former glory. And so, Ephrem sang, may it be for us: "Glory be to Him who traced this model for each [subsequent] penitent."

Though Nebuchadnezzar's contrition and confession became models for Western Christians, there is no evidence that the specific discipline this king underwent was ever copied. Contrition in the West involved prayer, fasting, putting on sackcloth, and abstention from sexual relations, but it did not require roaming the fields like an animal.

Such was not the case in the East. In Syria, just a few decades after the death of St. Ephrem, we read of certain holy men who followed in the footsteps of our Babylonian king. These holy men roamed the steppes and forests, foraging among the roots and tubers, drinking from streams, and allowing their hair and nails to grow, wild, like the animals.

Though it is unlikely that Ephrem himself knew of such persons, it is clear that his writings were a source of inspiration for those who would follow this path. In a composition entitled *Letter to the Mountaineers*—attributed to Ephrem, but certainly not written by him—we see the transformation of Adam and Nebuchadnezzar into model Christian penitents:

> [Nebuchadnezzar] was like Adam who went forth from Paradise and dwelt with the animals and ate grass and made his dwelling with the wild asses. Now you surely know to what location God cast that king and you have heard that his sins were forgiven in the wilderness, amid the dwelling of the beasts. From there he was taken back to his royal palace and his glory returned to him. You have run to the wilderness like him. And in the grass of the earth you have made a dwelling so that you might effect reconciliation. From there you shall be transferred to Paradise and the glory of Eden will be returned to you.

Holy Men and Women

This tradition of Adam's foraging among the roots and tubers of earth as a form of penance had a long chronological reach in Syrian Christianity. Bar Hebraeus, a twelfth-century Syrian theologian, said this about Adam's punishment, to eat the "grass of the field" (*Scholia on the Old Testament*, 27): "[From this] it is known that the house of Adam lived an ascetic life until the Flood, without fat and strong drink." Adam's life, understood in this fashion, formed the theological basis for the ascetic practices of those religious virtuosi we call holy men and holy women.

The importance of the holy man should not be underestimated. As Peter Brown put it, whereas the high Middle Ages put a premium on the great cathedrals, for earlier Christian thinkers "the *locus* of the supernatural was thought of as resting on individual men."

The two great centers of ascetic activity were Egypt and Syria. The former produced the infamous figure of Anthony, immortalized in the *Life of Antony*, penned by the Egyptian bishop St. Athanasius. The latter produced not just the foragers of the Syrian steppe, but also that peculiar breed of holy man who preferred to dwell on the top of a tall pole, exposing his body directly to the elements.

The best-known of these pole dwellers was St. Simeon "the Stylite" (born 389 C.E.), whose fame instantly spread around the known world. Theodoret, the fifth-century theologian, wrote that the pilgrims came to visit Simeon from as far away as Armenia in the East and Britain in the West (*Monks of Syria* 26). "In death," Sebastian Brock, a contemporary historian, observed,

> the saint was even less safe than he was in life from the attention of pilgrims, eager for relics, and the various parts of his body eventually ended up in a large number of different places.

In the eyes of their adorers, these holy men and women had anticipated in their manner of living (Syriac: *dibore*) the life Adam had known in Paradise. This was no easy life to be sure. And it will come as no surprise that the image of an athlete in training frequently served as a metaphor; the ascetic was "in training" to "compete in contests" as a "mighty athlete." Martyrdom was also a frequent metaphor, for like the martyr, the ascetic was preparing to risk all for the rewards of the kingdom.

What is striking, however, is that the language chosen is almost always the language of glory. These holy men and women were not, however, simply depriving themselves in hope of a future glory. They were enjoying, already in this life, the fruits of the world to come. They were not models of the old Adam but the new. "This style of life," Brock concludes,

> was in fact a return to . . . the life of Adam in Paradise before the Fall: the ascetic was thus entirely free to be in perpetual conversation with God, while he was in complete peace and harmony with his sole companions, the wild animals.

Brock's conclusion struck me, when I first encountered it, as somewhat odd. The sort of life that defines these holy men does not seem to fit a *redeemed* Adam, who has reentered Eden. Brock continues:

> [The holy man] lives out in the open, completely exposed to the elements and extremes of heat and cold; he eats roots and wild fruits, his clothing—that is, if he had any at all, and many had not—consisted of straw or leaves tied together; his hair was so shaggy, and his nails so long that he resembled a bird of prey more than a human being.

This description fits Adam *outside* of Paradise, not within. How could Adam's penitential behavior, in which he was likened to an animal, be reconciled with his earlier life of angelic glory?

The Story of a Hasidic Holy Woman

I must confess that I puzzled over this matter for some time until I stumbled upon a short story written by the modern Israeli novelist Shai Agnon. The story is titled "Tehillah," and it is about a holy woman of the same name. She hails from somewhere in Eastern Europe or Russia and immigrates to Israel in the mid-nineteenth century prior to the advent of Zionism.

Tehillah is a woman of considerable wealth when she arrives in Israel, but in a short time she dissipates all her wealth, giving it out in the form of charity to those who she believes are most deeply in need. Having exhausted her material wealth, she becomes equally lavish with her time and energy, spending it on the needs of Jerusalem's poor and destitute. Day and night she roams the city seeking new causes for her concern.

The protagonist of the story—by whom the entire story is narrated but about whom we learn almost nothing, including his name—meets her in the very opening of the story as he seeks out the home of a wise scholar and friend. Evidently lost, he bumps into Tehillah, who is carrying a bucket of water. He asks her about the whereabouts of his friend, and she volunteers to take him there personally. He initially refuses, for he does not wish to trouble her further. She politely upbraids him by asking,

> "Why do you care if this old lady has the possibility of fulfilling a commandment?" I said to her, "Well, if it's a matter of a commandment, then fulfill it! But at least let me take the bucket of water." She smiled and said, "You want to lessen the value of the commandment?"

The conversation is typical of the entire story. Tehillah operates in a world of holiness; she seeks at every opportunity to shower deeds of loving-kindness on those she meets, and the more difficult the deeds, the more meritorious they become. The protagonist, on the other hand, lives in a less holy world, a world bound by the conventions of propriety and politeness. No need to be overly solicitous of a stranger, he reasons; no need to underestimate my desire to serve, she answers. His position is not morally unsound. Her position is simply on a different moral level altogether.

Tehillah's attitude toward goodness is rooted in her sacramental sense of *mitzvah* or "commandment." For many Christians the commandments found in the Bible are nothing more than a list of do's and don'ts. At their best, they tell us the minimal expectations God has for his creation. But in Jewish tradition the commandment embodied much more than this. It was a gift of God given to his people so that they could openly display their love and devotion to him. Fulfilling a commandment is like offering flowers to a new-found love; though the lover is following a social convention the deed springs from a far deeper font. Tehillah, like a young lover, delights in the opportunities she finds to shower those she meets with these signs of her devotion to God.

But Tehillah is more than her good deeds. Our protagonist is captivated by her person and cannot grasp just what motivates her. In a conversation with the Talmud scholar, he asked just who she is. He was told,

"What is there to say about her, she is a saint, a saint pure and simple. If you can go see her, go! But I doubt that you will find her at home. Either she is visiting the sick, or attending those who are beyond cure or attending to some other commandment that is not required of her. Maybe you will find her at home for in between doing these commandments she goes home and sits down to mend clothes for the orphans and the poor. When she was wealthy she used her money for charity, now she does charity with her person."

And as these good deeds accumulated over time, they transformed the person who did them. Though Tehillah was a model of pious self-effacement, her transformative power was considerable. Once, while standing near the Western Wall, the protagonist laments the fact that the return to Palestine during the British mandate has not improved Jewish life. He, Tehillah, and other Jewish brethren watch hopelessly as a British soldier ruthlessly kicks a chair out from under an elderly woman, knocking her to the ground.

This brutal act was founded on a silly legalism: she had violated a law set down under the mandate that disallowed any stools near the Wall. As the protagonist saw it, the Jews who milled around were helpless: "Those praying grew silent; who is able to bring judgment upon the stronger one?" But Tehillah was undaunted; the protagonist relates: "That same elderly woman whom I had recognized came and looked at [the British soldier]. The officer lowered his eyes and returned the stool." With a presence stronger than any words, Tehillah stilled the wrath of the enemy.

A preternatural aura surrounds the person of Tehillah from the very beginning of the tale. In the very opening sentences we learn that "she was a righteous woman, wise, graceful and humble. The light from her eyes was that of loving kindness and mercy, the lines upon her face were those of blessing and peace. If it were not for the fact that women cannot be compared to angels, I would have thought her to be an angel of God."

Her angelic stature emerges frequently over the course of the book. Most striking is the fact that she does not age in the conventional fashion. Although she is over one hundred years old she appears to have aged only half that many years. And in the end, her death is unlike that granted to most mortals. One almost gets the impression that like Enoch or Elijah she was simply taken into heaven. As the protagonist greets her on her last day, the day she knows will be her last, he remarks at the clean and brilliant character of every detail in her room. She either stayed up all night to clean this space, the protagonist imagines, or angels came and did it for her. On the morning after her death, her room is vacant. The story ends as mysteriously as it began: "A peaceful silence filled the room just like in a prayer-room after prayer. On the floor of the room were the remains of the water used by those who purified Tehillah."

A Holy Life Spun from Tragedy

If we knew only this external structure, we might imagine this story to be a charming but somewhat naive piece of folklore. A testimony for the moral life to be sure, but marred by a strong streak of improbability. But there is a darker side to Tehillah.

She begins to tell her story to the protagonist when she realizes that her death is approaching. As the city of Jerusalem begins to change and the patterns of twentieth-century life overtake the rhythm of the life she once knew, it becomes apparent that her days are numbered. It is not the case that she casts a disfavoring eye on these changes; rather she realizes the city no longer reflects who she is. As the old city draws to a close, so must her life. She invites the protagonist to her house to write a letter.

It seems that Tehillah had been betrothed, at the age of twelve, to a man named Shraga. Her father was outraged when he later discovered Shraga was a member of a Hasidic sect and annulled the plans for marriage. So despised were the Hasidim, that they were evicted from the synagogue; it was as though they were not part of the people Israel. Because of this, the father made no attempt to seek forgiveness. He quickly made arrangements to marry Tehillah to another man.

Tehillah soon forgot this tragedy; she and had two sons and then a daughter. Moreover, the tide of history had now turned, and the ire toward Hasidism cooled. Tehillah's family hired a Hasidic teacher for the children, and they all soon adopted Hasidic customs. Shraga, on the other hand, left Hasidism. In Tehillah's view this shift was more than ironic; it was providential. *"If the matter was not for purpose of atonement for sin,"* she said, *"then I have no idea why it happened."*

The irony grew deeper and turned tragic. Her first-born son died at the end of the Sabbath, just thirty days before his bar mitzvah. Tehillah's betrothal to Shraga had also been broken at the end of the Sabbath, thirty days before the marriage. Then her second-born son died, and finally her daughter became an apostate. Tehillah had lost all her children. Noting the necessity of seeking Shraga's forgiveness lest more tragedy befall them, Tehillah's husband set out in search for him but died in transit. Tehillah was now completely alone.

Tehillah emigrated to Israel to seek a holy life within the blessed land. Her entire life of virtue was set in motion by a sin over which she no longer had any control. As she approached death, she wished to write a letter seeking Shraga's forgiveness. She intended to put that letter in a sealed clay jar and take it with her to the grave. In the world-to-come she would find Shraga and deliver the letter of apology to him.

Tehillah's stature as a living saint is forged in the crucible of human error and tragedy. Through her deeds of loving-kindness she is not seeking "satisfaction" for past sins, for this cannot be achieved without Shraga's consent. Instead, she has simply given her life wholly over to her maker. Out of the horror of her past she creates a life that becomes near angelic. From the ashes of her grievous past she rises, phoenix-like, to enjoy a life in which she is spared the agony of conventional aging.

The Paradox of Penance

When I finished reading the story of Tehillah, I recognized at once that I had solved the puzzle of Adam's condition outside of Eden. He was reduced to an animal by virtue of his transgression. But in taking on this new condition as a means of penance rather than enduring it solely as punishment, Adam was on the road to deification. Adam's way to God was through the comportment of a beast, just as Tehillah's trail of tears become in the end a moment of beatification.

The Syrian monks attempted to model their own behavior on the figure of Adam. This is no surprise. The religious life has frequently been defined as an *imitative* one. You must seek out a saint and study his or her ways with the goal of implanting them in your own life. Thus King Manasseh, who was the worst sinner known in the book of Kings, became a *figure* of the penitent in the book of Chronicles, and a *model* for the same in the *Prayer of Manasseh*. If Manasseh could be forgiven, the Jewish and Christian tradition has claimed, then so can you. Act contritely and pray as fervently as he did.

By copying the model laid down by Adam outside of Eden, early Christian monks were assuring themselves of a place inside Eden.

The medicine of such penance works like other healing agents known to the ancient world. The medicinal herb known as a *pharmakon* to the ancient Greeks (*samma* in Syriac) possesses a Janus-like character. Administered improperly it not only would not heal, but it could deal a graver blow, that of a lethal poison. The image of the pharmakon has always been a profound one in the religious life. It inscribes indelibly within the texts of the penitential life the paradoxical quality of self-abnegation.

Where moderns see signs of pathological self-denial, ancient Christians saw the tokens of a life lived after the pattern of Christ (*imitatio Christi*). Such suffering was not enervating or defeatist; it was empowering and triumphalist. The stylites of ancient Syria used the improbable instrument of their pole as a fulcrum upon which to move nations. For Tehillah the occasion of an unforgivable sin became the basis for near angelic transformation.

Adam will be saved through eating the grass of the field just as King Nebuchadnezzar was. Those unusual athletes of virtue who took to the hills and streams of ancient Syria to model themselves after Adam were both leaving Eden and returning there. The irony is this: *the more profound their remorse over what they found without, the more surely they established themselves as citizens within.* Of course this is an irony well known to members of twelve-step programs as well. Nothing could be more difficult to do than to confess the failures of one's past and present to a group of peers. But however hard this may be, nothing can be more healing.

This is exactly the type of irony that Milton's Satan could not understand when the command was issued to worship God's Christ. The economy of heaven, Satan thought, was a zero-sum world. What he gave, someone else took. Confession, in this view, is a sign of human weakness rather than a source of spiritual prowess.

But Abdiel, Satan's interlocutor prior to his eviction from heaven, saw things differently. To do obeisance would bring elevation not demotion. And so for repentance. To confess and make amends for past error does not humiliate; it honors. In the story of the Prodigal Son it is the wayward son who returns that merits the grand show of joy by the father. Or, in a midrash cited in the name of Rabbi Abbahu, God will speak words of peace and blessing *first* to those who have repented and stand near, and only afterwards to the righteous who stand at a distance. Those who have been forgiven much are also those capable of the deepest love and appreciation.

Chapter 8

The Genesis of Perfection

Satan showed Christ the signature of Eve and Adam and said:
"Take note: Your parents signed and sealed this. Read and
understand.
A bond Adam wrote me in Eden, because he succumbed to sin;
he could not repay, so he pledged his sons as interest.
From the beginning, I have possessed authority over man;
not in secret were they enrolled and enslaved as debtors."

—Narsai, *Hymns on the Resurrection*

If the introduction of evil into the world thwarts God's intentions
for human life, why doesn't God just eliminate it? He is God
Almighty, after all. Here we are thrust into one of the thorniest the-
ological problems of the Bible. On the one hand, there is the prob-
lem of free will. God must honor our tendency to steer clear of the
good and pursue evil. On the other hand, God is not so patient as
to let the entire human project go to waste. He enters the drama
of human history to correct these problems and in so doing pays
a high price. Reconciliation with humanity comes at considerable
cost.

The Harrowing of Hell

At the beginning of the *Divine Comedy*, when Dante enters the shadowy abyss of Limbo, he meets the greatest of all Latin poets, Virgil. Virgil's masterful epic about the founding of Rome, the *Aeneid*, was well known to Dante as it would have been to any educated medieval person. Yet Virgil lived just prior to the advent of Christ and therefore was not privy to the preaching of the gospel. "For such

155

defect and no other offense," Virgil confesses to Dante, "[w]e are lost, and only so far amerced; [t]hat without hope we languish in suspense."

Dante was greatly grieved at this discovery but hastened to press an urgent question to this esteemed man.

> "Tell me, my Master, tell me, Sir!" I said,
>   Seized with a longing wholly to be assured
>   Of that faith wherein error cannot tread,
> "Did ever any of those herein immured
>   By his own or other's merit to bliss get free?"
>   (*Inferno*, Canto 4:46–50)

The question appears cryptic to modern readers, but those of Dante's day knew exactly what the subject was. *According to a widespread and quite ancient tradition, Christ was thought to have descended into Hades during his three days in the grave and retrieved the righteous dead among the Israelites.*

Virgil, already a denizen of Limbo when Christ was crucified, provides Dante with the objective confirmation he seeks:

> And he, aware what meant my covert word,
> Answered: "I was yet new in this degree
>   When I saw one in power crowned appear
>   On whom the signs of victory were to see.
> He took from us the shade of our first sire;
>   Of his son Abel, and Noah of that same seed;
>   (*Inferno*, Canto 4:51–56)

In Limbo the holy name of the redeemer is not pronounced, but there can be no doubt that the "one in power crowned" was Christ. He had entered Limbo and restored Adam ("the shade of our first sire") along with other worthies from the Old Testament. "And I would have thee know," Virgil divulges,

> "that, before these,
> There has been no human soul that he atones."
>   (*Inferno*, Canto 4:62–63)

The Crucifixion was a cosmic turning point among the dead. Only at the descent of Christ was anyone redeemed.

Lift Up, Ye Princes, Your Heads

Dante has drawn on a long-standing tradition, widespread in both Eastern and Western Christianity, of Christ's descent to the underworld to redeem Adam. In the West, this tradition is best known in dozens of apocryphal narratives about "the harrowing of hell." Perhaps the most well known and influential of this genre was a tale known as the *Gospel of Nicodemus*. The story, which appears in nearly every language known to early Christianity, is notoriously difficult to date. So popular and beloved was the tale that it was not only copied and recopied dozens of times, but as it was recopied it was often changed and "improved." When pressed for an actual date, scholars generally attribute its composition to the fourth century. But nothing precludes the possibility that the tradition already existed in the third or perhaps even the second century.

In this story, the righteous dead are awakened during the last moments of Christ's life by the noisy and desperate efforts of Hades and Satan to prevent Christ from storming their door. They had bickered endlessly as to whether they should finally kill this figure on the cross. Hades feared his death would do them more harm than good. Satan was resolute; he demanded that Christ's life be taken. But at his death, both had to concede they had made a colossal mistake. Like the centurion at the foot of the cross, they recognize that this was no ordinary man; he was the Son of God.

Quickly they attempt to bar the gates and reinforce their stronghold. Christ arrives at the door and demands to be let in: "Lift up, ye princes, your heads, and let the King of Glory enter!" The famous words of Psalm 24 become the libretto of this final operatic act. Satan replies, "Who is this king of glory?" To whom an answer was quickly returned: "The Lord strong and mighty, the Lord mighty in battle." Then straightway the gates of brass were shattered, the bars of iron were ground to powder, and the dead were loosed from their chains. The King of Glory entered the realm of the dead, Sheol, and retrieved his bounty, Adam and Eve.

As testimony to its importance in the West, one need only point to the way Handel used this psalm in his Easter oratorio, *Messiah*. He set this psalm exactly between the accounts of the crucifixion and the ascension into heaven. Handel's audience would have known very well why this psalm was placed precisely in this location, a detail that is lost on nearly every modern listener.

This tradition of Christ's descent to and ascent from Hades was so deeply woven into the traditions of Easter that it has informed numerous liturgical celebrations. To this day in many Orthodox services in the East, the congregation gathers outside the doors of the church at the service of the Easter Vigil and knocks on the doors demanding that the King of Glory be ushered in. The celebration of Easter is founded on a dramatization of this moment of infernal combat.

This motif was equally important in the religious iconography of the East. The depiction of Christ's despoliation of Hades, entitled the *anastasis* or "resurrection" in Greek, became a standard means of interpreting the mystery of Easter. An excellent example of this image can be found in the contemporary Greek Orthodox Church, St. George's in Toronto (fig. 19). Here, the enormous figure of Christ stands on the broken-down doors of Hades while grasping the wrists of Adam and Eve and pulling them into the *mandorla*, or shield of light, that surrounds him. By their postures, we can tell that they are being pulled from their graves. Christ is the active agent in this drama; Adam and Eve enjoy the benefits. The righteous dead watch in wonder as Christ lifts Adam and Eve out of their respective sepulchers and tramples on the gates of Hades. The bolts and bars used to block Christ's entry, as well as Hades himself, lie scattered below.

Even a brief glance at the icon of the *anastasis* will confirm its attractive power. Christ, like an epic hero, has courageously crossed enemy lines, vanquished his opponent, and restored those so sorely oppressed.

But alongside the appeal of the tale is a narrative morsel that many readers have choked on. It seems that one of the reasons that Christ appears so gallant in these images of his forceful entry into Hades is that he has a formidable opponent—*Satan, or Hades as our antagonist is sometimes identified, seems to be in possession of a kingdom that has some claims to legitimacy.* God is not free to simply step in and dethrone this tyrant. He needs a strategy, and it needs to be successfully carried out.

Satan's Legitimate Rights over Humankind

The strategy devised by the Godhead cannot be understood without some sense of how the problem itself took shape. For early Christian theologians the dramatic narrative of the Bible could be condensed into four acts. In the first act, the peace of Eden is disturbed. Adam and

Figure 19
Anastasis
From the ceiling fresco, St. George's Greek Orthodox Church, Toronto.
(Copyright, Board of Directors, St. George's Greek Orthodox Church, Toronto)

The title *Anastasis* means "resurrection." In this famous icon of the Orthodox tradition, Christ breaks down the doors of Hades to redeem Adam and Eve. They are the pledge of what is to come. As Paul had said that all fell sway to Adam's death, so all will raised up as a consequence of the resurrection.

Notice that Christ grabs Adam and Eve by their wrists—their hands go limp—and literally pulls them forth from their sepulchres. All glory redounds to *Christus Victor* who redeems Adam and Eve of his own accord.

Eve sin and bring into creation the penalty of death. Unlike many acts of disobedience, the penalty of death does not fall on the perpetrators of the trespass alone. Because all humankind descends from this couple, *all* bear the marks of their punishment, whether deserved or not.

The second act begins at their expulsion; the powers of sin and death are quickened, and the kingdom of the underworld is founded. From now on, Hades has the *legitimate* right to take each and every human being. (Some writers prefer to identify Hades as Satan himself, whereas others identify Hades with Death; this is no small difference, as we shall see.) In some respects, God must acquiesce to this tragic picture. The death of each and every man and woman is the just outcome of the command and penalty God has imposed in Eden.

Yet the love that God feels towards his most favored creatures and the power of His merciful nature will not allow him to stand by idly as all creation meets its ignominious end. He must devise a way to retrieve man from Hades so that the just claims of Hades over all humankind are respected. In order to accomplish this he decides to send his Son in human flesh into the world.

And so the third act takes shape. The divine Son, born of the Virgin Mary, does not fall under the legal terms of Hades' contract. Hades is entitled to all those descended from Adam and Eve, but not to a God-man born of a virgin. We, as spectators in this drama, know this fact, but the human and demonic participants are clueless. Herein lies the dramatic tension of the gospel story.

Hades remains puzzled during Christ's entire earthly life about who Christ is. Christ's miracles, especially the raising of the dead, are those of a divine being. Yet his experience of hunger, his need for sleep, his weeping over the dead, and his sweating of blood in Gethsemane indicate a human being, subject to the passions of mortal life. Hades cannot resist the temptation; on Good Friday, he takes Christ.

With Christ in the kingdom of Hades, the fourth and final act begins. When Christ is put to death, his power—much to the shock of Hades—is revealed. *It is a power that can only be activated through weakness.* Hades is not entitled to take him; he has overreached the terms of his contract over human life. As a result, his just claims are abrogated, and man, through the figures of Adam and Eve, can be redeemed.

This perspective on the atonement has been enormously popular and abhorred at the same time. The popularity stems from the compelling portrait it paints of the character of God's mercy. Distraught over the sin of Adam and Eve, God laments the fact that in accord with the principles of justice, they must die. And with them will follow the rest of creation that he so deeply adores. So great is his love for the men and women he has fashioned that he will do nearly anything to redeem them from this tragic fate.

And herein begin the problems. God's love for humanity is thwarted by the lamentable but *just* kingdom of Hades. The legitimate rights of Satan over the human race must be respected but at the same time circumvented. *God overturns the power of Hades by an act of deception.*

Does God lie? This question has bothered many interpreters of this drama, even some of its most vigorous defenders. And this charge cannot be lightly dismissed. But before addressing it directly, I will need to digress briefly and account for the imagery used in this highly mythological tale. For we cannot handle the problem of the deception unless we have grasped the significance of the specific mythic images the tale deploys.

The Prince of This World Shall Be Cast Out

The Gospels themselves, as many have noted, say *nothing* about what happened between the burial of Jesus and his miraculous appearance on Easter. And some readers of the biblical text have urged us to respect this silence.

Such silence seems logical, but pressing the matter too far will leave us speechless about the larger contours of the salvific drama. The problem here is that the Gospel writers are loath to ascribe *any* cosmic significance to the death of Christ. If all we possessed was the Gospel of Mark, we would think that no one, save the centurion at the foot of the cross, knew who Christ was. The disciples were in the dark, Mark believes, because they have the wrong perspective on what kind of kingdom Christ planned to inaugurate. For Mark, Christ's messianic office was to be manifest in his suffering. On this point he is crystal clear, but Mark takes no pains to describe *how* this was so.

The closest we can get to a dramatic confrontation between Christ and Satan is in the Gospel of John. On the eve of his death, Christ announces (John 12:31), *"Now is the judgment of this world; now the prince of this world shall be cast out."*

For the fourth-century theologian St. Chrysostom, these two brief clauses in John's Gospel were a sufficient toehold that allowed him to anchor the drama of Christ's cosmic victory in scripture.

> It is as if Christ said, "[N]ow shall a trial be held, and a judgment be pronounced. How and in what manner? He [the devil] smote *the first man*, because he found him guilty of sin; *for it was through sin that death entered in.* But he did not find any sin in me; wherefore then did he fall on me and give me up to the power of death? ... How is the world judged in me? It is as if the devil was addressed in a court of law: 'You smote them all because you

found them guilty of sin. For what reason did you not strike Christ? Is it not evident that you did this unjustly? *Therefore the whole world shall become righteous through him.'"* (*Homilies on John, ad loc.* John 12:31)

Chrysostom's interpretation of John 12:31 draws on more than just the bare Gospel narrative. The picture drawn here is dependent on the theology of St. Paul, particularly Romans 5:12–21 and Colossians 2:14. In Romans, Paul argues that it was *through the first man that sin and death entered the world* (5:12–13). Through Adam all men and women will die. But Adam's sin was undone by the arrival of the second man. For Paul, the death of Christ secured the release of all Adam's progeny and through him *the whole world was made righteous* (5:19).

Erasing the Bond of Indebtedness

In Romans, Paul provides us with a vivid contrast: through Adam comes death—through Christ, life. But Paul does not supply the *mechanism* for this transformation. Yet it is precisely this issue that drives Chrysostom to ask, *"How* is the world judged [through Christ]?"

And to answer this he provides us with a supporting narrative that imagines the human condition in legal terms. The devil appears as an overly zealous prosecuting attorney. He has smote everyone *justly* for being *guilty of sin.* When he turns to Christ, a being who is *completely innocent of sin,* he continues to smite. In so doing, he overreaches and proves himself unfit for office.

This effacing of the devil's legal authority is not stated in Romans but can be found in the writings ascribed to the apostle Paul. According to Colossians 2:14, God redeemed man through Christ by "erasing *the bond of indebtedness* that stood against us with its legal demands."

New Testament scholars have spilled much ink on this text. For them, the background of this metaphor of human indebtedness has proved difficult to pin down. But such was not the case for early Christian readers. According to Chrysostom, it was the guilt of Adam writ large over all humanity. *Adam had signed a bond in Eden, and over the millennia the interest due on this ancient note had grown unabated* (fig. 20). We have all become debtors in its wake.

So we have found a biblical basis for the story of Christ's victory over the devil. By reading John's Gospel ("Now is the judgment of this world; now the prince of this world shall be cast out") in light of

Figure 20
The Bond of Adam, drawing after a Moldavian church mural, Vorone, Moldavia. (From P. Henry, *Les Églises de la Moldavie*)
In this remarkable image, Adam is seated before Satan and dutifully signs a bond of indebtedness that deeds over to Satan all his offspring.

Colossians ("Christ erased the bond of indebtedness that stood against us") the basic building blocks of the tradition fall into place. The prince of this world held a bond of indebtedness against us. At the passion of Christ, this evil prince brought this bond to the divine law court, to plead his case. Christ, he argued, has died and must descend to Hades and take up residence with the dead. But, the divine law court argued, Christ, being both man and God, did not fall under the terms of this contract. Satan had overplayed his hand; at long last, the bond he legitimately held could be torn up.

A good story to be sure, but questions still abound. Many have been bothered by the concreteness of the image. Comparing the human condition to a mortgage note may be a bit too much. But even if we grant this metaphor its due, we might ask why God didn't just dismiss the interest due on the note as a token of his mercy. If God is truly God, his purposes should not be hindered by a banknote held by the devil.

The Scapegoat Shall Bear Away All Their Iniquities

Perhaps we can get some further purchase on this problem by digging a little deeper into the biblical text. *It so happens that the Bible almost always speaks of sin in terms of some concrete metaphor.*

In the Old Testament, the dominant idiom for the sinner was one who labored under a heavy weight or burden. The sinner was said "to bear a sin" (*nasa' 'avon*) by which the writer meant "to carry on one's back the accumulated weight of wrongdoing."

Forgiveness was, consequently, understood as the removal of this onerous weight from the shoulders of its bearer. Most sins were light enough that they could be born for a while, at least until atonement was made; other sins were so heavy that they were lethal at impact. All sins, if left unattended, became so unbearable that they ultimately destroyed the person who bore them. And once a year, on the Day of Atonement (Yom Kippur) the collective sins of Israel were loaded onto the back of a scapegoat, which was then sent forth into the desert, carrying those sins to oblivion (Leviticus 16).

Forgive us our Debts

During the time of Jesus, a conspicuous change occurred in the Hebrew language. The metaphor of "debt" replaced that of "burden." In postbiblical Hebrew (and Aramaic) one speaks of sin as an obligation to pay off some form of debt (*hova*). And from this Jewish context the famous line from the Lord's prayer—"forgive us our debts as we forgive our debtors"—issued.

The imagery of debt was very influential in how the early church understood Paul. When Paul says, "Christ erased the bond of indebtedness that stood against us," the thought naturally arose, just *where* did this bond come from? *How* did it originate?

The answer was as immediate as it was obvious: if death and sin derive from Adam (Romans 5) then certainly this bond of indebtedness must as well (Colossians 2). Early Christian interpreters presumed that these letters attributed to Paul exhibited a consistent picture of the salvific act. We all die (Rom. 5:12–14) because of the enormous debt (Col. 2:14) that has accumulated in the wake of Adam's sin. The interest that had accumulated over several millennia had accumulated to the extent that no person could clear the account. Like a mortgage run amok, the interest payments were almost beyond calculation.

God Bore a Hole in the Firmament to Hear a Plea for Mercy

So far so good. We have established the New Testament foundations for this imagery of indebtedness, and we have pushed the metaphor back to the beginning of time. If Jesus forgives debts, our interpreters reasoned, then those debts must have begun with Adam and Eve. But there remains a more fundamental concern. If the bond of indebtedness that we inherit from Adam was laid down justly, and God subsequently deceived Satan in order to overturn it, then the character of God that emerges is not too flattering.

To get a handle on this issue, we must go back to the Bible. And here our initial guides will be the Rabbis. According to these Jewish sages, the Bible characterizes God as having two conflicting attributes: the principle of justice (*middat ha-din*) and the principle of mercy (*middat ha-rahamin*).

When God heard a prayer or plea for help, he weighed the request against these two principles before issuing his answer or edict. In rabbinic texts this tension was sometimes portrayed as residing within God himself. But quite frequently this double aspect of the divine personality was externalized in the figures of his attending angels. One group would represent justice, the other mercy; and God would be the arbiter between the two.

Sometimes the case for mercy was not so compelling. The God of Israel did not acquiesce, however, to such circumstances. Frequently, the unruly forces of justice would have to be tamed or even silenced in order for a favorable verdict to result. Consider the jam in which King Manasseh found himself:

[When King Manasseh was being led in chains to Assyria
(2 Chron. 33:1)], he saw that his troubles were great and there
was no form of idolatry in the world that he had not tried. When
none of this proved useful he said, "I remember my father [the
righteous King Hezekiah] would read to me in synagogue the
verse, 'When you are in distress and all these penalties come upon
you, at the end of days you shall return to the LORD (YHWH),
your God and obey his voice. For the LORD your God is a God
of love. He will not abandon or destroy you; he will not forget
the covenant he made with your fathers [Deut. 4:30–31].'" So I
now shall call to you, if he answers me then it will be fine; if not
then this God and that of the idols are the same (i.e., of no value).

Then the ministering angels closed the portals of heaven so
that the prayer of Manasseh could not ascend to the Holy One,
blessed be He. The ministering angels said before the Holy One,
blessed be He, Lord of the World, "Will you accept the repentance of a man who has practiced idolatry and set up idols in the
Temple?" He answered them, "If I don't accept his repentance,
then I shall close the door before all penitents! What did the
Holy One, blessed be He, do? He bored a hole beneath the
throne of his lordship and heard his prayer. That is what is written, "He prayed to him and the Lord consented. He heard his
prayer and returned him to Jerusalem and his kingdom"
[2 Chron. 33:13]. (J. Talmud, *Sanhedrin*, 10.2)

This particular midrash pushes the power of penitence almost to its
limit. King Manasseh's appeal to God is hardly an act of contrition.
He returns to the religion of his father only because all other avenues
have been closed and solely as a calculated gamble. If it works, he
thinks, great; if not, well, no harm done.

Yet the text he cites from memory ("when you are in distress . . .")
emphasizes that the biblical God (YHWH) is defined by mercy ("your
God is a God of love") and bound by his obligation to his chosen people ("he will not forget the covenant he made with your fathers"). The
angels naturally take umbrage at the thought that this villain will be
heard and attempt to block his prayer. God, who represents the power
of mercy, does not contest the position of the angels. The narrator has
conceded that the angels have the better side of the argument. And so
the surprise: *God cannot win this case by argument but only by a ruse.* So
desirous is God to be merciful that he dismisses the weighty argu-

ments of his angelic host and bores a hole in the firmament just below his throne. The words of King Manasseh's prayer find his waiting ear and the verdict instantly turns in his favor.

God Tipped the Scales to Thwart Satan

In the story of King Manasseh, the angels represent the power of justice whereas God represents that of mercy. But there were other ways of telling such a story. In some circumstances Satan, the archnemesis of Israel, could represent the powers of justice. To this end, God had to respect Satan's legal case. But at the same time God sought some means of redress. Consider this tale found in a ninth-century collection of homiletic midrashim:

> "An instruction of David. Happy is the one whose wrongdoing is born away, whose sin is covered over" [Ps. 32:1]. This is what David means: you have borne away the wrongdoing of your people, all their sins you have covered up.
>
> Once, on the Day of Atonement, Satan came to accuse Israel. He detailed her sins and said, "Lord of the Universe, as there are adulterers among the nations of the world so there are in Israel. As there are thieves among the nations of the world, so there are in Israel." The Holy One, blessed be He, itemized the merits of Israel. Then what did he do? He took a scale and balanced the sins against the merits. They were weighed together and the scales were equally balanced. Then Satan went to load on further sin and to make that scale sink lower.
>
> What did the Holy One, blessed be He, do? While Satan was looking for sins, the Holy One, blessed be He, took the sins from the scale and hid them under his purple royal robe. When Satan returned, he found no sin as it is written, "The sin of Israel was searched for, but it is no longer" [Jer. 50:20]. When Satan saw this he spoke before the Holy One, blessed be He, Lord of the World, "You have borne away the wrongdoing of your people and covered over all their sin" [Ps. 85:3]. When David saw this, he said, "Happy is the one whose wrongdoing is born away, whose sin is covered over" [Ps. 32:1]. (*Pesikta Rabbati*)

It is important to note that Satan is not a figure of complete evil here. He represents the principle of justice and wants to make the claim that

Israel does not deserve forgiveness. "In this midrash," the scholar of rabbinic Judaism Peter Schäfer argues, "the principles of justice and mercy are evenly balanced—the one personified in Satan, the other concretized in the robe of God—and justice was overtaken by mercy." God atones for Israel's sin by "bearing it away" and "covering it up." These two clauses from the Psalter are not morally neutral. When Satan turns his back, God removes the evidence against Israel. The rules of fair play do not apply. *God has deceived Satan.*

The theme of angelic rivalry is hardly rare in rabbinic literature; Schäfer has compiled a massive catalogue of examples to demonstrate this. In some stories the angels are punished; in others they are deceived. But whatever narrative turn is taken, it is clear

> that the angels speak for God himself when they represent the principle of divine retribution. . . . Even though the Rabbis never express this problem abstractly, nevertheless it cannot be doubted that they make clear that in all of the polemic against the angel's arguments, *the argument in the end is grounded in God himself.*

Mercy would have no value unless it was calibrated against a strict measure of justice. But a world that is just, through and through, would allow no room for humans. God must, in a certain sense, *deceive himself.* Were God simply to flatten his opposition he would, by this very act, falsify the claims of justice. Yet this doctrine cannot be stated in unvarnished form—God is a self-deceiver—for fear of making a mockery of the deity. To preserve the mystery of God's *unknowable* being and his unfathomable rulings, the midrash avails itself of the closest alternative; it tells a *story* of how God's mercy can be *likened* to the deceit of a just but overly zealous prosecutor.

Moses Stood in the Breach
and Battled with God

This exposition of the mystery of God's ways with sinful humanity is, strictly speaking, not the creation of the Rabbis. It is deeply rooted in the Bible itself, especially those narratives that concern repentance.

The paradigmatic moment in the Bible when God's wrath is turned toward mercy occurs immediately after Israel has begun to worship the golden calf (Exodus 32). Moses is at the end of his forty-day sojourn at the peak of Mt. Sinai. God has just finished revealing to him the details of the tabernacle where the Israelites are supposed to house his divine glory on earth (Exodus 25–31).

The irony of what has happened should not be lost on the reader. As this heavenly structure is being revealed, Israel is already in the midst of erecting her own countertemple, a shrine to a lifeless golden calf. "I am the LORD your God who brought you out of Egypt," God had announced from the heights of Sinai as the people trembled below (Exod. 20:1); "These are your gods, O Israel," Aaron had responded after the calf had emerged from its mold, "who brought you up out of the land of Egypt" (32:4).

The hubris of such a declaration was not lost on God. "Go down at once!" he commanded Moses. "Your people, whom you brought up out of the land of Egypt have acted perversely" (32:7). Wasting no time, Israel's God came right to the point: "I have seen this people, how stiff-necked they are. Now let me alone, so that my wrath may burn hot against them and I may consume them; and of you I will make a great nation" (32:9–10).

The entire mystery of election was poised to unravel. No longer was YHWH the God of Israel; the people of Israel belonged to Moses ("*your* people, whom *you* brought up"). And this very God, who had promised never again to send a flood to destroy the whole world, was on the brink of destroying the entire chosen nation (a world in miniature) and rebuilding their foundation from the single figure of Moses. Perhaps the promise to Noah was not being broken—the world at large, after all, was in no danger—but the parallels to the flood were ominous indeed. God was ready to destroy an entire people and refashion them anew from the likes of a single righteous man.

Moses clearly perceives the seriousness of the situation, both the gravity of Israel's sin and the burning rage of divine wrath. Yet as God's chosen prophet, Moses does not simply acquiesce to the script that lies before him. He does not kneel in obedience to the whims of the deity. He stands in the breach between God and his people and attempts to make amends. "O LORD, why does your wrath burn hot against your people," he begins, echoing the words of God himself, "whom you brought out of the land of Egypt with great power and with a mighty hand" (32:11). These are not my people, Moses counters, they are *yours*, those whom *you* led out of Egypt.

But Moses does not stop here; this is not a matter of linguistic precision about the status of the elected nation. *He launches a frontal attack on the very character of God.*

"Why should the Egyptians say, 'It was with evil intent that he brought them out to kill them in the mountains . . .]'? Turn from your fierce wrath; change your mind. . . . Remember Abraham, Isaac, and Israel, your servants, how you swore to them by your own self saying to them, 'I will multiply your descendants like the stars of heaven, and all this land that I have promised I will give to your descendants, and they shall inherit it forever.'" (Exod. 32:12–13)

With this, Moses rests his case. And the verdict? "The LORD *changed his mind* about the disaster that he planned to bring on his people" (32:14).

The audacity of Moses' words should not be minimized. He reminds God of what it means to be the God of Israel. Moses appeals to the stature of God among the nations ("What will the Egyptians say? You led this people to the desert simply to kill them?") and the promises made to the patriarchs ("You swore to give the land to their descendants"). And with this, the proposal to destroy the entire elected nation was tabled.

A God Who Turns toward Man

The Bible, I should underscore, does not frame its portrait of God with theological abstractions. We learn about the nature of God through the medium of narrative. The Bible contains no reflection on the principles of justice and mercy; there is no detailed account of how the heavenly host adjudicates the affairs of mankind. God reveals himself through the stories told about him.

But we can infer something about this process through the relationship of God to his prophet Moses. As the Jewish biblical scholar Yohanan Muffs has observed, Moses' resistance to God's just decree is not summarily dismissed. Quite the contrary, *God raises up prophets so that they can press the case of the accused.* God's will is only arrived at through a vigorous, and sometimes heated, exchange. If the prophet must use what looks like moral blackmail to defend Israel ("What will the nations think?"), so be it.

For those not familiar with prophetic narrative, the idiom of intercessory prayer may appear disrespectful at best, irreverent or even blasphemous at worst. The biblical prophet appears to have some sort of moral advantage over God. But what, we must ask, is the alternative to this? The God of Aristotle may be a more appealing figure. But this God's clearest characteristic, Muffs reminds us, is *indifference*. Such a god "would not have been moved by such an egoistic and human argument [as that of Moses]." On the contrary, it is only "a God Who turns toward man and is interested in man's destiny and in man's reaction to His commandments [that would] leave Himself open to such intimidation."

Death Confesses Christ
as the First-born of All Creation

It has been a long road to travel, but I think that we are now in a position to get some purchase on the tale of Christ's redemption of Adam and Eve. We have seen several biblical and Jewish correlates to the overall plot line. In all of these it has become clear that *forgiveness in the Bible is a contested event. It costs God something.* God desperately desires to show mercy, but he also must remain just. To map this cleavage between desire and character, the Bible pits the prophet against God. Moses *must* stand up to God and remind him of his promises. God, in turn, can be talked out of his wrathful inclinations, but he needs someone to make the case against him.

To the Rabbis, this contest between God and prophet is shifted to the heavens. The angelic host, or sometimes Satan, represents a portion of God's character that God himself must get the best of. So important is this task that God will even stoop to deception to redeem his people. But given the fact that the angels represent a portion of God's being, the deception is not as morally troubling as one might think. God, after all, is deceiving himself.

In the end, the emphasis in these tales is not on the means or even the fact of deception. Rather these acts of deception are exempla that point out God's all-consuming love for those he has fashioned and raised up.

Nearly all these points come home to roost in the thought of St. Ephrem. He expounds the passion of Christ by attending to a single but weighty detail:

> Our Lord tore asunder [the forces of] Error in Sheol
>   So as to teach through the visible, what was hidden.
> For as he visibly tore asunder Sheol,
>   So he burst open Error in hidden fashion.

> Many saw the graves ripped open,
>   They did not see that Satan was defeated.
> By what is close at hand he demonstrated
>   what is hidden [and] far away.
>   (*Hymns on the Unleavened Bread* 4:3–7)

His reference to graves that were ripped open refers to a portion from Matthew's Gospel:

> At that moment [when Christ breathed his last] the curtain of the temple was torn in two, from top to bottom. The earth shook, and the rocks were split. The tombs also were opened, and many bodies of the saints who had fallen asleep were raised. (Matt. 27:51–52)

Through these formidable events, Ephrem concluded that Satan (or "Error" as he calls him) had been defeated. Christ's resurrection was anticipated on the cross through the raising of some of the just.

The contents of Sheol could be compared to the molten lava that lies below the earth's crust. Though invisible most of the time, its existence is proven whenever there is a volcanic eruption. Ephrem, like a diligent geologist, pondered what this surface eruption of resurrected bodies revealed about the world below.

For Ephrem, the name of the foe below was known from scripture: Death. It was he who meted out justice in accord with Adam's sin. And he discharged the affairs of his office with utter resolve and fairness. "I despise the money of the rich," Death asserted, "their gifts cannot bribe me. . . . A hater of persuasion I am called by all men; I do only what I am commanded" (*Carmina Nisibena* 36:5).

Satan, on the other hand, was more immoral; he was the great tempter. But even his evil had its limits. After all, Satan had been charged by God with the task of testing human virtue. "I am an oven of testing for mankind," he boasted, "by me, their thoughts are put to proof" (*Carmina Nisibena* 40:7).

When Ephrem tells the story of Christ's life and passion, he follows a well-trod path. Death and Satan are fooled by the signs of Christ's human nature. As Christ lies dying on the cross, Death cries out,

> If you are God, show your strength
> if you are man, test our strength.

If it is Adam that you seek, be gone!
He is bound for his sins here. Neither Cherub
    nor Seraph . . . can pay his debt.
                                (*Carmina Nisibena* 36:2)

Though Death and Satan remain puzzled about Christ's identity to the end—is he god or man?—Christ's deception has had its effect; Death decides to risk all and slay him (35:18).

When Christ descends to the gates of Sheol, Death recognizes that he has made an enormous mistake. Unlike Satan, Death was not a disobedient rebel opposed to the reign of God. He was installed as king over Sheol due to Adam's sin, and he paid no respect to persons as he executed his duties there. "It is God that I serve," he confesses (38:3), "for there is no partiality before him."

Though his name was besmirched by virtue of his office, his character was redeemable. As Christ enters his kingdom he need not break down its doors. Death runs forward to open his gates and announce the arrival of the Messiah just as John the Baptist had done several years earlier. "I am your servant forever," Death declares on bended knees (38:6).

Death, who had previously reviled Christ because of his body, which had "veiled [his] divinity," now begs for mercy. It was Christ who was the true first-born, and through him everything in creation had its ground. Others had been raised prior to Christ, but Christ was still the true "first-born of Sheol" (38:7):

Those who were first have become last,
The recent-born have become first-born. If Manasseh was the first born,
How did Ephrem assume his rights?
If a child born later could precede him,
How much more should the Lord and Creator be first at resurrection.

This confession of Christ as the true first-born should not strike us as a complete surprise. Its significance is grounded in the story of Satan's fall told in the *Life of Adam and Eve*. There, Satan refused to worship Adam, on the grounds that Adam was born last. Satan himself was the true first-born, and Adam should have prostrated himself before Satan rather than the other way around. In Ephrem's retelling of this tradition, it has been moved from the moment of creation to that of Christ's entry to Sheol. And here Death is found worthy of the test. He recognizes Christ's role as the first-born of all creation and pays him laud and honor.

Is Death a Part of God's Being?

The overcoming of Death was not, strictly speaking, the vanquishing of a purely external enemy. *In the figure of Death, we have represented an aspect of the deity himself.* As in the rabbinic midrashim, Death represents the just nature of God's being, whereas the work of Christ represents his mercy. *In deceiving Death through the act of incarnation, God is deceiving himself.* This can be shown by comparing the story of Christ's descent into Limbo to Ephrem's interpretation of Cain and Abel:

> In your mercy you entrusted Abel as the first into the depths of Sheol. [This was] in order that Sheol would be compelled *in justice* to cast him forth from its depths. . . . For, if Adam had been the first to enter [Sheol], which was his deservedly, it would have been meted out to him to remain there forever. (*Commentary on the Diatessaron*, 339)

This remarkable text dispenses with the figures of Satan, Death, Error, and the other countless characters that Ephrem is so fond of animating and giving voice. The issue at hand has been foreshortened to a conflict between mercy and justice. Abel, the victim of a brutal murder, dies first in order to precede Adam to the grave.

The logic of this interpretation, though compressed, is clear and compelling. Had Adam gone to Sheol first, Ephrem reasons, he could never have been redeemed. For he had violated a command that had attached to it a clear and unalterable penalty: "The day you eat of that fruit you shall certainly die." But history did not work out this way. Instead, Abel died first, and consequently the mouth of Hades was opened for the first time *unjustly*. Henceforth the legal foundation of the underworld rested on shaky grounds. Since Abel died first and unjustly, God has full authority to evacuate those held prisoner there at the end of time.

A further irony is the salvific role played by the innocent death of Abel. Since Abel was considered by Ephrem, and nearly all early Christians, as a type of Christ, the miracle of the incarnation was inscribed into the very beginning of Genesis. Because the innocent

Abel (a.k.a Christ) dies unfairly, Adam (all humanity) will be justly cast forth from Sheol.

Finally, we should note that Ephrem's use of the categories of justice and mercy look strikingly similar to their use in rabbinic literature. God has worked into the fabric of creation's beginnings not only the dispute between justice and mercy but also its resolution. Though the contention of justice is ultimately trumped, it is never fully removed from God's inscrutable being.

The Genesis of Perfection

It is worth noting that the role of Adam and Eve in the iconography of the *Anastasis* is, in a formal sense, exactly the same as it was at creation. When Adam and Eve sin, they create the conditions of their own mortality and of all those that will be born of them. According to patristic writers, the dominion of Hades comes into being at the moment of expulsion; it was not in the blueprint of creation. Because everyone is related ultimately to this first couple, all will enter the gates of this nether-kingdom. But similarly, just as Christ lifted Adam and Eve out of Hades in 30 C.E., so he shall return at the end of time to raise all those that remain. Adam and Eve are but the firstfruits of a much larger, more universal, salvific intent.

Death was just following orders when he took every person born of the womb. But death will also obediently follow Christ's directive when he gives up all his reluctant citizens at the moment of the general resurrection. In giving up Adam and Eve at Easter, he is making a down payment on a larger sum he must and will repay. The theology of Romans 5 is worked out in this iconographic tableau: just as death and sin entered into creation through the first Adam, so through the second Adam comes life and righteousness.

I should also emphasize that in the iconic representation Adam and Eve are *pulled* from Hades; they do not climb out by their own power. Some decisive *divine action* is required to lift humanity from death to life. Some scholars have compared the ascent of Christ and his elect to pagan myths of retrieval from the underworld or to theurgic ascents to the heavenly realms. Although the parallels have some merit, they should not mislead the reader into thinking that the resurrection of Adam and Eve involves some magical action on their own part. As the iconography clearly depicts, Christ grabs Adam and Eve by their wrists—their hands are limp—and frees them from the realm of death.

Though the patristic tale of the *Christus Victor* is absent from the Gospel narrative itself, the essential pieces of the plot line are stitched together from different salvific moments in scripture. In this tradition, God's actions to redeem his people episodically in the Bible are writ large over the cosmos as a whole. What the iconographer wants us to see is not simply the raising of Adam and Eve, but our raising as well.

The story of Adam and Eve is tied to the story of Christ's death and resurrection because the account of creation cannot conclude without its completion. By drawing Adam and Eve into the passion narrative, a broad, universal dimension to the story is depicted that does not exist within the Gospels themselves.

Afterword: Adam, Eve, and Us

Better is the Torah to the one who observes it and walks in the paths of the way of life than the fruit of the tree of life.
— *Targum Pseudo-Jonathan, ad loc.* Gen. 3:24

Religious texts are not just for reading and rereading; they are meant to be lived. Crucial to every piece of Jewish and Christian interpretation that we have encountered is some sort of dramatic enactment, be it liturgy, prayer, or almsgiving. How we perform the scriptures is just as important a vehicle for understanding as how we read them.

The Torah's Conclusion

The narrative of the Torah, in its final canonical form, has two principle foci: entering the land of Israel and keeping the commandments given by God at Mt. Sinai. The former theme becomes, over time, strongly eschatological, or future-oriented, in tone. Throughout the Second Temple period—after the return of Ezra, Nehemiah, and many of those banished to Babylon—many Jews continued to pray for an end to the exile. When Israel is finally gathered into the Promised Land, the Messiah will arrive, the Temple will be properly rebuilt, and the nations of the earth will stream to Zion to give honor to God for what he has done. The commandments, on the other hand, remain the focus of daily life, albeit with a future orientation. Many of them can only be fulfilled when Israel is in full possession of her land.

According to rabbinic teaching, this messianic destiny will happen when Israel has successfully repented of those sins that brought on the exile. There remains within talmudic thought, however, a significant difference as to how this repentance will come about. According to Rabbi Eliezer, Israel will one day of *her own accord* choose to return with all her heart, soul, and might to faithful obedience to the covenant. Rabbi Joshua disagrees. In his opinion, Israel *is not capable*, as an entire nation, of making such a choice. Her repentance will come about only when God wills it into being.

This debate, which raged throughout the rabbinic era, made a considerable impression on the framers of the rabbinic canon.

> Rabbi Eliezer says: If Israel repents, she will be redeemed, and if not, she will not be redeemed. Rabbi Joshua replied, "If they do not repent, they won't be redeemed?! Rather, the Holy One, blessed be He, will establish a king over them whose decrees will be as harsh as those of Haman [the man in the book of Esther who wished to exterminate the Jews in Persia]. Then Israel will repent and God shall restore her to what is blessed.
>
> Rabbi Eliezer says: If Israel repents, she will be redeemed for it is written, "Return, O wayward children, that I might heal your apostasies" [Jer. 3:22]. Rabbi Joshua replied, "Isn't it also written, 'you were sold for naught and without money you shall be redeemed'?" [Isa. 52:3]. The meaning of 'for naught you were sold' is for idolatry; 'without money you shall be redeemed' means without repentance or good deeds." (Babylonian Talmud, *Sanhedrin* 97b)

Joshua's position is strikingly close to that of Augustine. It is not within the capacity of the human will to work out its own salvation. This is a deed that rests solely in the hands of God.

This grand eschatological moment of messianic redemption was linked to the conclusion of the Torah's epic narrative. As modern biblical scholars have noted, the Torah ends prematurely and in a highly unnatural manner. God had promised Abraham his descendants would lay hold of the land of Canaan (Gen. 12:1–4). This promise was, in turn, repeated to the other patriarchs, Isaac (26:3–5) and Jacob (28:13–15). And the nation Israel, at the base of Mt. Sinai, spent a long time preparing to fulfill this dream (Numbers 1–10). Nevertheless, Israel's sins in the wilderness prevented them from reaching this goal. (Numbers 13–14; compare Exodus 32–34). Israel was condemned to march for forty years in the wasteland until the previous generation had died out and a new one arose.

So the Torah ends with Israel poised to enter the Promised Land, but not yet there. This editorial decision had a profound effect on the people Israel. It meant that every subsequent generation would place themselves in that wilderness moment and imagine themselves as hearing Moses' final exhortation to covenantal obedience (Deuteronomy). Perhaps in our day, one prays, God will see fit to bring the promise made to Abraham to closure.

Such is the prayer of every observant Jew. Modern Zionism, of course, complicates this somewhat as there now exists a gathered body of Jews in the land of Israel. But this modern secular state is still bereft of Temple and certainly is not constituted around the principles of the rabbinic Torah. However it is to be understood, it cannot be equated with the messianic kingdom spoken of in Jewish tradition.

Eden through the Lens of Sinai

Not surprisingly, the entrance into the Holy Land is imagined as a return to the glories of Eden. But not simply Eden as at creation, but an Eden *deepened* through the revelation of and obedience to God's Torah. A simple equation—last things equals first things—cannot and should not be drawn. Last things assume and *go beyond* first things. The end recasts the beginning, not the reverse.

Let us consider what Nachmanides, a justly famous thirteenth-century commentator on the Torah, had to say about Leviticus 26. In this chapter, Moses speaks about the blessings that will accrue to Israel should she keep the Torah in the Promised Land and contrasts them with the curses and eventual exile that will dog her should she prove disobedient.

Nachmanides observes that in Leviticus 26 God promises to put an end to the marauding swords of foreign armies and the vicious teeth of wild animals (26:6). This leads Nachmanides to conjecture that this is exactly the situation that Adam enjoyed in Eden prior to his sin. For at that time, there were no carnivorous animals (Gen. 1:30); all of creation was at peace. If Israel is faithful to her mandate, Nachmanides reasons, these Edenic conditions will return. Israel will bask in the effulgence of her Torah—a glory like that of Eden but beyond it as well—when she is gathered into the Promised Land.

Targum Pseudo-Jonathan, the Aramaic paraphrase of the Torah, makes the same sort of correlation. Just after Adam has been driven from Eden (Gen. 3:24) but prior to his establishment of a life outside the Garden (Gen. 4:1ff.), there is a rather long digression, a rare event in the literary form known as the Targum.

The targumist notes that God created the Torah and the Garden of Eden *prior* to the rest of the world. Though Adam was the first to dwell in Eden, this Garden was, in fact, intended for *all* the righteous. Those who would live according to the eternal mandates of the Torah and keep them, to the best of their abilities, are to enjoy the blessings of paradise in the world to come.

The valley of Gehinnom, on the other hand, was prepared for the wicked who would openly spurn what God had so graciously offered. The last sentence of this digression reads, "Better is the Torah to one who observes it and walks in the paths of the way of life than the fruit of the tree of life; for the word of the Lord prepared it for humanity to keep, that they would be established in the world to come."

In this text three moments of time are brought together: creation, Sinai, and the end of time. But they are not understood to be coequals; there is an advance. The revelation of the Torah completes and supersedes that of Eden and prepares one for the full enjoyment of what is prepared at the end of time. By keeping Torah in this life, one improves on the lot of Adam ("*Better* is the Torah . . . than the fruit of the tree of life").

Moreover, the beatific moment at Eden or Sinai is not merely a time that one labors for solely through anticipation. It is *also a moment that can be experienced in the present.* In tending to God's word, honoring his Sabbath, and acting justly, the beatific moment of the primal revelation can be quickened anew. This impulse that appears so mystical does not wait until the advent of the medieval mystical movements. It is already present in the rabbinic era.

Standing with Moses at Sinai

As we have seen repeatedly over the course of this book, God descends to Mt. Sinai to give Israel his Torah and to establish a life with Israel similar to the life Adam and Eve knew in Eden. Israel lost this blessed state when she venerated the calf. But she can reappropriate it now by her faithful obedience.

According to the Talmud (Babylonian Talmud, *Sukkah* 28a), while Rabbi Jonathan ben Uzziel was sitting and poring over the Torah in fervent study, "every bird that flew over his head was immediately burned up." Just as at Mt. Sinai the revelation of God's holy Torah was

accompanied by fire and smoke (Exod. 19:18) so it is in these liturgical dramatizations. When one treads the path of Torah study, one does
not so much embark on a trip to the past, but enters the dwelling of
an eternal and sacramental present.

The author of the book of Proverbs claims that "wisdom is a tree
of life to those who lay hold of her" (3:18). And the Rabbis, having
identified wisdom with Torah, glossed the verse: "Torah study is both
the way to the Tree of Life and the enjoyment of the Tree itself." With
a heart properly directed toward heaven, Eden and end-time are
brought into planetary alignment. Chronological time, with its restless advance, grinds to a halt, and God's eternal rest is momentarily
entered. Such was the experience of Ben Azzai, as he

> was sitting and interpreting the scriptures. Suddenly a flame
> was burning round about him. They said to him, "Are you per-
> haps studying the mystical chariot?" [Ezekiel 1]. He answered:
> "No, rather I am finding in the Torah parallels to expressions in
> the Prophets, and in the prophets parallels to expressions in the
> Writings [Torah, Prophets, and Writings are the three main
> rubrics of the Jewish Bible]. The words of the Torah are as joy-
> ful as they were on the day they were being given at Sinai. They
> were originally given amidst fire, as it is said: "The mountain
> burned with fire" [Deuteronomy 4:11]. (*Leviticus Rabbah* 16:4)

The very same Torah offered to Moses, a text that incorporated Moses
into the mystery of the divine life, can be reexperienced by the reli-
giously devout. The benefits of Eden are not restricted to a hoary
antiquity or a distant future. The *living* tradition of Judaism offers the
opportunity to bring them into the present.

Many of the midrashic interpretations of Eden/Sinai that we have
encountered in this book have this *lived* trajectory in mind. It is not
simply Adam and Eve who are joined in marriage in Eden; their ceremony becomes a template for the future redemption and the *present*
celebration of the joining of husband to wife. The rebel angels
opposed the giving of the Torah to Moses, and similarly resisted the
practices of the great mystical adepts who laid claim to Mosaic powers.
In short, the midrash is not simply learned by rote; it is experienced.
Adam and Eve, Moses and Israel are as much our contemporaries as
they are figures of the past.

Baptism and the Exaltation of Adam

In Christian sources it is also important to attend to the environment in which Adam and Eve are interpreted. For them, there is a very specific *liturgical context* in which this story is retold, interpreted, and expanded.

One important consequence of this liturgical context is the very idea of the *felix culpa*, or happy fault. Because the *coming redemption* of men and women is the defining feature of the Lenten season, the elaboration of the sin of Adam and Eve was never meant to lead to despair. Quite the opposite; it underscores the audacious mercy shown toward humankind. As any good novelist or screenwriter knows, the more perilously the protagonist's situation is drawn the more remarkable will the redemption appear. A tepid plot inscribes a lukewarm God.

But there is another key concept to bear in mind. Just as Torah giving is not a one-time event, so the passion is not a singular moment, limited to the figure of Jesus of Nazareth. In the liturgy of Easter, it is continually reappropriated in the life of the church. Already in the New Testament, the apostle Paul says that baptism is a participation in the *gloria crucis*, "the glory of the cross."

> Do you not know that all of us who have been baptized into Christ Jesus were baptized into his death? Therefore we have been buried with him by baptism into death, so that, just as Christ was raised from the dead . . . so we too might walk in newness of life. (Rom. 6:3–4)

At baptism, the Christian descends to the dead with Christ in order to rise with him and claim that high calling for which humanity was created. This lived liturgical cycle had profound impact on how the church understood the historical event of Christ's own baptism. According to the Gospel of Matthew, the baptism of Christ was questioned by John. "Shouldn't I be baptized by you?" he asked. To which Christ replied, "Let it be so for now; for it is proper for us in this way to fulfill all righteousness" (Matt. 3:14–15). In the life of the church, the baptism takes on even deeper importance; it *anticipates the Passion.* And if baptism is an initiation into Christ's death, early Christian thinkers reasoned, then Christ's own baptism must have foreshadowed this death.

Indeed, in the iconography of the Passion in the Orthodox church, the descent of Christ into the Jordan parallels that of Christ's descent into Hades. As in our discussion of Eve in early Christian art, where we saw how hard it was to figure out whether we were looking at the first woman or her antitype Mary, so in the baptism it is hard to know whether the primary point of reference is a descent into Sheol or the River Jordan. Each event bleeds into the other. The "end" of the gospel reinscribes its beginning.

Satan's Appearance at Baptism

At baptism *the entire cosmic cycle of redemption is compressed within the individual life of the catechumen.* As Theodore of Mopsuestia makes clear in his account of the church's liturgy, it was at baptism that the full stature of men and women as creatures made in the image of God is restored. It is for this reason, Theodore asserts, that Satan appears on the scene and offers such resistance. The baptismal liturgy begins with the exorcisms, because Satan represents the claims of justice waged against the power of God's mercy. Our image of Satan in these rites should not be the young girl in the movie *The Exorcist*, vomiting green spittle across the room. Rather the image should be those numerous midrashim and apocryphal tales that detail how mercy must outwit justice in order for the bloom of true human personhood to blossom and flourish. Satan contests the baptism just as he contested the elevation of Adam and Christ. Satan *must* be renounced to bring creation to closure.

Baptism, in the early church, began at the start of Lent, with the candidates coming forward to register their names with the priest at the church. Theodore likens the moment of enrollment into the cat-echumenate to a census in which you are about to establish "legal title to a land fertile in corn and rich in good things, in which there is much happiness to those who registered for it" (*On Baptism*, II, 27). Previously this land belonged to an enemy who envies you the happiness he had once enjoyed. He appears before you, arguing that you have no rightful claim to this land. So, Theodore concludes, "it behooves [you] who are about to be registered . . . to go to a magistrate and make use of the title which he possesses, and show the supposed owner of the land . . . that he is desirous of bringing the matter before a judge." (Ibid.)

And so for the drama of baptism. When Satan hears of the pending enrollment of the catechumen, he shows the same hostility he had formerly shown towards the exaltation of Adam and the resurrection of Christ.

> [He] tries and endeavors to bring us to the judgment hall as if we had no right to be outside his ownership. He pleads that from ancient times and from the creation of the head of our race we belong to him by right; he narrates the story of Adam, of how he listened to his words and by his will rejected his Maker and preferred to serve him; of how this kindled the wrath of God, who drove him out of Paradise [and] pronounced the sentence of death upon him." (Ibid.)

Having pledged to resist Satan, the candidates were urged to "stand with outstretched arms in the posture of one who prays, and look downwards and remain in that state in order to move the judge to mercy." And they were then told, "Take off your outer garment and stand barefooted" (*On Baptism*, II, 31). In some contexts the catechumens stood on animal skins while they prayed, symbolizing the taking off of the garments of skin they had inherited from Adam. By stripping themselves of this mortal skin, they were preparing to put on those heavenly garments with which humanity was first clothed.

This drama of Satan's ire toward the catechumen is almost exactly identical to the rage he shows toward Christ during his passion. Consider the account of Narsai, a Syriac theologian who lived a generation or so after Ephrem. In Narsai's view, when Christ descends to Hades, Satan holds forth adamantly about the justice of his claim over all humans. He shows Christ the bond (cf. Col. 2:14) on which appears the handwriting of Adam and Eve. "Behold," he charges, "Your parents have sealed and delivered this over. Read and understand it." This bond, Satan reasons, dooms Christ himself to eternal perdition.

The similarity of Narsai's depiction of the Passion to the liturgy of baptism is striking. Indeed it would be hard to determine the direction of influence. Did the account of the Passion derive from the libretto of the liturgy, or did the liturgy simply act out the denouement of the Passion? In the affairs of Adam and Eve, the lines between liturgical enactment and historical reconstruction become blurred.

This is brought out graphically in a twelfth-century medieval church in Cyprus (fig. 21). The baptismal font was located immediately below a fresco that depicts Christ's descent into Hades to retrieve Adam and Eve. As one looks carefully at the image, it appears that the lower frame of this (upper) fresco is broken by Christ's sharp descent so that he appears to be on the verge of entering the space below.

Figure 21

Anastasis

Fresco from the west bay, north wall, Church of Panagia tou Arakou, Lagoudera, Cyprus (ca. 1192). (Dumbarton Oaks, Washington, D.C.)

Below this depiction of Christ descending into Hades (upper register) to retrieve Adam and Eve is a painting of Christ's baptism in the Jordan (lower register). Directly in front of this lower panel there would have sat a baptismal font. Just as Christ descends into Sheol to retrieve the first man and woman, so he descends with the catechumen (person seeking entry to the church) to die and rise with him or her. And similarly, just as Christ was tempted by Satan and then renounced him at baptism (in actuality, just after his baptism) and at his passion, so for the newly minted Christian.

Paul's notion of baptism as a participation in the death of Christ (Romans 6) is no metaphor; it is the stage and script of redemption. In short, the Passion of Christ was not a one-time affair—it was continually relived in baptism.

Creatio ex Nihilo or *Creatio Continua?*

It has long been observed that the doctrine of creation is subject to two different descriptions in the Bible. According to Genesis 1, the creation of the world appears to be a single and once-in-a-lifetime action. God laid the foundations and set creation in motion. No further maintenance was required, thus the teaching of *creatio ex nihilo*, "creation out of nothing."

But alongside this we have numerous examples, especially in the Psalms, of an ongoing battle on the part of God to uphold creation. The forces of evil wage war against the divine will, and creation must be continually shored up against these onslaughts. This notion of *creatio continua*, "an ongoing creation," is most at home in the Psalms, the prayer book of ancient Israel. In the liturgy, God's creative task is never at an end. The same analogy holds for the Passion. In the Gospels and creeds it is presented as a single moment in historical time, but at baptism the drama comes to life time and again.

At baptism, the envy of Satan toward the status God wishes to confer on men and women returns with a vengeance. This reveals an aspect of angelology that is not often appreciated. The angels serve as an important category that marks off human life from the divine. One might expect that the resulting hierarchy would be a simple pyramid, with men and women on the bottom, angels in the middle, and God at the top.

For both Jews and Christians this was not the case. One of the functions of the angelic host is to be supplanted by humans! We saw how the Rabbis described Israel's election as God's choice of Israel over the other nations and over the angels themselves. Not surprisingly the angels contested this election and had to be put down for their efforts. As a consequence of this election, the angels in heaven began their praise of the deity *after* Israel. Similarly, in Christian writings we have seen that the angels were commanded to prostrate themselves to Adam and Christ. Some angels resisted this command, and they were eternally damned for their efforts.

What I would like to underscore is that this angelic resistance, whether to the election of Israel or to the resurrection of Christ, *per-*

sists. Earlier we examined a midrash in which God thwarted the designs of Satan by removing the sin of Israel from the scales and hiding it within his robe. What I did not emphasize then was that the occasion of this encounter was the Day of Atonement; it was the day on which Israel repents before her God and is restored to the status she had at Sinai prior to venerating the golden calf.

This restoration of Israel to her former glory enrages Satan, and the midrash begins with his calling into question the fairness of Israel's election itself. Satan begins by asking God whether Israel's sins are any fewer than the sins of other nations of the world. Nothing about Israel's moral capacity seems to warrant the favors God has cast their way. As in many other (but not all) traditions about the election of Israel, the moral question is left unanswered. Israel is not chosen because of her moral nature; she is chosen solely by the grace of God. Christian baptism shows striking similarities to the Jewish Day of Atonement. Both rites are penitential; both restore humans to their status before the Fall, and both stimulate the renewed contest between the justice and mercy of God.

The story of Adam and Eve begins with sin in paradise and ends with redemption on Easter Sunday. The Orthodox churches saw the redemption of Adam and Eve from Sheol as of such consequence that they canonized this image, the *anastasis*, and so made it a permanent witness to the work of Christ. What the Gospels passed over in silence, the iconographer filled in.

But this story of Adam and Eve was never narrated as a simple, objective account of human beginnings, as a story that could take its place alongside modern theories of the "Big Bang" or evolution. Instead, the story of Adam and Eve has always been subject to liturgical enactment. It derives its meaning from the world of penitence and restoration. A more pertinent parallel than Darwinian evolution is the parable of the Prodigal Son, a favorite Gospel reading in the Lenten season.

The story of the Fall had value in the early church because every Christian was called to situate his or her life in between the contours of Adam and Christ as well as Eve and Mary. The arc that extends from Adam to Christ defines a horizon of mercy.

Jews and Christians read Genesis in very different ways. Adam and Eve, from a Jewish perspective, reflect the glory that was to shine on Israel. Adam was already a keeper of Torah; Moses recaptures the effulgence of Eden. For the Christian, Adam points toward Christ; at baptism the glories once appointed for Adam are claimed by the catechumen. But behind all this difference is a larger structural unity: Both Jews and Christians understand themselves as elected peoples given respective narratives that have coherent beginnings, middles, and ends. These ends are carefully and continuously pondered and eventually affect the way creation's beginning is re-told. This broad and supple story-cycle embraces the life of each and every reader. In the liturgy of synagogue and church both traditions situate the penitential reenactment of history's opening act within a larger drama of cosmic significance, and both ultimately portray a relationship with a God whose justice is revealed through mercy and whose love is the true font of all wisdom.

Glossary

Abdiel. One of the major angelic figures in Milton's *Paradise Lost*. His name, significantly, means "Servant of God." He is one of the members of Satan's band of angels who retire to the north after Christ has been designated King over the Heavens. Satan says that his intentions are to prepare a fit celebration for this event, but in actuality he is plotting rebellion. Abdiel, alone among Satan's many allies, defies this rebellious intention and quits Satan's fold.

Annunciation. The moment when the Archangel Gabriel comes to announce to the Virgin Mary that she is to conceive the Christ child. It is only recorded in Luke's Gospel but becomes the paradigm event for all Christian obedience to the call of the gospel. As such, it was the subject of hundreds upon hundreds of artistic depictions and homiletic expansions. It is celebrated on March 25 of the church year.

Apocrypha. A term capable of many definitions. In its most narrow sense it refers to those books in the Roman Catholic Bible that were deemed of questionable significance to the Reformed churches (such as Judith, Tobit, Ecclesiasticus/Ben Sira, among others). In this book, the term is used in a more generic sense: books that were treasured by Jews and Christians in antiquity but stand outside the official canon or list of the biblical corpus.

Aramaic. The official language of the Persian empire (538 B.C.E. until 333 or so) that remained very important for commerce and literature in Syria-Palestine until well into the Common Era. It became the standard colloquial tongue of Jews and Christians who lived in classical Mesopotamia, or what now would be considered modern Iraq and Syria. It is still a living language in parts of the Middle East and remains the liturgical dialect for Syrian Christians of a variety of types.

Augustine (354–430 C.E.). Perhaps the most important thinker of the Latin patristic period for the Christian West. His best-known works include his *Confessions* and the *City of God*. Long entranced by the book of Genesis, he wrote several commentaries on it. His thought became the standard fare of theological curricula throughout the cathedral schools and universities of the Middle Ages and remained (and remains) highly influential among most Protestants. The classical definition of the concept of "original sin" in the West comes from Augustine.

Before the Common Era (B.C.E.). See Common Era.

189

Catechumen. A Greek word referring to a person who declares an interest in becoming a baptized Christian. In the rite of the early church the formal process began at the beginning of Lent with the registration of the person and a renunciation of Satan. The catechumen kept the Lenten regime, attending services regularly to hear the scriptures read and expounded but being excused from attendance when the Eucharistic mystery was celebrated. On Holy Saturday, otherwise known as the Easter Vigil, the catechumen was baptized at midnight, clothed with white garments and anointed with oil. He or she became a new creation.

Church Fathers. Those theologians that shaped what became the thinking and structure of the early church. Those who received this title usually lived after the apostles (thus, the so-called postapostolic era), or roughly the mid-second century. The period of the church fathers, also identified as the patristic era (from the Latin *pater,* "father"), concludes with the rise of the Middle Ages.

Conceptio per aurem. This term literally means "conceiving through the ear." It refers to Mary's miraculous conception of the baby Jesus through her obedience at the annunciation. Mary's obedient hearing and conception of the Christ Child was regularly contrasted with Eve's gullible submission to the suggestion of the serpent and her conception of Cain, the first murderer. In early Christian art, the serpent frequently has his mouth directly in Eve's ear, whereas at the annunciation Mary or Gabriel (or both!) point at the Virgin's ear.

Common Era (C.E.). A more neutral manner of referring to those centuries that follow the birth of Christ. The more common identification, A.D., poses a problem for Jews, as it amounts virtually to a faith affirmation: *anno domini,* "in the year of [our] Lord."

Cotton Genesis. An important manuscript of the Septuagint that contained a set of illustrations of the biblical story. It dates to the fifth or sixth century. Its name derives from Robert Cotton, who bought the manuscript in the early seventeenth century. The manuscript was badly burned by a fire in 1731. This important text is one of the earliest illustrated Bibles and an important witness to early Christian artistic conventions. Enough of the document remains to show that it provided the basis for the mosaics that now adorn a cupola in the San Marco Church in Venice. This church, in turn, has become an important witness to artistic conventions of early Christianity.

Election. The central theological affirmation of the Old Testament: God chose the Jewish people as his very own and vouchsafed to them his most prized possession, the Torah. The stories about the patriarchs in Genesis (Abraham, Isaac, Jacob, and his sons) are all centered on this doctrine and the difficulties it posed for the individuals who fell under the claim of the divine hand. Those who fall under the claim of the elect are also designated "first-born." Hence, Exodus 4:22–23 identifies Israel as God's first-born son.

Ephrem (306–73 C.E.). Perhaps the most important thinker in the Syriac theological tradition. He lived in the late fourth century and composed most of his theology in liturgical poetry. Known as "the Harp of the Holy Spirit," he was arguably the greatest poet of the patristic period. Little is known about his biography other than that he was born and spent his early years in Nisibis. Later he moved to the city of Edessa, where he spent his remaining years. He became and remains quite significant in Orthodox circles. The Roman church celebrates his feast day on June 18.

Exile. The state of being estranged from the land of Israel. Israel was exiled from her land in 587 B.C.E. with the promise that she would one day return. Some of the exiles returned in 538 under the edict of Cyrus (see the book of Ezra), but many remained in Babylon. Because these exiles failed to construct a culture and temple that matched the prophetic promises for this return, many writers believed that the exile never ended. In 70 C.E., with the destruction of the Second Temple by the Romans, there was another dispersion of the Jewish people. In Jewish liturgy and memory the events of 587 and 70 are collapsed into nearly a single event; on the fast day of the ninth of Av, both are mourned. To this day, Jewish daily, Sabbath, and festival prayers are punctuated by pleas that God will gather in his peoples from the ends of the world.

First-Born. According to biblical law, the first-born son was the beloved son and received a twofold share of the family patrimony (Deut. 21:15–17). Although the title is firmly defined in legal corpora, it is used more flexibly in the book of Genesis. There the boundary between "first-born" and "chosen" becomes somewhat fuzzy. This is because the book of Genesis wishes to show how God's electing hand subverts human expectation. As a result, later-born sons are, more often than not, preferred. The Jewish prayer book remembers Jacob as "first-born" even though, technically, he was born after Esau.

Garment of Skin. According to a widespread Jewish and Christian tradition, Adam and Eve were clothed in resplendent glory at creation, like unto the angels. When they sinned, they immediately lost this divine form and were rendered like the animals. Outfitted with a perishable body, they left Eden to toil on the earth. The Orthodox tradition prefers to refer to the fallen state of humanity under the rubric "garments of skin" as opposed to the Western concept of "original sin." Although the differences are exaggerated by some, it is fair to say that East puts a premium on the fact that Adam brought death into the world, while the emphasis in the West, due to Augustine, is on sin.

Genesis Rabbah. An important fourth-century composition from the land of Israel. It reads like a continuous line-by-line commentary on the Genesis text. But its appearance is deceiving. Like all rabbinic texts it is made up of small pieces of disparate rabbinic teaching that have been sewn together by later editors to appear as a single book. Much of the midrashic interpretations found in this important collection are far older than the fourth century; this date simply designates the time when all these traditions were collected and edited.

Golden Calf. Almost immediately after Israel received the Torah at Mt. Sinai (Exodus 19–24), she builds the golden calf (Exodus 32). According to one rabbinic tradition Israel began planning this calf the moment she heard the injunction against it (*Exodus Rabbah* 42:7–8). Another rabbinic tradition declares that every tragic event that has been visited upon creation since that time has had rolled into it some element of punishment for the veneration of that calf (Babylonian Talmud, *Sanhedrin* 102a). Thus two elements dear to the Christian notion of original sin are present in this Jewish tradition: the *sin was nearly instantaneous* after the moment of beatitude, and the *consequences of that sin were uncontainable;* they rebounded across many generations. So heinous and well known were the effects of this idolatrous moment that the entire biblical scene could be captured in the brief Hebrew phrase, *oto ma'aseh,* "that deed."

Gregory of Nyssa (d. 394 C.E.). A very important church father who lived in a region of Central Turkey known as Cappadocia. A contemporary of St. Ephrem, he lived just a few hundred kilometers away from Edessa. Though the linguistic-cultural gulf between the two was enormous (Greek versus Semite), there are numerous points of theological continuity. Though a married man, he wrote one of the most famous treatises of the early church defending the monastic virtue of virginity. He, his brother Basil, and his good friend Gregory of Nazianzus along with his erudite sister Macrina are known as "the Cappadocians."

Happy Fault. An English translation of the Latin phrase *felix culpa.* It occurs in the famous song of the Easter Vigil, the *exultet,* a song sung over the paschal candle at the beginning of the liturgy. In recounting the history of salvation that will culminate in the death and resurrection of Jesus Christ, the song stops midway to exclaim, "O *necessary* sin of Adam, that Christ has blotted out by his death; O *happy* fault [*felix culpa*] which has earned for us such a great redeemer." In *Paradise Lost,* among Adam's final words before departing Eden we find this important theological theme (11:469–478).

Imitatio Christi. In the early church, Christian faith was not so much an affirmation of creedal principles as it was a *way of life.* Already in the book of Acts, when Stephen is martyred, his last words to the crowd recall those of Christ on the cross (7:54–60). Eventually, in the second century, numerous other acts of the apostles were composed, and the theme that tied them together is the desire to define the Christian life as an imitation of Christ's life. Ephrem, in his *Hymns on Julian Saba,* an early monastic adept consistently lauds Julian for his *dibbore,* or "virtuous ways of living." Because Christ himself was not married, the celibate state became an honored way of imitation.

Jubilees. This is an extremely important document, for it is our earliest attested example of a rewritten Bible. The earliest forms of biblical commentary were not line-by-line compositions as we know them today but complex and quite learned retellings of the biblical original. Sometimes the book of *Jubilees* takes great liberties in its wandering from the biblical original, while at other times it reproduces the text almost verbatim.

Kenosis. A Greek word meaning "emptying." It was used in Philippians to define the Christological mystery: Christ emptied himself of his divine attributes to come to earth and take on human life for a time. Because Christ was obedient to this vocation and humbled himself to the point of death, God "highly exalted him / and gave him the name / that is above every other name" (2:9). In this perspective, power and glory in the end only come to those who renounce them from the start. This theological mystery, which is at the heart of the Christian life, remained unintelligible to Satan in *Paradise Lost.*

Michelangelo. The justly famous sixteenth-century artist and sculptor from Florence, Italy. A highly devout man, he took on religious assignments not merely for the stipend they afforded but for the theological opportunity they provided. The frescoes that adorn the ceiling of the Sistine Chapel are worthy of the most intense theological analysis.

Midrash. The method (or methods) used by the Rabbis to expound the Jewish scriptures. Though it is impossible to give an adequate summary in just a few sentences, midrash begins with a sense that something is problematic in the biblical text ("Why does God say, 'Let *us* create man?'") and turns to another part of the biblical canon to see if it might shed light on the same. The result is often the creation of a third biblical narrative that it is not quite the same as either of the first two.

John Milton (1608–74). Puritan thinker and poet of the seventeenth century. He wrote *Paradise Lost* near the end of his life while blind. Though much of this composition derives from his individual genius, Milton was also an accomplished student of theology, and many of the building blocks of this massive epic can be traced back to biblical, patristic, medieval, and Reformation sources.

Mishnah. A compilation of rabbinic legal dicta of various dates that were assembled into a single document around 200 C.E. At first most of this composition circulated in memorized form. We can thus understand why it was called "Oral Torah," for unlike the written scrolls of the Bible, it was transmitted by word of mouth.

Mother of God. A translation of the Latin *mater dei* and Greek *theotokos.* This title was made binding on all Christians at the Council of Ephesus in 431. It became instantly famous and inspired many homilies. Its origin was in the Christological controversies of the late fourth and early fifth centuries. A certain Nestorius found the term objectionable, for he believed that only the human nature had been born of Mary, not the divine. In denouncing this move, the church solidified that Jesus was *indivisibly* God and man. As John of Damascus put it, "If she who bore him is the *Theotokos*, then certainly he who was born of her is both God and man" (*Orthodox Faith* 3:12).

Original Sin. In its most narrow sense the term identifies a theological notion that derives from Augustine: At conception each person *inherits* a drive toward sin from the *improperly ordered conjugal relations* of the parents. Unaware of genetic theory, Augustine explained the principles of heredity through the act of copulation. Augustine arrived at the general idea of original sin from liturgical practice. At that time, the church baptized infants. Because baptism absolves original sin and infants have not yet sinned in their own person, they must have inherited sin from their parents.

Paradise Lost. The epic composition of John Milton. It comprises twelve books, each made up of some thousands of lines of verse. The work is not written in chronological order. It begins with Satan in Hades after his fall, turns to the story of creation, then tells of Satan's fall, the fall of humankind, their eviction from Eden, and their hope for restoration.

Paul. The most important figure in the New Testament after Jesus. His letters—which antedate the composition of the Gospels—formed the basis of all subsequent Christian reflection on the nature of the gospel message. In Romans 5 and 1 Corinthians 15 he established the relationship between the first and second

Adam, one of the most productive theological moves in all of Christian thought. In Colossians 2:14, a letter attributed to Paul but probably written in his name, the early church found both the basic principle of its theory of atonement and the overturning of the baneful legacy of Adam.

Pelagius. Born in Britain in 354, he was baptized some thirty years later in Rome where he became a very influential voice. He is best known as an important theological opponent of Augustine. Pelagius opposed Augustine's notion that Adam's fall deprived human beings of free will. Rather than inherit a fallen state from Adam, every person has chosen to imitate him. Pelagius had a much more optimistic view of human nature and believed that the perfection of the monastic adept was within the scope of human possibility.

Protevangelium of James. A text from the mid-second century that records the life of the Virgin Mary up to and including the moment of her delivery of the Christ child. Though there is no historical or scriptural basis for most of the narrative, it became the basis of a good bit of latter Mariology.

Purity. According to biblical law, certain bodily states such as menstruation, sexual emissions, and the handling of corpses rendered one unfit to enter the Temple. Sometimes the impurity was of sufficient strength that it could be passed on by contact. Different rituals were employed to purify a contaminated person or object. Being impure is not the same as being in sin. In fact, becoming impure was often natural (a result of sexual relations) and even obligatory (tending to the dead, especially immediate relatives).

Rabbis. A technical term used to identify a group of Jewish sages who expounded the scriptures and passed on a series of oral traditions or laws. Almost every subsequent Jewish group traced their lineage back to these figures. The rabbinic movement is responsible for the Mishnah, the Talmud, and the various midrashic compilations such as *Genesis Rabbah*.

San Marco. See Cotton Genesis.

Santa Maria Maggiore. A church in Rome that was built in the wake of naming Mary the "mother of God." A famous depiction of the annunciation is found therein on a triumphal arch in which Mary is seated on her throne with distaff and spindle, preparing to weave the body of the incarnate God.

Satan. Originally a good angel, he fell because of his hatred of God or humanity. In some traditions he was head of the entire angelic assembly and was titled the firstborn of the heavenly host. According to the *Life of Adam and Eve*, he lost his position of primacy with the creation of Adam. After his rebellion he was evicted from heaven, and according to Christian tradition, Satan alone out of all creation is offered no possibility of repentance.

Septuagint. A translation of the Hebrew text of the Old Testament into Greek. Though the translation was made by Jews in Alexandria, Egypt, a couple of centuries before Christ, it became identified as a Christian text when it was taken up by the nascent Christian movement.

Shekinah. A Hebrew noun that derives from a verbal root (*shakan*) meaning "to tabernacle, to tent among." It refers to the deposit of a portion of God's being within the community of Israel. According to rabbinic tradition, God's *Shekinah* departed Jerusalem after the destruction of the Temple and now resides with Israel in the Diaspora. It will not be fully gathered into the land of Israel until all of the Jews are similarly regathered.

Mount Sinai. The location where Moses received the Ten Commandments and the rest of God's Torah. It also marks the spot where God formally "elected," or chose, Israel as his very own. Almost immediately after this moment of election, Israel rebelled and built the golden calf.

Sistine Chapel. See Michelangelo.

Syriac. A dialect of Aramaic spoken in classical Mesopotamia. It was probably only slightly variant in pronunciation and grammar from the Aramaic dialect spoken by the Jews in the same locale. Written in its own distinctive script, it became the liturgical language of the third major branch of ancient Christianity (that is, the so-called "Oriental" or Syro-Armenian traditions).

Talmud. A commentary on the Mishnah that includes many interpretive glosses on the Bible. It exists in two forms, one from Palestine (the Jerusalem Talmud) and one from Babylon (the Babylonian Talmud). The Babylonian is the later of the two and became the more studied and important version. The Talmud, along with the Bible, is the most important sacred text in Jewish tradition. Talmudic traditions can predate the Mishnah, but the date of its final composition is usually placed in the fifth century.

Targum. An Aramaic translation—and sometimes interpretive expansion—of the Hebrew Bible. Dozens of Targumim (plural of Targum) existed in Late Antiquity, of which about a half dozen survive. The most important text forms are *Onkelos*, *Neophyti*, and *Pseudo-Jonathan*. Although all postdate the rise of the rabbinic movement, there are many very ancient interpretive traditions embedded within these translations.

Telos. A Greek word meaning "end." Its technical definition in theological literature refers to either the purpose of human existence or the end of time when God will bring his creation to consummation.

Virgin Mary. The mother of Jesus. In early Christianity, due to the influence of Paul, Jesus was often described as the "second Adam," meaning the one who brought Adam to his completion. And so with Mary; she became the "second Eve." In early Christian interpretation, this allowed literary motifs of Mary (such as the *conceptio per aurem*) to attach themselves to Eve and vice versa.

Appendix A

Biblical Origins and the Fall

*Rabbi Abbahu said: I led Adam into the garden of Eden and com-
manded him and he transgressed my commandment, whereupon I
punished him by dismissal and exile. . . . Similarly, I brought his
descendants into the land of Israel and commanded them, and they
also transgressed my commands whereupon I punished them by dismissal and exile.*

—*Genesis Rabbah* 19:9

This book has been almost entirely about the *reception* of Genesis
2 and 3 in early Judaism and Christianity. From time to time I
have considered the work of modern biblical scholars and their interest in the *formation* of that text. But for the most part, this has not been
my focus. I thought, however, that my efforts would not be complete
without some attention to this modern problem. And so I would like
to address the issue of original sin in the Bible and the problems it has
posed for a reading of the first few chapters of Genesis. As we have
seen throughout this work, the key to a solution is the ability to locate
that end toward which creation points.

The Problem

The modern age has not been kind to the traditional interpretation of
the story of Adam and Eve. Since the rise of modern biblical studies
in the early part of the eighteenth century, more than a modicum of
doubt has been cast on the standard Christian understanding of that
story as "the Fall." If the transgression of Adam really does usher in
the reign of sin and death from which the rest of the biblical odyssey
will seek redress, why is Adam's sin and its consequences *never* mentioned until the writings of Paul? Could the story really have such

intrinsic significance and yet be completely ignored by the rest of the Old Testament and the teachings of Jesus?

The problem is a real and profound one and must be addressed. On the one hand, I am in clear agreement with most of my biblical colleagues that the story of Adam and Eve, on its own terms, does not lead inevitably to the Christian notion of "the Fall." Yet I do not believe that focusing on the *bare narrative* of Genesis 2–3 is the proper way to approach this doctrine. If we wish to place this doctrine on solid biblical grounds, we will need to expand our notion of what creation entails in the minds of our biblical authors. And armed with this datum, I think we will be better prepared to understand, with some sympathy, why the fathers of the church read Genesis 2–3 in the manner that they did.

Two Creation Stories

Reading the Bible's story of creation has never been a simple matter. Modern readers have puzzled over the relation between these ancient descriptions of the world's beginnings and the alternative accounts provided by scientific investigation. But there are other, even more basic problems. Consider, for example, the long-known fact that the Bible contains not one but two accounts of creation. And both these accounts are presented back to back at the very beginning of Genesis.

The earliest interpreters of the Bible, both Jewish and Christian, thought that both accounts came from the hand of Moses. In the first story (Gen. 1:1–2:4a), Moses provided only the barest essentials about creation. His diction was grand and majestic; God creates the world through the power of his word. "Let there be light" God commands, "and there was light." "Let us make man in our image," God suggests (to whom?!), and he was so made. If this first chapter were set to music, one would expect its setting to include a large chorus and orchestra.

In the second story of creation, Moses dispenses with these broad brush strokes and gives a far more detailed presentation (Gen. 2:4b–3:24). The impersonal and majestic portrait of God is displaced momentarily in favor of a more informal approach. "The Lord God formed every animal of the field," Moses writes, "and brought them to Adam to see what he would call them." Later, when Adam and Eve have sinned, God appears in the cool of the day to pass judgment (Gen. 3:8), but before he sternly evicts the couple from his garden of delights he pauses to clothe them with "garments of skin" (Gen. 3:21).

If the first story provides the reader with a majestic conception of creation in its entirety; the second is a far more intimate examination of a detail or two within that created order. The tone is tragic, yet homespun. It eschews the elaborate structure of the first story in favor of a more impressionistic, and consequently incomplete, presentation of the events.

The author of the first creation story uses language that is similar to that found in the priestly legislation of Leviticus. He takes great interest in the division of all life into its various species; he asserts that the task of the sun and moon is to order the calendrical cycles of humans; and he grounds Sabbath rest in the created order. All these characteristics are developed in elaborate detail in Leviticus. Genesis 1 is but a brief foretaste or précis of what is to follow. Because of the numerous parallels between this account of creation and the book of Leviticus, modern scholars have named the writer of Genesis 1 "P," a convention that signifies a school of priests.

The author of the second story uses a unique name to identify the deity, YHWH Elohim. This writer, unlike the priestly source, does not show the same fastidiousness about the personal name of Israel's God. He feels free to use the name YHWH prior to its formal revelation to Moses. As a result, he is identified as the circle of "J," a convention that comes from the German form of YHWH, JHWH. There is profound disagreement as to whether or not J was supplemented by another source (often abbreviated "E") and whether J preceded or followed the writing of P. We need not worry about these details; for our purposes the first four books of the Bible are divisible into priestly (P) and epic (J or perhaps, better, "JE") sources. What is agreed on, however, is that in the final editing of the Torah there was a conscious decision made to place the P story first. It was intended to introduce the story that followed.

The Priestly Story of Creation

The modern discovery of the sources of the Pentateuch has revolutionized the way the Bible is read. Outside of religious fundamentalists who have an a priori commitment to the notion of a single Mosaic author for the Pentateuch, nearly all accept the thesis that Genesis 1–3 comes from two different literary sources. Still, the division of these chapters into two different literary sources should not obscure the responsibility of the interpreter to account for their assemblage into a single text. The final editor of the Bible clearly intended these two stories to be read together. The question is, how?

The first thing to be noted is that the biblical writer does link his account of creation's beginnings with the end toward which creation points, although the links are only apparent after the whole story has unfolded. Our own conceptions of creation are far more scientific in outlook, and we expect creation stories merely to disclose the rudiments of nature's origins. Not so the ancients. They told creation stories with the primary purpose of providing a cosmic foundation for the meaning and purpose of human life. Creation of human life could not be understood fully without relating creation to its appropriate *telos* or end. Because the Babylonians imagined the building of great cities and temples as the supreme task of the human being, it should be no surprise that their stories of creation culminated in the building of Babylon and the descent of the office of the king from heaven.

The P writer makes a similar move but achieves it in a *very* different fashion. In between the opening narratives about the creation of human beings and the end toward which this points—the election of Israel at Mt. Sinai—we find a lengthy set of stories about Israel's pre-Sinaitic ancestors. Unlike other myths of origin, the biblical story takes a long time before it discloses its ultimate aim. No doubt this delay is intentional; it allows Israel's appearance in the story—like her election itself—to emerge as a surprise, a completely unexpected event from the perspective of Genesis 1–11.

At Sinai the purpose of creation comes into focus. Moses ascends that mountain in the presence of his fellow Israelites. "The glory of the LORD settled on Mount Sinai," the P writer reveals, "and the cloud covered it for six days; on the seventh day he called to Moses out of the cloud." (Exod. 24:16) While he is protected within this cloud-covered peak, God reveals directions for the sanctuary he will inhabit (Exodus 25–31). Having heard this revelation, Moses descends the mountain. His face is aglow as a result of his close audience with the Creator (Exod. 34:29–35). When he reaches the Israelites, Moses discloses the plans for the sanctuary, and the people proceed to construct it (Exodus 35–40).

As scholars have long noted, the building of this sanctuary parallels the creation of the world. Like Genesis 1, the story of the tabernacle's construction is patterned after a sevenfold activity. The sevenfold activity begins immediately after Moses ascends to Mt. Sinai. He waits there for six days and then on the seventh God draws him near to his very presence (Exod. 24:15b–18). The initial plans for the tabernacle are given to Moses in a set of seven addresses that conclude with the command to observe the Sabbath rest of the seventh day (Exod. 25:1; 30:11, 17, 22, 34; 31:1, 12). The fashioning of priestly vestments is marked by the sevenfold refrain "he did as the Lord had commanded him," (Exod. 39:1, 5, 7, 21, 22, 27, 30) as is the erection of the tabernacle itself (Exod. 40:19, 21, 23, 25, 27, 29, 32).

The narrative describing the construction of the tabernacle ends with the remark "Moses finished the work." This recalls the conclusion of creation in Genesis 2:1–2 where almost the exact same terminology is used to describe the completion of creation by God himself. Just as Genesis 1 ends with divine rest on the Sabbath, so at the end of Exodus 40 when God's glory descends and fills the tabernacle. The indwelling of this shrine after seven works of construction parallels the sacralizing of the Sabbath day on the seventh day of creation. The "rest" to be provided by the sanctuary is an apt and fitting parallel to Sabbath rest. Just as the Sabbath is both within time and stands outside of it, so the hallowed ground of the sanctuary is situated on earth yet points beyond earth's finite contours.

But there is a significant advance in this Sinaitic moment. Whereas in creation God's sacralizing of the Sabbath takes place apart from human knowledge and participation, *at Sinai God involves man in the process of creation itself*. It is striking that whereas God finishes the creation of the world in seven days, it is Moses who constructs the tabernacle through seven deeds. At Sinai, unlike creation, God approaches Israel and draws her near to himself. The Rabbis caught the high valuation of this human act of world building when they describe the purpose of Moses' action as causing the divine presence (*Shekinah*) to dwell within *a work of human hands*. As Peter Shäfer summarizes the rabbinic position, "the creation of the world is not, if one accepts this view, solely the work of God but also the work of man: only when the man Moses erects the tabernacle is God's created order brought to completion." Subsequently, when explaining why the completion of the tabernacle was necessary to complete creation itself, Schäfer concludes, "The world, from its beginning onward, requires that God be in relationship with mankind; without such a relationship between God and man, the creation of the world would be senseless and superfluous."

Creation has been mimed in the building and consecration of the tabernacle and its priestly attendants. But the point is more profound than that of mere literary parallel. *The construction of the tabernacle is the climax of creation.* At Sinai, God descended to earth and drew Israel to himself. Creation remained unfinished until the day the tabernacle was completed. It should not surprise that Christian interpreters, from the patristic era forward, saw the tabernacle as similar to the womb of the Virgin Mary. Both tabernacle and womb became the "bearers of God," and both were seen as the focal point of God's creative design.

The Heart of the Jewish Bible:
Lighting the Sacrificial Pyre

According to the theology of P, once the tabernacle and its altar had been consecrated by Moses, the preparatory work of the liturgy was finished. And this point must be underscored: when the daily sacrifices began (Exod. 29:38–42 = Leviticus 9) *the goal of all creation would be consummated.* The promise of God is now on the verge of realization: "*I will dwell among the Israelites, and I will be their God*" (Exod. 29:45). The people, in turn, offer a public response to God's decision to reside in the tabernacle. Rather than pledging words of obedience to the Torah, as they do in J, the people fall on their knees in praise and trembling at his awesome appearance:

> As [Moses and Aaron] came out from the tent of meeting, they blessed the people and the glory of the LORD appeared to all the people. Fire came out from the LORD and consumed the burnt offerings and the fat on the altar. When all the people saw it, they gave a loud shout and fell on their faces. (Lev. 9:23–24)

The moment of lighting the sacrificial pyre is the very apogee of the Torah. And, as such, this moment of wonder and glory has ample parallels in the ancient Near East. In these texts, the moment of temple building *always* ushers in an age of peace and tranquillity. Because the Temple was in microcosm what the world was in macrocosm, ancient Near Eastern texts are quite happy to compare the erection of a temple to the act of creating the world. Some scholars have reconstructed an earlier form of P that would make the biblical tale look very much like these ancient Near Eastern models. Moses received a divine blueprint of the tabernacle and its founding rites (Exodus 25–31) that he then put in place (Exodus 35–40; Leviticus 8); having finished the installation of the building, the altar was lit amid great festivity and joy (Leviticus 9).

But our biblical writer does not honor this script in the final form of the story; a detail that is nearly always lost on those scholars who content themselves with reconstructing more primitive versions of the canonical story. *For as soon as the sacrificial pyre has been sanctified by fire, it is profaned.* Or, to put it in a slightly different way: this foundational moment did not culminate in beatitude but cultic error. Just as fire issued from the Temple to consume the first sacrifices, so fire miraculously and immediately issues forth and devours the first offenders of the liturgy.

> Fire came out from the LORD and consumed the burnt offering and the fat on the altar. . . ." (Lev. 9:24)
> Fire came out from before the LORD and consumed them. . . ." (Lev. 10:2)

It is easy to see from the parallelism of these two texts why the Jewish medieval commentator Rashbam argued that it was one and the same fire that both consumed the sacrifices and incinerated Nadab and Abihu.

Nor is this the end of the matter. A sacrificial rite is not concluded until all of the flesh of the animal has been properly disposed of. This can be done by incineration on the altar, disposal outside the camp, or consumption by a qualified person, the specific means depending on the type and grade of sacrifice. It turns out that Aaron's other two sons, Elazar and Ittamar, had failed to eat the purification sacrifices they had prepared in Leviticus 9:15. And so the story of the founding of the cult ends with guilt distributed among the entire priestly family: Aaron and his four sons have been found negligent of their duties, and Moses must conclude this episode with a harsh rebuke (Lev. 10:16–20). It is not until Leviticus 16, the first rite of atonement, that these priestly sins are rectified. Israel's first public penitential moment is motivated by the errors of her cultic beginnings.

The Chasm Between Leviticus 8 and 9

Let us pursue the issue of priestly error from a slightly different angle. We have set this story against its ancient Near Eastern environment, but its placement within the literary framework of Leviticus is also revealing. Most readers of Leviticus do not notice the major disjuncture that exists between Leviticus 8 and 9. In Leviticus 8 Aaron and his sons have been, more or less, passive participants in a seven-day rite of consecration. It is Moses who brings them forward to the altar and washes and clothes them; and it is Moses who supervises and performs nearly all the rites at the altar. We should also add that Moses performs all these actions according to the precise decrees given in Exodus 29:1–37; nothing in Leviticus 8 is left to human improvisation or chance. Seven times, the narrator underscores, Moses completes a portion of the ritual "just as the LORD had commanded." This sevenfold refrain, which is repeated over seven days, ties the entire ceremony back to creation itself, which was also completed over a seven-day sequence.

Enter Leviticus 9 and the mold is broken. The foundation rites end as do the sequences of seven-fold cultic actions. Moreover, unlike Leviticus 8, the ritual narrated in Leviticus 9 has no corresponding command section, so *it is the first act since the arrival at Sinai that P has not pre-scripted.* The period of careful design, oversight, and execution through the agency of Moses and the Deity has drawn to a close. Yet as soon as the closely superintending hand of God is removed and a space is created for human autonomy, things begin to unravel.

The picture drawn by P is striking. Although creation began with an account of what took place during the first six days in Genesis 1, it did not reach its true climax until Moses and the Israelites had arrived at Mt. Sinai. When the priesthood was consecrated and the altar lit, God's purpose for the world was completed. He had elected the nation Israel and commanded them to draw near to his presence and tend his daily needs. But no sooner has creation come to closure than its very centerpiece, the tabernacle, was violated. In consequence of this, the Day of Atonement served to set creation aright.

Let me summarize this interpretation of Leviticus 10 by underscoring what the text does not say. Although P will not allow the story of the founding of the cult to end in utter beatitude, he is also loath to assert in any dogmatic way that the error of Nadab and Abihu was an act of obstreperous rebellion against, or even wanton disregard for, the God of Israel. We are left completely in the dark about the motivation of these two wayward priests and the specific nature of their sin. God's presence in the tabernacle, P seems to imply, is elusive. Ritual prescriptions seek to safeguard the practice of the cult, but they do not eliminate all danger. To house even a portion of God's being on earth (his *Shekinah*, in rabbinic vocabulary) is a daunting task, and no code of cultic law, however detailed, can head off all dangers.

But this ambiguity about the motives of Nadab and Abihu should not blind us to the structural significance of their error. In P's view, the prescriptions for behavior around sancta are not graded as to weight of sin or level of human intentionality.

The Story of the Golden Calf in J

The structural significance of Leviticus 10 has been lost on many readers of the Bible, both ancient and modern. The reason for this is easy to uncover. The final editors of the Torah were not content to leave the story of the founding of the tabernacle in the form that P had bequeathed them. Instead of moving in a seamless fashion from the blueprint (Exodus 25–31) to its completion (Exodus 35–40), a catastrophe intervenes—the building of the golden calf and the beginning of idolatry. The foundation narrative of the cult was marred by human sin even before the first tent peg had been secured. This textual insertion had grave consequences for the understanding of Nadab and Abihu's sin as set forth by P. In the eyes of most, the sin of the golden calf was by far more serious than the improper offering of the two sons of Aaron. To commit a wanton act of idolatry at the foot of Mt. Sinai was to show such disregard for the covenant that the very election of Israel itself might be called into question. Indeed, for a moment God thought to destroy the entire nation and start over again with the figure of Moses (Exodus 32:9–10).

Peter Kearney has argued that the introduction of the golden calf into the middle of the tabernacle narrative has resulted in the following sequence: creation (Exodus 25–31), fall (32–34), and then restoration (35–40). If we exclude Leviticus 8–10 from our picture, this reading would be attractive but still troublesome. In spite of a brilliant job of editing, there is no evidence that the priestly narrative about the construction of the tabernacle (Exodus 35–40) "knows" a tradition about the calf. Kearney has not done justice to what Geoffrey Hartman has aptly called the "frictionality" of biblical narrative. It is easier and simpler to understand the placement of the calf as an editorial act of upping the ante of original sin. *If the P narrator had placed the act at the conclusion of the tabernacle cycle, the shapers of the canon were determined to do him one better: the act of original sin would precede the ceremony of installation.*

Israel constructed this bovine idol at the very moment Moses received the final instructions for the heavenly tabernacle and in direct violation of the commandments received just a few weeks previous. By attending to how the biblical story expanded over time, we can see that the text is more interested in establishing the *immediacy* of human disobedience than in creating a seamless whole that can be read with a minimum of friction.

Indeed, "immediacy" may be the best way to define "original sin" in its Old Testament context. As soon as Israel receives the benefaction of her election, she offers not praise and gratitude but rebellion. This pattern defines not only the narrative of Israel's election but also that of other founding moments in the Hebrew scriptures. Consider the establishment of the Northern Kingdom under King Jeroboam. At the close of Solomon's reign, the prophet Ahijah announced that all the tribes of Israel save one shall be ripped from the house of David and given to Jeroboam and his successors (1 Kings 11: 26–40). Indeed the only reason David's house will be able to keep even Judah and Jerusalem is because of an earlier promise God has made (11:32).

The granting of this new kingdom to Jeroboam is truly a wonderous affair. The character of his royal office—*in potentia*—looks every bit as grand as that of David (11:38). And like David, as soon as Jeroboam is elected king, he is driven from the land. He takes refuge in Egypt (11:40). When Solomon dies, his son Rehoboam assumes the throne and puts the entire nation under harsh slave-like labor. Jeroboam is subsequently called out of Egypt to redeem the Israelites from these oppressive conditions. The parallels to an earlier story of departure from Egypt are patent.

But no sooner has Jeroboam come forth from Egypt and liberated his people than he erects golden calves and demands that his citizens worship them rather than worship at the altar in Jerusalem (1 Kings 12:25–33). Jeroboam's words of instruction exactly match those of Aaron: "Here are your gods, O Israel, who brought you up out of the land of Egypt" (1 Kings 12:28; cf. Exod. 32:4). The punishment is swift and sudden; a prophet denounces the act and declares that the Northern Kingdom of Israel is henceforth doomed to destruction as a result of this apostasy (1 Kings 13:1–2). And certainly not by accident, Jeroboam's two sons, Abiyah and Nadab—recalling the sons of Aaron—die tragic deaths. The entire cycle of Exodus has been relived. Jeroboam's opportunity to realize another Davidic dynasty ends as quickly as it begins.

Rabbinic interpreters were very attentive to the theme of Israel sinning immediately upon reception of a benefaction. According to one rabbinic elaboration (*Exodus Rabbah* 42:7–8), the thought of building such a calf was entertained within just moments of hearing the command that forbade it. The biblical prophet Ezekiel was even more extreme: he put the moment of original apostasy all the way back in Egypt (20:6–10). Another well-known tradition declared that the veneration of the calf was a sin whose consequences were eternal: "No retribution whatsoever comes upon the world which does not contain a light fraction of the sin of that calf" (Babylonian Talmud, *Sanhedrin* 102a). Had Israel not venerated the calf, her status would have been like that of the angels (*Exodus Rabbah* 32:1): "There would have been no exile, nor would the angel of death have had any power over them." "You were like gods," Psalm 82 asserts, a state that Israel had entered as a result of her pledge to keep the Torah. Having violated that pledge so soon after making it, the penalty of death was laid upon her (*Exodus Rabbah* 32:1,7): "Nevertheless you shall die like Adam."

Let me summarize. I have argued that a reading of Exodus 19 through Leviticus 10 will be deepened if we have some sense of how the previous writings were put in final canonical form. The earliest tradition was a cult-foundation legend that ended with the successful lighting of the sacrificial pyre in Leviticus 9:24. This is the legend that Hurowitz claims to find in his study of the ancient Near Eastern materials. Later, the supplementary narrative about Nadab and Abihu's "strange fire" was added. This changed the complexion of this foundation narrative from festal joy to somber reflection on the improper treatment of the altar and its sacrifices. Even later still, when the Torah was being assembled into its final form, the tabernacle narrative was cut in half and the story of the calf was placed in the middle. This move undercut the severity of the priestly error in Leviticus 10 but made the moment of original sin more immediate and universal.

Eden and the Fall

The story of Adam and Eve in the J source shows a striking number of parallels to Israel's larger national story. We might say that the entire narrative of the Torah is in a tersely summarized form. As Joseph Blenkinsopp has observed, the establishment of humans in

Eden recalls the experience of "rest," which is very much at home in the stories of conquest as well as building the tabernacle and enjoying the Sabbath. "Permanency in that environment," Blenkinsopp observes, "is contingent on obeying a commandment, and death is threatened as punishment for disobedience." By framing the story of creation in this way, the J writer has "recast the national experience in universal terms by learned use of familiar mythic themes and structures, and [by] placing it at the beginning as a foreshadowing of what was to follow." Indeed it is difficult not to see the influence of a theology very similar to that of Deuteronomy. For in that book God sets life and death before the Israelites and says the choice is theirs: Obey my Torah and you shall have life in the land; disobey it and you shall die in exile. Eden is Torah in miniature.

But there is more. By placing the story of Adam and Eve after the creation account of P, the editor of Torah has said something very profound about the propensity of human nature toward disobedience. The story of Adam and Eve according to our J source stands in a very awkward relationship to the narrative that precedes it. And this awkwardness is not to be understood simply as the result of poor editorial work on the part of the editor who stitched together these two sources. On the contrary, there is real and evident literary and theological artistry here. In P's story we get a glimpse of the high hopes that attended the creation of the world. All was set in order by a just and orderly God. Man, the very image of God, was established as ruler over all. At the conclusion, God took his seat to rest and enjoy the wonders of this cosmos he had set in motion. In J's account things turn sour, and quickly. The first portion of J's account takes us over ground that P had already covered in the first chapter; we watch as man, woman, the beasts, as well as all the rest of creation take their places upon the earth. The second portion of J's account begins to strike new ground. No sooner is this new territory entered when tragedy occurs. We are not told what happened between the introduction of Eve to Adam (Gen. 2:21–25) and the approach of the snake (3:1), but Adam and Eve had hardly a moment's leisure within the Garden of Eden before the snake drew near. If there was a period of time in which Adam and Eve enjoyed the splendors of Eden, we, as readers, are not privy to it. Adam and Eve fall at the first and only command given to them. And like the nation Israel, the consequences of their disobedience is exile from a land of blessing.

St. Paul and Original Sin

How then does the idea of original sin get attached to the figures of Adam and Eve, to the detriment of the golden calf? This is the distinctive move made by early Christianity. And the person responsible for this is St. Paul. Adam is central to Paul's argument for two different but complementary reasons. The first we find in his first letter to the Corinthians; the second in his Letter to the Romans.

Paul's First Letter to the Corinthians can be dated to within a couple of decades after the death of Christ (56 or 57 C.E.), not too long after Paul's own conversion to the movement. In the fifteenth chapter he takes up the problem of certain members of the community who lack a clear conviction about the bodily resurrection of Christ. Paul begins his argument by acknowledging that his own teaching is simply a handing on of what he had received. Christ, Paul declares, was buried and "rose on the third day in accordance with the scriptures. He appeared to Cephas, then to the twelve. Then he appeared to more than five hundred brothers and sisters at one time. . . . Then he appeared to James, then to all the apostles. Last of all, as to one untimely born, he appeared also to me" (1 Cor. 15:4–8). From this brief resume we can see that Paul has established the fact of Christ's resurrection on evidence greater than his own personal authority. The teaching is founded on a tradition for which Paul is merely a conduit, and, more important, Jesus' appearance is an event whose witnesses number in the hundreds.

Paul's interest is not to establish merely the truth of the resurrection. Taken on its own, the event of Jesus' bodily resurrection would seem a wondrous miracle that befell one particular person. For Paul, the event was epoch-making and had cosmic significance. In order to underscore the universal dimensions of this event, Paul introduced the figure of Adam:

> But in fact Christ has been raised from the dead, the first fruits of those who have died. But since death came through a human being, the resurrection of the dead has come through a human being; for as all die in Adam, so all will be made alive in Christ. But each in his own order: Christ the first fruits, then at his coming those who belong to Christ. (1 Cor. 15:20–23)

Paul was aware, as any Jewish reader of the Bible would be, that Adam was both the personal name of a literary figure in Genesis and a noun designating humankind more generally. What happened to Adam in Genesis 2–3 was not limited to him alone; by virtue of his name ("mankind") it had ramifications for all persons. If the first (*protos*) Adam died, Paul reasoned, then all must die through him. Since Christ was the second or final (*eschatos*) Adam, his death and resurrection must also have had universal dimensions. The resurrection was not an isolated or singular event in world history, for it did not involve one man alone but all humanity.

And it is exactly this type of argumentation that Paul returns to in his Epistle to the Romans. Now, however, his point is slightly different. Rather than arguing for the cosmic significance of the resurrection, he wishes to establish the universal nature of human sin. "Therefore, just as sin came into the world through one man," Paul argues, "and death came through sin, so death spread to all because all have sinned" (Rom. 5:12). Why this desire to make all persons culpable for death? Because the burden of Paul's apostolic office is to show that the benefits of Christ's resurrection extend to all persons, Jew and Gentile. And to do this, Paul must show that all are in need of this great benefaction.

If Paul were to look solely at the central Old Testament narratives about Israel's proclivity for sin and rebellion, he would not be able to say much about the state of the Gentiles. Paul's turn to the figure of Adam as the parade example of a biblical sinner is not in accord with the basic thrust of the Old Testament. The Hebrew scriptures put their primary focus on the example of Israel herself. But if the elected nation is so prone to sin, and those sins continue to rebound across generations, then certainly it is not a great leap to extend this insight to humanity at large. What is revealed in microcosm through the nation Israel can be extended, in macrocosm, to all peoples.

Appendix B

Genesis 1–3: Annotated Text

In what follows, I have attached a brief set of annotations to the running text of Genesis. My annotations are not intended to be complete in any respect. Their purpose is far more circumspect: They highlight those parts of the biblical text that the commentators I have discussed in this book found difficult or troubling and worthy of more extensive elaboration. I have added a brief reference at the close of each annotation to that place in the book where the reader can find a larger discussion of the problem.

Creation Story: Part I (Gen. 1:1–2:4a)

In the **Image** of God (Gen. 1:26–28)

[26]Then God said, "Let us make humankind in our image, according to our likeness; and let them have dominion over the fish of the sea, and over the birds of the air, and over the cattle, and over all the wild animals of the earth, and over every creeping thing that creeps upon the earth."

[27]So God created humankind in his **image,** in the image of God he created them; male and female he created them.

[28]God blessed them, and God said to them, "Be fruitful and multiply, and fill the earth and subdue it; and have dominion over the fish of the

Image: God refers to himself in the plural: "Let *us* make humankind." This is usually taken as a reference to the angelic host. God inquires of the angels about his intention to make human beings in his image. For some of the angels this special status (in his image, after his likeness) was an affront to their honor and they resisted the divine plan. (See chapter 1.)

sea and over the birds of the air and over every living thing that moves upon the earth."

Allocation of **Food** (Gen. 1:29–31)

[29]God said, "See, I have given you every plant yielding seed that is upon the face of all the earth, and every tree with seed in its fruit; you shall have them for **food**. [30]And to every beast of the earth, and to every bird of the air, and to everything that creeps on the earth, everything that has the breath of life, I have given every green plant for food. And it was so. [31]God saw everything that he made, and indeed, it was very good. And there was evening and there was morning, the sixth day.

Sabbath (Gen. 2:1–4)

[1]Thus the heavens and the earth were finished, and all their multitude. [2]And on the seventh day God finished the work that he had done, and he rested on the seventh day from all the work that he had done. [3]So God blessed the seventh day and hallowed it, because on it God rested from all the work that he done in creation. [4]These are the generations of the heavens and the earth when they were created.

Creation Story: Part II (Gen. 2:4b–3:24)

Creation is told in two separate accounts. For biblical scholars in the modern era, this is seen as evidence of two distinct authors who were unaware of each other's tradition. They used different vocabularies and plot lines to frame their stories; their stories unfold in a contradictory fashion. In the first story the world is created from chaos. Plants appear first, then fish and fowl, and last the animals and humankind, as male and female. In the sec-

Food: God allots cereals for food to human beings ("every plant yielding seed," v. 29); the animals are given the wild grasses as pasturage ("every green plant for food," v. 30). But, many early interpreters presume, Adam and Eve live an angelic life in Eden and don't require such food. Genesis 1:29 must look beyond life in Eden and anticipate the transgression and its plan for human agriculture ("you shall eat the plants of the field. By the sweat of your face you shall eat bread." 3:18–19). (See chapter 7.)

Sabbath: This is the goal of the first creation story. Strikingly, there is no mention of Adam or Eve enjoying the Sabbath, only God. We have to wait until the covenant at Sinai (Exod. 20:8–11, the Ten Commandments) to see human beings—more accurately, the favored nation Israel—drawn into this aspect of the divine life. (See Appendix A: "Biblical Origins and the Fall.")

ond account, Adam is created first, then the animals and birds (no reference to fish), and finally Eve.

Creation of **Adam** (Gen. 2:46–7)

In the day that the Lord God made the earth and the heavens, [5]when no plant of the field was yet in the earth and no herb of the field had yet sprung up—for the LORD God had not caused it to rain upon the earth, and there was no one to till the ground; [6]but a stream would rise from the earth, and water the whole face of the ground—[7]then the LORD God formed man from the dust of the ground, and breathed into his nostrils the breath of life; and the man became a living being.

Adam: Adam is a common noun in Hebrew meaning "man;" it is not a personal name. Adam is so named because he was created from the dust (*adamah*). With the inbreathing of the divine breath, this clay vessel comes to life, a moment regularly identified as when Adam is designated "the image." (See chapter 1.)

Eden (Gen. 2:8–9)

[8]And the LORD God planted a garden in Eden, in the east; and there he put the man whom he had formed. [9]Out of the ground the LORD God made to grow every tree that is pleasant to the sight and good for food, the tree of life also in the midst of the garden, and the tree of the knowledge of good and evil.

Eden: Hebrew word that is normally translated as a place name. It could also be understood as a common noun meaning a "luxuriant or fertile [garden]" and was translated as such in the Greek and Latin Bibles. Because water, the source of fertility, was thought to originate from the Temple (see Ezekiel 47 for this notion), Eden was sometimes thought of as a holy place. (See chapter 2.)

Four Rivers (Gen. 2:10–14)

[10]And a river flows out of Eden to water the garden, and from there it divides and becomes four branches. [11]The name of the first is Pishon; it is the one that flows around the whole land of Havilah, where there is gold; [12]and the gold of that land is good; bdellium and onyx stone are there. [13]The name of the second river is Gihon; it is the one that flows around the whole land of Cush. [14]The name of the third river is Tigris, which flows east of Assyria. And the fourth river is the Euphrates.

Commandment: The tree of life, though set in the very center of the Garden (2:9), is not revealed to Adam. For Ephrem, the tree of life was at the center of the Holy of Holies and the tree of knowledge guarded its port of entry, consequently Adam and Eve were ignorant of it. (See chapter 2.)

Adam is told not to eat the fruit (v.17), but Eve believes the command forbids both eating and touching (3:3). Did Eve mishear the command or did Adam improvise on the original? The answer to this question had enormous consequences for assessing who was to blame for the Fall. (See chapter 5.)

Creation of Eve: Adam appears to play a passive role. It is God who notices Adam's lack of a mate (v. 18) and solves it (v. 21). Yet the scene ends with Adam's cry of joy over the creation of Eve (v. 23): "This one, *at last!*" This suggests that *Adam* has been the one in search of a mate, not God.

God's creation of the animals (v. 19) in response to Adam's loneliness (v. 18) is unusual. Didn't he know this would not do (v. 20b)? If we presume that Adam plays an active role in looking for a mate, however, then the creation of the animals is no longer problematic. By parading them two by two before Adam (vv. 19b–20), God realizes Adam's lonely state. (See chapter 2.)

The text concludes with a reference to marriage (2:24). Does Adam rejoice over his newly won spouse? If so, consummation of this marriage should follow. Yet the very next verse says that the two were naked without shame. If so, they were both prepubescent and not capable of sexual congress. (See chapter 2.)

Commandment (Gen. 2:15–17)

[15]The LORD God took the man and put him in the garden of Eden to till it and keep it. [16]And the LORD God commanded the man, "You may freely eat of every tree of the garden; [17]but of the tree of the knowledge of good and evil you shall not eat, for in the day that you eat of it you shall die."

Creation of Eve (Gen. 2:18–24)

[18]Then the Lord God said, "It is not good that the man should be alone; I will make him a helper as his partner." [19]So out of the ground the LORD God formed every animal of the field and every bird of the air, and brought them to the man to see what he would call them; and whatever the man called every living creature, that was its name. [20]The man gave names to all cattle, and to the birds of the air, and to every animal of the field; but for the man there was not found a helper as his partner. [21]So the LORD God caused a deep sleep to fall upon the man, and he slept; then he took one of his ribs and closed up its place with flesh. [22]And the rib that the LORD God had taken from the man he made into a woman and brought her to the man. [23]Then the man said,

"This at last is bone of my bones
    And flesh of my flesh;
This one shall be called Woman,
    For out of Man this one was taken."

[24]Therefore a man leaves his father and his mother and clings to his wife, and they become one flesh.

Naked **Without Shame** (Gen. 2:25)

[25]And the man and his wife were both naked, and were not ashamed.

Transgression (Gen. 3:1–7)

Now the serpent was more crafty than any other wild animal that the LORD God had made. He said to the woman, "Did God say, 'You shall not eat from any tree in the garden.'?" [2]The woman said to the serpent, "We may eat of the fruit of the trees in the garden; [3]but God said, 'You shall not eat of the fruit of the tree that is in the middle of the garden, nor shall you touch it, or you shall die.'" [4]But the serpent said to the woman, "You will not die; [5]for God knows that when you eat of it your eyes will be opened, and you will be like God, knowing good and evil." [6]So when the woman saw that the tree was good for food, and that it was a delight to the eyes, and that the tree was to be desired to make one wise, she took of its fruit and ate; and she also gave some to her husband, who was with her, and he ate. [7]Then the eyes of both were opened, and they knew that they were naked; and they sewed fig leaves together and made loincloths for themselves.

Interrogation (Gen. 3:8–13)

[8]They heard the sound of the LORD God walking in the garden at the time of the evening breeze, and the man and his wife hid themselves from the presence of the LORD God among the trees of the garden. [9]But the LORD God called to the man, and said to him, "Where are you?" [10]He said, "I heard the sound of you in the garden, and I was afraid, because I was naked; and I hid myself." [11]He said, "Who told you that

No Shame: This verse was commonly glossed: Adam and Eve lacked conventional shame toward their naked bodies because they were not clothed in human clothing but vested with ineffable glory. (See chapter 6.)

Augustine went his own way and tied the theme of shame to the faculty of the will. Prior to sin, they knew no shame because their sex organs obeyed their will just like their hands and feet. After the transgression, the sex organs rebelled and shame was felt. Romans 7:14–25 was instrumental for Augustine's interpretation. (See chapter 3.)

Transgression: The snake approaches Eve, who appears to be alone (v.1). Eve reveals the commandment, whereupon the snake denies the validity of the warning ("you shall *not* die"). The story makes no effort to clarify the motive of the serpent. Does he tempt of his own volition or is he put up to it by an angel who opposes the creation of humankind? (See chapters 1 and 4.)

According to one very important line of interpretation, Adam and Eve lost their garments of glory when they ate the forbidden fruit (v. 7; compare 2:25 and 3:21). At the very same time they lost these garments they sewed on fig leaves and were expelled from the Garden. Most artistic depictions show Adam and Eve leaving the Garden dressed in fig leaves. (See chapter 7.)

Interrogation: Does God take walks in the Garden? Is he uncertain where Adam is? The Rabbis projected the horizontal image of walking vertically: it marked the first stage in the departure of the divine presence from the world. (See the Introduction.)

Didymus saw God's question— "Where are you Adam?"—as deeply ironic. Adam, when he sinned, was instantly expelled from Eden in such a way that he finds himself already on earth when God comes to question him. God's question, then, is an statement of judgment as to what Adam has lost. (See chapter 6.)

Only the snake is not questioned as to motive. (See chapter 7.)

Judgment: If Adam and Eve were stripped of their angelic nature as soon as they ate, then what further purpose do these particular punishments play? Adam and Eve have already lost their biggest prize—their glorious vestments—and have suffered their largest loss—their immortality. In the wake of this, the punishments of Adam and Eve became a means of penitential renewal. The snake, on the other hand, is given no second chance.

Adam eats the grass of the field (v. 18). This was understood to be a reversal of the intentions of Genesis 1. Adam, initially, is given animal food (1:30) instead of human (1:29). Like Nebuchadnezzar (Daniel 4) this was to teach Adam the means of penance. Once he repents, he is given seed to sow grain (v. 19). (See chapter 7.)

you were naked? Have you eaten from the tree of which I commanded you not to eat?" [12]The man said, "The woman whom you gave to be with me, she gave me fruit from the tree, and I ate." [13]Then the LORD God said to the woman, "What is this that you have done?" The woman said, "The serpent tricked me, and I ate."

Judgment of the Serpent, Eve, and the Snake (Gen. 3:14–19)

[14]The LORD God said to the serpent,
"Because you have done this,
    cursed are you among all animals
    and among all wild creatures;
upon your belly you shall go,
    and dust you shall eat all the days of
        your life.
[15]I will put enmity between you and
        the woman,
    and between your offspring and hers;
he will strike your head,
    and you will strike his heel."
[16]To the woman he said,
    "I will greatly increase your pangs in
        childbearing;
    in pain you shall bring forth children,
yet your desire shall be for your husband,
    and he shall rule over you."
[17]And to the man he said,
    "Because you have listened to the voice
        of your wife,
    and have eaten of the tree
about which I commanded you,
    'You shall not eat of it,'
cursed is the ground because of you;
    in toil you shall eat of it all the days of
        your life;
[18]thorns and thistles it shall bring forth
        for you;

and you shall eat the plants of the field.
¹⁹By the sweat of your face
   you shall eat bread
until you return to the ground,
   for out of it you were taken;
you are dust,
   and to dust you shall return."

The Naming of Eve; the **Garments** of Skin (Gen. 3:20–21)

²⁰The man named his wife Eve, because she was the mother of all living. ²¹And the LORD God made garments of skins for the man and for his wife, and clothed them.

Expulsion (Gen. 3:22–24)

²²Then the LORD God said, "See, the man has become like one of us, knowing good and evil; and now, he might reach out his hand and take also from the tree of life, and eat, and live forever"—²³therefore the Lord God sent him forth from the garden of Eden, to till the ground from which he was taken. ²⁴He drove out the man; and at the east of the garden of Eden he placed the cherubim, and a sword flaming and turning to guard the way to the tree of life.

Adam Knew Eve (Gen. 4:1–2)

Now the man knew his wife Eve and she conceived and bore Cain, saying, "I have produced a man with the help of the LORD." ²Next she bore his brother Abel.

Adam Lived **Nine Hundred Thirty Years** (Gen. 5:3–5)

³When Adam had lived one hundred and thirty years, he became the father of a son in his like-

Garments: This is perhaps the most important verse in the whole story for the Orthodox tradition. After the punishments, we have what appear to be two extraneous actions prior to expulsion, the naming of Eve and the donning of garments of skin. Many early interpreters believed that the narrative order of scripture did not follow the strict sequence of historical events. Eve must have been named at the close of chapter 2 when the rest of creation received their names (2:20, 23). If so, then Genesis 3:21 occurred immediately after Adam and Eve eat the fruit (3:7). Upon transgression, they take on mortal flesh, that is, flesh prone to sickness, decay, and death. (See chapter 6.)

Expulsion: God, who alone knows about the tree of life and planned to reveal it to Adam and Eve, does not believe that Adam and Eve are worthy of it after they sinned. In this way, the role of this tree is parallel to the role of the sabbath in Genesis 2:1–4. It was intended for human beings but not given to them at creation. Adam and Eve's status at creation is without error but still not complete. Offering the fruit of the tree of life is an *advance* and would have attended the moment of completion. Subsequently the tree of life is identified with the Torah by Jews and with Christ by Christians. (See Afterword.)

Adam knew Eve: It appears that the first thing that happens outside of Eden is the consummation of marriage. This would seem to settle the matter of sexuality that was raised at the close of Genesis 2. But the grammar of the Hebrew original also allows a translation in the pluperfect: Adam *had already known* Eve in the Garden. If so, Adam knew Eve at the moment of her presentation (Gen. 2:23). The verse could be translated as a simple past (Adam knew Eve); then the first moment of sexual congress occurs outside Eden. (See chapter 2.)

Nine Hundred: Adam's longevity is an enormous problem. God threatened Adam with death (2:16–17), but he lives for nearly a millennium. (See chapter 6.)

ness, according to his image, and named him Seth. [4]The days of Adam after he became the father of Seth were eight hundred years; and he had other sons and daughters. [5]Thus all the days that Adam lived were nine hundred thirty years; and he died.

Appendix C

Life of Adam and Eve (Armenian version*)

Adam and Eve Repent Outside Paradise (cf. Gen. 4:1)

1:1 It came to pass, when Adam went forth from the Garden with his wife, outside, to the east of the Garden, they made themselves a hut to live in and went inside. Their tears fell ceaselessly and they spent their days in unison of mind, weeping and saddened, and they said to one another, "We are far from life." 2:1 Then, after seven days, they grew hungry and looked for food. 2:2 Eve said to Adam. "My lord, I am hungry. Arise, seek food so that we may live and know that God is going to come and bring us to the Garden, to our place."

Searching for Suitable Food (cf. Gen. 1:29–30; 3:18–19)

3:1 They arose and went about upon the earth, and they did not find food like the food by which they had been nourished in [the Garden]. 3:2a Eve said to Adam, "I am dying of this hunger. It would be better if I were dead, my lord; perhaps (then) they would bring [you] into the Garden, for because of me God is angry." 3:2b Adam said, "Great wrath has come upon us, I know not whether because of you or because of me." 3:2c Eve said, to h[im], "Kill me if you wish, so that the wrath and anger may abate from before you—for this has come about because of me—and they will bring you into the Garden." 3:3 Adam said to her. "Eve, do not (even) mention this matter; lest God bring upon us even greater evils and we become contemptible. How, indeed, can I do you any evil, for you are my body?" 3:4 Eve said "Arise, so that we may seek vegetable food."

---

*The text is the updated version of Anderson and Stone, *Synopsis*; for the original publication, see Stone, *Penitence of Adam*.

219

Forty Days of Harsher Penance

4:1 [They sought] and they did not find [vegetable] food [like that which was in the Garden]. 4:2 [Eve said "...] because God established this vegetable food as food for the beasts that they might eat on the earth, but our food is that which the angels eat. 4:3 Arise, let us repent for forty days; perhaps God will pity us and give [us] food which is better than that of the beasts so that we should not become like them."

5:1 Adam said to Eve, "In what fashion will you repent? How many days can you endure toils? Perhaps you will begin and be unable to repent, and God will not hearken, 5:2 so that we will not be able to keep that which we originally received." 5:3 Eve said, "Set me the number of days which I might think to repent; perhaps the days will be too long—for I brought this penitence upon you."

Adam and Eve, Submerged in Water, Appeal for Mercy

6:1a Adam said, "You cannot endure the same number of days as I, but do what I tell you and abide by [this] instruction." Adam said, "I shall be [in penitence] for forty days, six days more than you, because you were created on the sixth day [of those upon which] he accepted his works. 6:1b Now, therefore, arise, go to the T[i]gris river and take a stone and place it under your feet and stand in the water up to your neck, in your clothes. Let no word of supplication to God escape your mouth, for we are unworthy of [soul] and our lips are impure and unclean, because of the transgressions which we committed in the Garden when we ate of the tree.

6:2 Stand silent there in the middle of the water until [you] have done penitence for thirty-four days, and I will be in the Jordan river, until we learn that, behold, God has hearkened to us and will give us our food." 7:1 Then Eve went to the Tigris and did as Adam had instructed her, 7:2 and Adam [went] to the Jordan. And the hair of his head was uncovered.

8:1 He prayed and said, "I say to you, waters of Jordan, be fellow sufferers for me and assemble all the moving thing[s] which are in you, and let them surround me and bewail me, 8:2 not for their own sakes, but for mine. Because God did not withhold their food from them, which God appointed from the beginning, but I have been withheld from my food and from life." 8:3 When Adam said that, all moving things which were in the Jordan gathered to him and stood around him like a wall. And the waters of the Jordan stopped at that time and became stationary from their flow. Adam cried to God and he set apart six hundred orders of them to call to God in prayers all the days.

Second Temptation of Eve

9:1 When eighteen days of their weeping were completed, then Satan took on the form of a cherub with splendid attire, and went to the Tigris river to deceive Eve. 9:2 Her tears were falling on her attire, down to the ground. Satan said to Eve, "Come forth from the water and rest, for God has hearkened to your penitence, to you and Adam your husband, 9:3 because we beseeched God. 9:4 And God sent [me] to lead you forth from there and to give you your food, on account of which you repented. 9:5 Since just now I went to Adam and he sent me to you and said, 'Go, son, summon my wife,' now come, let us go to Adam and I will lead you to the place where your food is."

10:1. When Eve came forth from the water, her flesh was like withered grass, for her flesh had been changed from the water, but the form of her glory remained brilliant. 10:2 [When she came forth from the water] she fell down and remained upon the ground in great distress for two days, for she was quite unable to move from the spot. Then she arose and Satan also led her to where Adam was. 10:3 When Adam saw Satan and Eve who was following him, he wept loudly and called out with a great voice and said to Eve, "Where is my command of repentance, which I gave you? How did you go astray, to follow him by whom we were alienated from our dwelling?"

11:1 When Eve heard this, she knew that he who dec[ei]ved her was Satan; she fell down before Adam. From that time Adam's distress increased twofold when he saw the sufferings of his wife, for she was overcome and fell like one dead. 11:2 He was sad and called out great lamentation and said to Satan, "Why have you engaged in such a great conflict with us? What are our sins against you, that you have brought us out of our place? 11:3 Did we take your glory from you? Did we reject you from being our possession, that you fight against us unnecessarily?"

Satan's Account of His Fall

12:1 Satan also wept loudly and said to Adam. "All my arrogance and sorrow came to pass because of you; for, because of you I went forth from my dwelling; and because of you I was alienated from the throne of the cherubs who, having spread out a shelter, used to enclose me; because of you my feet have trodden the earth." 12:2 Adam replied and said to him,12:3 "What are our [sins] against you, that you did all this to us?"

13:1 Satan replied and said, "You did nothing to me, but I came to this measure because of you, on the day on which you were created, for I went forth on that day. 13:2 When God breathed his spirit into you, you received the likeness of his image. Thereupon, Michael came and made you bow down before God. God said to Michael, 'Behold I have made Adam in the likeness of my image.'

14:1 Then Michael summoned all the angels, and God said to them, 'Come, bow down to god whom I made.' 14:2 Michael bowed first. He called me and said. 'You too, bow down to Adam.' 14:3 I said, 'Go away, Michael! I shall not bow [down] to him who is posterior to me, for I am former. Why is it proper [for me] to bow down to him?' 15:1 The other angels, too, who were with me, heard this, and my words seemed pleasing to them and they did not prostrate them-selves to you, Adam.

16:1 Thereupon, God became angry with me and commanded to expel us from our dwelling and to cast me and my angels, who were in agreement with me, to the earth; and you were at the same time in the Garden. 16:2 When I realized that because of you I had gone forth from the dwelling of light and was in sorrows and pains,16:3 then I prepared a trap for you, so that I [might] alienate you from your happiness just as I, too, had been alienated because of you.'

Eve Decides to Go to the West to Die

17:1. When Adam heard this, he said to the Lord, "[Lord, my soul is in your hand.] Make this enemy of mine distant from me, who desires to lead me astray, I who am searching for the light that I have lost." 17:2 At that time Satan passed away from him. 17:3 Adam stood from then on in the waters of repentance, and Eve remained fallen upon the ground for three days, like one dead. Then, after three days, she arose from the earth,

18:1 and she said to Adam, "You are innocent of the first sin and of this second one. Only me alone did Satan overcome, as a result of God's word and yours." Again Eve said to Adam, "Behold, I shall go to the west and I shall be there and my food (will be) grass until I die;

for henceforth I am unworthy of the foods of life." 18:2 Eve went to the west and she mourned and was sad; 18:3 and then she made a hut for herself in the west, and she was advanced in her pregnancy and she had Cain, the lawless one, [in] her womb.

The Onset of Birth Pains (Gen. 3:16)

19:1 When the times of her parturition came, she began to cry out in a loud voice and said, 19:2 "Where is Adam, that he might see this pain of mine? Who, indeed, will relate my afflictions to Adam? Is there a wind under the heavens that will go and tell Adam, 'Come and help Eve'?!" And she said, "I implore you, all luminaries, when you come to the east, tell my lord Adam about my pains."

The Gift of Seeds for Growing Grain (Gen. 1:29; 3:19)

20:1a Then Adam, in the river Jordan, heard Eve's cry and her weeping. 20:1b When God hearkened to the sound of Adam's penitence, he taught him sowing and reaping and that which was to come upon him and his seed.

Adam Intervenes on Behalf of Eve

20:1c Then Adam heard the sound of Eve's entreaty in the west, and Adam said to himself, "That voice and weeping are of my flesh. Let me arise and go to her and see why she is crying out. Perhaps the beast is fighting with her once more!" 20:2a Adam arose and followed the noise (to) where Eve was. When Eve saw him, she spoke and said to Adam, "Did you hear the sound of my crying? Did the winds inform you, whom [I] entreated concerning you? Did the luminaries of heaven inform you, who are in the [east]ern regions every day, in their courses? Did the birds of the heavens inform you, or the beasts of the earth whom I summoned and dispatched to you, to tell you? 20:2b Now arise, entreat your Creator to deliver me from these pains."20:3 Adam wept and prayed to God on her behalf.

21:1 And behold, two angels and two powers descended from heaven, came to Eve and stood before her. 21:2 The powers said to her, "Eve, you are blessed because of Adam, God's elect one, for his prayers are mighty and through him help from God has come to you.

Apart [from him], you would not be able to survive this birth." The angel said to Eve, "Prepare yourself, and I will be a midwife for you." 21:3a Then, when she bore the child, the colour of his body was like the colour of stars. 21:3b At the hour when the child fell into the hands of the midwife, he leaped up and, with his hands, plucked up the grass of the earth near his mother's hut; and infertilities became numerous in that place. 21:3c The angel said to him, "God is just, that he did not make you fall into my hand, for you are Cain, the lawless one, who will be destroyer of the good and . . . and living [p]lant and adultery, bitterness and not sweetness." 21:3d And again the angel said to Adam, "Remain by Eve, so that she will do what I commanded."

(Abridged: Story of Cain and Abel [Gen. 4:1–16])

Adam's Death Bed (Gen. 5:3–5)

30:1 Then, after that, he had sons and daughters, thirty of each kind, and they grew up. Adam was upon the earth 930 years, 30:2 and then Adam fell sick with a mortal affliction, and he cried out in a loud voice and said, "Let all my sons come and gather by me, so that I may see them first, before I die." 30:3 All his sons who were in every part of the world gathered by him. [They assembled by him inside the place which Eve had entered,] and he prayed to the Lord God.

31:1 His son Seth said to Adam, "My father, did you remember the fruit of the Garden, of which you used to eat, and have you become sad from that longing? 31:2 If indeed [this] is the [case], tell me, so that I may go close to the Garden and cast dust upon my head and weep. For, perhaps God will give me of the fruit, that I might bring [it] to you, and this pain may be driven away from you." 31:3 Adam said to him, "It is not so, [my son, Seth]; rather do I have mortal sickness and pain." 31:4 Seth said to him, "Through whom did this pain come to you?"

Adam's Account of the Fall (Gen. 3:1–7)

32:1 Adam said to him, "When God made us, me and your mother, he gave us a command not to eat of that tree. 32:2 Satan deceived us at the hour when [the] angels [who] were guardians of the tree ascended to worship God. Then, Satan caused Eve to eat that fruit; 32:3a Eve gave [it] to me to eat when I did not know. 32:3b For, my son Seth, God divided the Garden between me and your mother Eve, that we might watch it. To me he gave the eastern portion and the [northern], and to your mother, the western and the [southern].

Adam is Separated from Eve at Transgression; He Eats the Fruit Unawares

33:1 We had twelve angels who went around with each of us, because of the guarding of the Garden, until the time of the light. 33:2 Since, every day they would go forth [to worship the Lord], at the time when they went to the heavens, at that time Satan deceived your mother and caused her to eat of the fruit. Satan knew that I was not with her, nor the angels, at that time he caused her to eat. 33:3 Afterwards, also, she gave [it] to me.

The Garment of Skins (Gen. 3:7 = 3:21)

34:1 I knew then, when I ate the fruit, that God was angry with us. 34:2 God said, 'Because you transgressed my commandment, I shall bring seventy afflictions [upon] your body, pain of the eyes and ringing of the ears and all the joints.' It will be reckoned for me [?] among the afflictions of sickness which are preserved in the treasuries, so that God might send them in the last times."

35:1 When Adam said this to his son Seth, he cried out and said, "What shall I do, for I am in great pains and toils." 35:2 Eve wept and said, "My lord Adam. Arise, give me some of your pain, so that I might receive and bear it, for these pains which have come upon you, came about because of me." 36:3 Adam said to her, "Arise, go with your son Seth, close to the Garden and there cast dust on your heads and weep before God. 36:4 Perhaps God will pity me and send his angel to the Garden, and he will go to the place where the olive tree stands, from which oil comes forth, and give you a little of it, so that you might bring it to me and I might anoint my bones and be separated from pain, 36:5 and I might teach you this way . . . which we were tried formerly."

(Abridged: Seth and Eve in Search of the Oil of Life)

Archangel Michael Tells Seth the Oil from the Tree of Life to Heal Adam Cannot Be Retrieved

40:1 Seth, [with] Eve, went close to the Garden, and they wept with loud lament and asked God to send an angel to help them. 41:2a God sent to them the angel Michael, who is prince of souls, and [he spoke these words to them], 41:2b "Seth, [man of God]: Do not labour to supplicate for the oil which issues forth from the tree—that oil of joy—to anoint your father Adam.

Prophecy of the Christ's Descent to Hades [see the *Gospel of Nicodemus*]

42:3a This cannot be now: but then, at that time when the years of the end are filled and completed, 42:3b then the beloved Christ will come to resurrect Adam's body, because of his sins which took place. 42:3c He will come to the Jordan and be baptized [by] him, and when he will come forth from the water, then Michael will come and anoint the new Adam with the oil of joy. 42:4 Then, after that, it shall happen in the same fashion to all the wild beasts of the earth, who will arise in resurrection and be worthy of entering the Garden. I shall anoint them with that oil.

Appendix D

*Gospel of Nicodemus**
or
The Harrowing of Hell

Setting: It is Good Friday and Christ is just about to die and descend into Hades. The righteous dead gather to consider what this event portends. Adam is called forth to tell what he learned from on his own deathbed (see the Life of Adam and Eve*).*

Adam's story [From the *Life of Adam and Eve*]

III: Now when John was thus teaching those who were in Hades, the first-created, the first father Adam heard, and said to Seth his son: "My son, I wish you to tell the forefathers of the race of men, and the prophets where I sent you when I fell into mortal sickness. And Seth said: Prophets and patriarchs, listen. My father Adam, the first-created, when he fell into mortal sickness, sent me to the very gate of paradise to pray to God that he might lead me by an angel to the tree of mercy that I might take oil and anoint my father, and he arise from his sickness. This also I did. And after my prayer an angel of the Lord came and asked me: "What do you desire, Seth? Do you desire, because of the sickness of your father, the oil that rises up the sick, or the tree from which flows such oil? This cannot be found now. Therefore go and tell your father that after the completion of 5,500 years from the creation of the world, the only-begotten Son of God shall become man and shall descend below the earth. And he shall anoint him with that oil. And he shall arise and wash him and his descendants with water and the Holy Spirit. And then he shall be healed of every disease. But this is impossible now. When the patriarchs and prophets heard this, they rejoiced greatly.

---

*Taken from Schneemelcher, ed., *New Testament Apocrypha*.

The Descent: Satan's Quandry and Puzzlement

IV: And while they all were thus so joyful, Satan the heir of darkness came and said unto Hades: "O insatiable, devourer of all, listen to my words. There is one of the race of the Jews, Jesus by name, who calls himself the Son of God. But he is [only] a man, and I heard him saying: "My soul is very sorrowful, even to death" [Matt. 26:38]. And he did me much mischief in the world above while he lived among mortal men. For wherever he found my servants, he cast them out, and all those whom I made to be maimed, or blind, or lame, or leprous, or the like, he healed with only a word, and many whom I had made ready to be buried, he also with only with a word made alive again."

Hades and Satan Discuss their Options

Hades said: "Is he so powerful that he does such things with only a word? And if he is of such power, are you able to withstand him? It seems to me that no one will be able to withstand such as he is. But whereas you say that you heard how he feared death, he said this to mock and laugh at you, being determined to seize you with a strong hand. And woe, woe to you, for all eternity."

Satan answered: "O all-devouring and insatiable Hades, did you fear so greatly when you heard about our common enemy? I did not fear him, but worked upon the Jews, and they crucified him and gave gall and vinegar to drink. Therefore prepare yourself to get him firmly into your power when he comes."

(Abridged: further conversation between the two)

Christ Enter Hades; Psalm 24
(see the setting for the same in Handel's *Messiah*)

V: While Satan and Hades were speaking thus with one another, a loud voice like thunder sounded: "Lift up, O rulers, your gates, and be lifted up, O everlasting doors, and the King of glory shall come in" [Ps. 24:7]. When Hades heard this, he said unto Satan: "Go out, if you can, and withstand him." So Satan went out. Then Hades said to his demons: "Make fast well and strong the gates of brass and the bars of iron, and hold my locks, and stand upright, and watch every point. For if he comes in, woe will seize us."

When the forefathers heard that, they all began to mock him, saying: "O all-devouring and insatiable one, open, so that the King of glory may come in." David the prophet said: "Do you not know, blind one, that when I lived in the world I prophesied that word, 'Lift up, O princes, your gates'" [Ps. 24:7]. Isaiah said: "This I foresaw by the Holy Spirit and wrote: 'The dead shall arise, and those who are in the tombs shall be raised up, and those that are under the earth shall rejoice'" [Isa. 26:19]. "O death, where is thy sting? O Hades, where is thy victory?" [1 Cor. 15:55].

Again the voice, sounded: "Lift up the gates." And when Hades heard the voice the second time, he answered as if he knew it not, and said: "Who is this King of glory?" [Ps. 24:8]. The angels of the Lord said: "The Lord strong and mighty, the Lord mighty in battle." And immediately at this answer the gates of brass were broken in pieces and the bars of iron were crushed, and all the dead who were bound were loosed from their chains, and we with them. And the King of glory entered in like a man, and all the dark places of Hades were illumined.

Defeat of Hades and Satan

VII: Hades at once cried out: "We are overcome, woe to us. But who are you, who have such authority and power? And who are you, who without sin have come here, you who appear small and can do great things, who are humble and exalted, slave and master, soldier and king, and have authority over the dead and the living? You were nailed to the cross, and laid in the sepulcher, and now you have become free and have destroyed all our whole power. Are you Jesus, of whom the chief ruler Satan said to us that through the cross and death you would inherit the whole world?"

Then the King of glory seized the chief ruler Satan by the head and handed him unto the angels saying: "Bind with iron fetters his hands and his feet and his neck and his mouth." And then he gave him to Hades and said: "Take him and hold him fast until my second coming."

VII: And Hades took Satan and said to him: "O Beelzebub, heir of fire and torment, enemy of the saints, through what necessity did you contrive that the King of glory should be crucified, so that he should come hither and strip us naked? Turn thee and see that not one dead man is left in me. All whom you gained through the tree of knowledge, you have lost through the tree of the cross. All your joy is turned into sorrow. You wished to kill the King of glory, but you have killed your-self. For since I have received you to hold you fast, thou shall learn by experience what evils I shall inflict upon you. O arch-devil, the begin-ning of death, the root of sin, the summit of all evil, what evil did thou find in Jesus that thou went about to destroy him? How did you dare to commit such a great wickedness? How were you bent on bringing down such a man into this darkness, through whom you have been deprived of all who have died since the beginning?"

The Raising of Adam

VIII: While Hades was thus speaking with Satan, the King of glory stretched forth his right hand, and took hold of our forefather Adam and raised him up. Then he turned also to the rest and said: "Come with me all you who have suffered death through the tree that this man touched. For behold, I raise you all up again through the tree of the cross." With that he put them all out. And our forefather Adam was seen to be full of joy and said: "I give thanks to thy greatness, O Lord, because thou hast brought me up out of the lowest [depth of] Hades." Likewise also all the prophets and the saints said: "We give thanks unto thee, O Christ, Saviour of the world, because thou hast brought up our life from destruction."

And when they had said this, the Saviour blessed Adam with the sign of the cross on his forehead. And he did this also to all the patri-archs and prophets and martyrs and forefathers. And he took them and leaped up out of Hades. And as he went the holy fathers sang praises, following him and saying: "Blessed is he who comes in the name of the Lord. Alleluia [Ps. 118:26]. To him be the glory of all the saints."

(Abridged: Adam taken into Paradise; meeting with Enoch, Elijah and the Thief [Luke 23:42–43]. Conclusion.)

Abbreviations

ACW   *Ancient Christian Writers.* Westminster, Md.: Newman
        Press.

ANF   *The Ante-Nicene Fathers.* Reprint, Grand Rapids, Mich.:
        Wm. B. Eerdmans Publishing Co.

CSCO   *Corpus Scriptorum Christianorum Orientalium.* Louvain,
        Belgium.

FC   *Fathers of the Church.* Washington, D.C.: Catholic
        University of America.

NPNF   *Nicene and Post-Nicene Fathers.* Reprint, Grand Rapids,
        Mich.: Wm. B. Eerdmans Publishing Co.

PG   *Patrologiae cursus completus, Series Graeca,* 221 vols. Edited
        by J. Migne. Paris: 1844–66.

SC   *Sources Chrétiennes.* Paris: Editions du Cerf.

Notes

Introduction

Quotations

Page 7: citation is from Leo Steinberg, "The Line of Fate," 440 and 441. Page 12: citation from Maimonides is from his commentary on Mishnah, *Sanhedrin*. The translation is taken from Jon Levenson, "Eighth Principle," 206.

General Bibliography

I am not an art historian, so my interpretation of the **Sistine Chapel** has been highly dependent on the work of others. For a general background to the Chapel, I have relied on O'Malley, "The Theology," and Partridge, *Michelangelo*. For the figure of Eve and her antitype Mary, I have consulted Steinberg, "The Line of Fate." An excellent background to the theology of **John Milton** can be found in Patrides, *Milton and the Christian Tradition*. For Milton's use of classical Christian sources see Evans, *Paradise Lost and the Genesis Traditions*. Perhaps the most insightful and concise guide to his theology is C. S. Lewis, *A Preface to Paradise Lost*. The literature on **Mary as second Eve** is staggering in scope. For a general introduction, consult Pelikan, *Mary*. On the matter of the Protoevangelium, see Laurentin, "L'interprétation de Genèse 3,15." The discipline of **literary theory** has spent much effort over the past few decades on the problem of narrativity. My work has been guided by the fine book of Brooks, *Reading for the Plot*. The influence of this recent interest in narrative has also spilled over into theology. For a brief statement on this, see Robert Jenson, "How the World Lost Its Story." For the impact of theories of narrative on the formation of the Creed, see Lash, *Believing Three Ways in One God*, and Blowers, "The *Regula Fidei* and the Narrative Character of Christian Faith." Part of the crisis in the field of biblical studies has been the loss of a sense for the final form of the Bible's story. The turn toward historical reconstruction as opposed to attention to narrative has been well documented by Frei, *The Eclipse of Biblical Narrative*. For an excellent introduction to **Jewish biblical interpretation,** see Kugel, *The Bible As It Was* and Levenson, "Eighth Principle." On the role of the story of the golden calf see appendix A, "Biblical Origins and the Fall," and Kaminsky, "Paradise Regained."

Chapter One

Quotations

Page 29: Wyschogrod, "Incarnation," 213. Page 29: that the beloved son must die, either in actuality or metaphorically, is the thesis of Levenson's entire book *Death and Resurrection*. For specific examples, see his treatment of the binding of Isaac (111–142)

233

or the Joseph story (143–172). Page 30: von Balthasar, *Mysterium Paschale*, 29. Page 35: Shäfer, *Rivalität*, 232–33.

General Bibliography
For a fuller discussion of all the texts cited in this chapter and many others, see Anderson, "The Exaltation and the Fall of Satan." On the matter of **election** and the role it plays in shaping the stories of Genesis, see Levenson, *Death and Resurrection*. The *Life of Adam and Eve* is one of the most important apocryphal texts in our possession. It was extraordinarily influential in both Eastern and Western Christianity. For a discussion of the text, the problem of its historical origin, and its influence on subsequent literature, see Stone, *A History of the Literature of Adam and Eve*. For the text itself, see Anderson and Stone, *A Synopsis*. For **Milton's** treatment of the fall of Satan and his reliance on previous material including the *Life of Adam and Eve*, see Evans, *Paradise Lost and the Genesis Traditions* and Hunter, "War in Heaven." I have been greatly aided in my understanding of Milton by my former colleague James Nohrnberg of the University of Virginia. It is to him I owe the insight that Christ's elevation in Book 5 of *Paradise Lost* was a means of "smoking-out" Satan's anger over the proposed creation of man. For a deeper consideration of the **Jewish legends** about fallen angels, see Anderson, "Exaltation"; Altmann, "Gnostic Background"; Bamberger, *Fallen Angels*; and Shäfer, *Rivalität*. The Christian materials have been ably assembled by a number of scholars. For consideration of a variety of nonstandard and apocryphal works, see Stichel, "Die Verführung der Stammeltern," and Rosenstiehl, "La chute de l'Ange." For the **church fathers** themselves, see Daniélou, *Angels and their Mission*, and Pagels, *Origin of Satan*. On the theology of the **happy fault,** see Anderson, "Necessarium."

Chapter Two
Quotations
Page 53: the reference to the "Letter of Holiness" comes from Feldman, *Birth Control in Jewish Law*. Page 58: Brown, *Body and Society*, 285.

General Bibliography
A deeper discussion of this entire topic, with the exception of the material on Gregory of Nyssa, can be found in Anderson, "Celibacy." The Jewish material has been treated subsequently in Boyarin, *Carnal Israel*. For the discussion of **Gregory of Nyssa,** I am dependent on the very insightful article of Hart, "Reconciliation of Body and Soul," whose approach contrasts sharply with scholarly convention; for the latter, see Brown, *Body and Society*. The topic of **purity** is one of the most difficult topics for scholars and laypersons alike. On the general nature of the problem, see Douglas, *Purity and Danger*. On purity in the Bible and post-Biblical sources, see Klawans, *Impurity and Sin*. For the relationship of purity to Eden, see Anderson, "Celibacy," and Wright, "Holiness, Sex and Death." The conception of **Eden as a temple** has been ably treated by Levenson, *Sinai and Zion*, and Stager, "Jerusalem and the Garden of Eden." For the significance of **celibacy in early Christianity,** see Brown, *Body and Society*; for the specific problem of avoiding baptism until older age when sexual temptation was no longer so problematic, see Murray, "Exhortation." Although there is no evidence of the honorific status of celibacy in rabbinic law, there were strains of **Jewish asceticism** that can be compared to early Christianity. For a review of this literature, see Fraade, "Ascetical Aspects of Ancient Judaism," and Guillaumont, "Monachisme et

éthique judéo-chrétienne." For the **geography of Eden** in early Christianity, see Daniélou, "Terre et Paradis"; for Ephrem, see Séd, "Les hymnes sur le Paradis."

Chapter Three

Quotations

Pages 64–65: Pagels, *Adam, Eve, and the Serpent*, 96. Page 66: Brown, *Augustine*, 342 and 350. Pages 66 and 69: Fredriksen, "Beyond the Body/Soul Dichotomy," 110 and 112. Page 67: Lewis, *Preface*, 70.

General Bibliography

The best **biography of Augustine** is Brown, *Augustine of Hippo*. A reliable introduction to the thought of Augustine can be found in Bonner, *Augustine of Hippo: Life and Controversies*. On Augustine's interpretation of Genesis 1–3, I have consulted Burns, "The Fall of Humanity according to Augustine." **Augustine's use of St. Paul**— especially chapter 7 of his Epistle to the Romans—to understand original sin is masterfully surveyed by Fredriksen, "Beyond the Body/Soul Dichotomy." A very solid treatment of Augustine's primary writings on **marriage** and a good introduction to their significance can be found in Clark, ed., *St. Augustine on Marriage*, and Clark, "Adam's Only Companion." For **Augustine and Milton**, see Lewis, *Preface*, especially chapter 10, "Milton and St. Augustine."

Chapter Four

Quotations

Page 82: Lipscomb, *The Armenian Apocryphal Adam Literature*, 109. Pages 84–85: Pelikan, *Mary*, 44. Pages 93–94: "Homily on the Annuciation," falsely attributed to Chrysostom, *PG* 755D-760D, my own translation. Pages 94 and 96: Constas, "Conceptio per aurem." The El Bagawat images can be seen and are discussed in Urbiank-Walczak, "Die 'Conceptio per aurem.'" Page 97: quotations from Cabasilas are from Constas, "Conceptio."

General Bibliography

The Jewish texts relevant to **Eve's culpability** are treated by Kimmelman, "The Seduction of Eve." For a striking Christian parallel, in St. Ambrose, to the Jewish treatment, see Poorthuis, "Who is to Blame?" On the mosaics of **San Marco** and their relationship to the Virgin Mary, see Jolly, *Made in God's Image?* These mosaics date from the twelfth century, but they go back to exemplars from the Cotton Genesis. This illustrated Septuagint (Greek translation of the Bible) dates from the fifth century. It is an outstanding resource for early Christian depictions of the Garden of Eden. For the theological significance of the *conceptio per aurem*, see Constas, "Conceptio," and for its iconographic significance, see Urbiank-Walczak, "Die 'Conceptio per aurem.' " For image of **Mary as a weaver**, see Constas, "Weaving the Body of God." For a discussion of Mary and the *Protevangelium of James*, see Gaventa, *Mary*.

Chapter Five

Quotations

Page 100: Hays, *Moral Vision*, 67–68. Page 103: the quotation of Gregory of Nyssa is taken from Pelikan, *Mary*, 220. Page 104: the citation of Ephrem is Brock's translation, *Ephrem's Hymns on Paradise*, 213. Page 115: H. C. Agrippa, *De Nobilitate*, 65–66.

General Bibliography

This chapter is almost identical to my earlier essay, "Is Eve the Problem?" Further documentation can be found therein. For the **biblical Eve,** see Meyers, *Discovering Eve,* and Trible, *God and the Rhetoric;* for Eve in Jewish sources, see Kimmelman, "The Seduction of Eve," and Bonner, *"From Eve to Esther."* Bassler, "Adam, Eve, and the Pastor," has treated the text from **1 Timothy** in its New Testament context. On **Michelangelo,** see the sources cited in the notes to chapter 1. Also worthy of note are Gilbert, *Michelangelo, On and Off the Sistine Ceiling,* and Dotson, "An Augustian Interpretation of Michelangelo's Sistine Ceiling." For the remarkable text of **Agrippa,** see Albert Rabil's introductory essay to his edition of the work by H. C. Agrippa, *Declamation* 3–38. Also compare the fine prefatory essay of Roland Antonioli found in the French edition of the Latin text, H. C. Agrippa, *De Nobilitate.*

Chapter Six

General Bibliography

Much of the material in the chapter has appeared in denser form in my article, "Garments of Skin." For the **biblical problem** of Adam's mortality as a result of his transgression, see Barr, *Garden of Eden;* Moberley, "Did the Serpent Get it Right?" and Blenkinsopp, *Pentateuch;* also note the parallels between Adam and Eve in Eden and Israel in the Promised Land. On the careful calibration between the **priestly garments** and the zones of holiness in the Temple, see Menahem Haran, *Temples and Temple-Service.* **Psalm 82** as a summary of Israel's "fall" at Mr. Sinai has recently been reviewed by Kaminsky, "Paradise Regained." On the **garments of glory** in Jewish and Christian writers, see Gottstein, "The Body as Image of God"; Brock, "Clothing Metaphors"; and J. Z. Smith, "Garments of Shame." For the theological implications in the Greek church fathers, see Peterson, "Theologie des Kleides," and for the function of this whole complex in Orthodox tradition, see Nellas, *Deification in Christ.* The ramifications for **baptism** are treated by Meeks, "The Image of the Androgyne," and Smith, "Garments of Shame."

Chapter Seven

Quotations

Page 148: Brown, "The Rise and Function of the Holy Man." Pages 148–49: Brock, "Early Syrian Asceticism," 16 and 12. I have used the Hebrew original of Shai Agnon's story, "Tehillah" in his *Kol Sippurav.* An English translation can be found by I. M. Lask, *Tehilla and other Israeli Tales.*

General Bibliography

On the **Jewish origins** of Adam's penance, see Anderson, "The Penitence Narrative." For the important relationship of this Jewish tradition for **early Syrian monastic traditions,** see Anderson, "Figure of Adam" and "The Original Form of the *Life of Adam and Eve,*" and Beck, "Asketentum."   Recently my student Matthias Henze has systematically gone through this material in his published dissertation, *The Madness of King Nebuchadnezzar.* The role of **Nebuchadnezzar as model penitent** in early Christianity has been masterfully studied by Satran in his Hebrew University dissertation, "Early Jewish and Christian Interpretation of the Fourth Chapter of the Book of Daniel," 1985. It remains unpublished, but a precis of the argument can be found in his *Biblical Prophets in Byzantine Palestine,* 82–91. This work became an important point of reference for Henze's *Madness of King Nebuchadnezzar*. On the issue of **penance** in the early Church, see Poschmann, *Penance and the Anointing of the Sick*, and Rahner, *Penance in the Early Church*. On early **Christian ascetic practice,** see Brock, "Early Christian Asceticism"; Griffith, "Julian Saba"; and Nagel, *Die Motivierung der Askese in der alten Kirche*.

Chapter Eight

Quotations
Page 168: Shäfer, *Rivalität*, 187. Pages 170–71: Muffs, *Love and Joy*, 12–13.

General Bibliography
Additional biblical texts that allude to Christ's descent into Hades include Ephesians 4:8–9 and 1 Peter 3:18–22. The Apostles' Creed also includes a reference to Christ's descent to the dead. A longer form of this essay, entitled "The Resurrection of Adam and Eve," will appear in a Festschrift for Robert Wilken, edited by Paul Blowers and Robin Young. On the **iconographic representation** of the descent of Christ into Hades to redeem Adam and Eve, see Kartsonis, *Anastasis*. For the liturgical reflex of these traditions in the rite of baptism, see Kelly, *The Devil at Baptism*. The **Gospel of Nicodemus** had an enormous afterlife in the Christian tradition, both East and West. For a survey of this elaboration, see MacCullough, *The Harrowing of Hell*, and Daniélou, *The Theology of Jewish Christianity*, 233–248. The theme of **Christus Victor,** i.e. the dramatic victory of Christ over Satan and the forces of Hades, was the focus of Aulén's justly famous work, *Christus Victor*. See the edition of 1968, which has an important prefatory essay by Pelikan that outlines the deep influence this book had on a previous generation of theological students. The thesis of Aulén has received more critical review in the past couple of decades; see the article of Young, "Insight or Incoherence." Von Balthasar, in his *Mysterium Paschale*, reviews the descent-into-Hades material but is less convinced than Aulén as to its theological value. On the role of **Colossians 2:14** in the formation of this tradition, see Best, *An Historical Study*. Adam's bond with the Devil as a theme in later apocryphal literature is treated in Stone, *Adam's Contract with Satan*. For the metaphor of "bearing sin," see Schwartz, "The Bearing of Sin." On God's intention to **outwit the angels** so as to forgive sinners, see Shäfer's, *Rivalität*, and Muffs, "Love and Joy."

Appendix

Quotations
Page 201: Shäfer, "Tempel und Schöpfung," 132–33. Page 205: P. J. Kearney, "Creation and Liturgy," and Hartman "Struggle for the Text," 13. Pages 207–08: Blenkinsopp, *Pentateuch*, 66.

Bibliography
For recent statements on **Genesis 1–3 among modern biblical scholars,** see Barr, *The Garden of Eden;* Moberley, "Did the Serpent Get it Right?"; and Di Vito, "The Demarcation of Divine and Human Realms." For a review of the source-critical problems in Genesis, see Blenkinsopp, *Pentateuch*. For the problem of **original sin and the Bible,** see, Sommer, "Expulsion as Intitiation," and Damrosch, *The Narrative Covenant*, 266–78. For the **Mesopotamian tradition** that concludes with the descent of kingship, see van Seters, "The Creation of Man and the Creation of the King." For temple dedication ceremonies in the ancient Near East, see, Hurowitz, *I*

Have Built You an Exalted House. On the correlation of **Genesis 1 and temple building,** see the studies of Blenkinsopp, *Prophecy and Canon,* 56–69, and Weinfeld, "Sabbath, Temple, and the Enthronement of the Lord." For the **septenary structure** of Leviticus 8, see Milgrom, *Leviticus 1–16,* 542–544. For a comparison of **Jeroboam and Leviticus 10,** see Damrosch, *The Narrative Covenant,* 266–78; Greenstein, "The Formation of the Biblical Narrative Corpus," 171; and Nohrenberg, *Like Unto Moses,* 280–96. On **Paul and the golden calf,** see Meeks "And Rose up to Play."

Selected Bibliography

Classical Sources

I. Jewish Texts
> When original works existed in a Hebrew original, the translations are, for the most part, my own. For a serviceable translation of the primary rabbinic materials, see the Soncino edition of the classical midrashim (*Genesis Rabbah* et al.) and the Babylonian Talmud).

A. Apocryphal Writings
The Book of *Jubilees*
> Charlesworth, James H., ed. *The Old Testament Pseudepigrapha*. Garden City, N.J.: Doubleday, 1985, 2:35–142.

Life of Adam and Eve (disputed origin; see below)
> Anderson, Gary and Michael Stone. *A Synopsis of the Books of Adam and Eve*, 2nd rev. ed. Society of Biblical Literature, Early Judaism and its Literature, vol. 17. Atlanta: Scholars Press, 1999.

B. Rabbinic Literature
Genesis Rabbah
> Theodor, J., and Ch. Albeck, eds. *Midrash Bereshit Rabba: Critical Edition with Notes and Commentary* [Hebrew], 3 vols. Berlin, 1903–36.

Exodus Rabbah
> Mirkin, M., ed. *Midrash Rabba: Shemot* [Hebrew], vols. 5–6. Tel Aviv, 1956.

Leviticus Rabbah
> Margulies, Mordecai, ed. *Wayyiqra Rabba* [Hebrew], 2 vols. New York: Jewish Theological Seminary, 1993.

Deuteronomy Rabbah
> Mirkin, M., ed. *Midrash Rabba: Devarim* [Hebrew], vol. 11. Tel Aviv, 1956.

Sayings of the Fathers
> Schecter, S., Ed. *Avot de Rabbi Natan* [Hebrew], Vienna, 1887. Translations into English: Judah Goldin, trans. *The Fathers According to Rabbi Nathan*. New Haven: Yale University Press, 1955. Anthony J. Saldarini, trans. *The Fathers According to Rabbi Nathan Version B: A Translation and Commentary*. Leiden: Brill, 1975.

Pesikta Rabbati
> Friedmann, M., ed. *Midrash Pesikta Rabbati* [Hebrew] Vienna.

Babylonian Talmud
> *Talmud Bavli* [Hebrew and Aramaic], 20 vols. Vilna: Romm, 1886. Reprint Jerusalem, n.d.

Jerusalem Talmud
> *Talmud Jerushalmi* [Hebrew and Aramaic]. Venice: Bomberg, 1523–24. Reprint, Jerusalem, n.d.

Targum Pseudo-Jonathan
Clarke, E. G., et al., eds. *Targum Pseudo-Jonathan of the Pentateuch: Text and Concordance.* [Aramaic] Hoboken, N.J.: Ktav, 1984.

II. *Christian Texts*
I have translated most of the texts that were written in Syriac and Greek. The few Latin writers I have used have been cited from translation.

A. Apocryphal Writings
Life of Adam and Eve (disputed origin; see above)
Anderson, Gary and Michael Stone, eds. *A Synopsis of the Books of Adam and Eve,* 2nd rev. ed. Atlanta: Scholars Press, 1999.
Gospel of Nicodemus
Schneemelcher, Wilhelm, ed. *New Testament Apocrypha, Vol 1: Gospels and Related Writings.* Louisville: Westminster/John Knox, 1991, 501–532.
Protevangelium of James
Schneemelcher, Wilhelm, ed. *New Testament Apocrypha, Vol 1: Gospels and Related Writings.* Louisville: Westminster/John Knox, 1991, 426–39.

B. Church Fathers
Augustine
City of God. Trans. by Henry Bettenson. New York: Penguin Books, 1972.
Bar Hebraeus
Sprenglin, Martin, and William C. Graham, eds. *Bar Hebraeus' Scholia on the Old Testament.* Part I: Genesis–II Samuel. Chicago: University of Chicago, 1931.
John Chrysostom
Homilies On Genesis, PG 53–54.
Homilies on John, *NPNF,* vol. 14:1–334. *PG* 59:23–482.
Pseudo-Chrysostom
On the Annunciation, PG 62:755D–760D.
Clement of Alexandria
Stromateis. In *Alexandrian Christianity: Selected Translations of Clement and Origin with Introduction and Notes,* edited by John L. Oulton and Henry Chadwick. London: SCM Press, 1954.
Didymus the Blind
Nautin, P., ed. *Didymus L'Aveugle sur la Genèse I. SC,* 233.
Ephrem the Syrian
Carmina Nisibena [Syriac], edited by E. Beck. *CSCO,* 240–41.
Commentary on the Diatessaron. Trans. by C. McCarthy. Oxford: Oxford University Press, 1993. For the Armenian with Latin translation, see Dom L. Leloir, *CSCO,* 137, 145 (1953–54); for the Syriac with Latin translation, see D. Leloir, *S. Ephrem, Commentaire de l'Evangile concordant.* Dublin, 1963. A French translation can be found in Leloir, *SC,* 121, 1966.
Commentary on Genesis = Most of the citations come from Brock's translation found at the back of his *St. Ephrem, Hymns on Paradise. Sancti Ephraem Syri in Genesim et in Exodium* [Syriac]. Edited by R. M. Tonneau, *CSCO,* 152–53.
Hymns on Unleaved Bread = *Des Heiligen Ephraem des Syrers, Paschahymnen* [Syriac]. Edited by E. Beck, *CSCO.*

Hymns on Paradise = *St. Ephrem, Hymns on Paradise.* Trans. by Sebastian Brock. Crestwood, N.Y.: St. Vladimir's Seminary Press, 1990. *Hymnen de Paradiso und Contra Julianum* [Syriac]. Edited by E. Beck *CSCO,* 174–75, 1957.

Pseudo-Ephrem
  Letter to the Mountaineers = *Des Heiligen Ephraem des Syrers, Sermones IV.* Edited by D. Beck, *CSCO,* 334–35, 1973.

Gregory of Nyssa
  On Virginity, NPF, 5:343–71; *De Virginitate, SC,* 71.
  Against Eunomius = *Contra Eunomium.* Edited by W. Jaeger, *Gregorii Nysseni Opera.* Leiden: Brill, 1921.

Gregory Nazianzus
  Theological Orations = *Grégroire de Nazianze, Discours 38–41.* Edited by C. Moreschini and P. Gallay, *SC,* 358.

Origen
  On First Things. ANF, 4:237–382.
  Homilies on Leviticus 1–16. Trans. by Gary W. Barkley. *FC,* 83, 1990.
  Commentary on the Song of Songs = *Origen: The Song of Songs, Commentary and Homilies.* Trans. by R. P. Lawson. *ACW* 26, 1957.
  Commentary on John. ANF 9:297–408.

Tertullian
  On the Apparel of Women. ANF 4:14–25.
  On Penance = W. P. Le Saint, *Tertullian: Treatises on Penance. ACW* 28, 1959.

Theodore of Mopsuestia
  On Baptism = *Commentary of Theodore of Mopsuestia on the Lord's Prayer and on the Sacraments of Baptism and the Eucharist.* Edited and trans. by A. Mingana, Woodbrook Studies. Cambridge: W. Heffer & Sons, 1933.

Theodoret
  Monks of Syria = *A History of the Monks of Syria.* Trans. by R. Price, Kalamazoo, MI: Cistercian Publications, 1985.

III. Later Writers
Agnon, Shai. *Kol Sippurav Shel Shmuel Yosef Agnon. Vol 7: Ad Hennah.* Tel Aviv: Shoken, 1994, 178–206.

H. C. Agrippa,
  Declamation on the Nobility and Preeminence of the Female Sex. Edited by Albert Rabil, Chicago: University of Chicago Press and H. C. Agrippa, *De Nobilitate et Praecellentia Foeminei Sexus.* Edited by Roland Antonioli, Geneve: Librairie Droz, 1990.

Chaucer
  Canterbury Tales. The Middle English text is available on-line at http://etext.lib.virginia.edu.

Dante
  Divine Comedy. Trans. by P. Milano in his *The Portable Dante.* New York: Penguin Books, 1947.

Herrad of Hohenbourg
  Herrad of Hohenbourg: Hortis Deliciarum. Edited by Rosalie Green et al., London: University of London Press, 1979.

John Milton
  Paradise Lost. Edited and annotated by Alistair Fowler, New York: Longman Books,
  1998.

Modern Works

Alexandre, Monique. *Le commencement du Livre Genèse I–V: La version grecque de la Sep-
  tante et sa réception.* Paris: Beauchesne, 1988.

Altmann, Alexander. "The Gnostic Background of the Rabbinic Adam Legends."
  Jewish Quarterly Review 35 (1945): 371–91.

Anderson, Gary A. "The Cosmic Mountain: Eden and Its Early Interpreters in Syriac Christianity." In *Genesis 1–3 in the History of Exegesis,* edited by Gregory Robbins, Lewiston, N.Y.: Edwin Mellen Press, 1988.

———. "Celibacy or Consummation in the Garden?: Reflections on Early Jewish
  and Christian Interpretations of the Garden of Eden." *Harvard Theological Review,*
  82 (1989): 121–48.

———. "The Penitence Narrative in the *Life of Adam and Eve,*" *Hebrew Union College Annual* 63 (1993): 1–38.

———. "The Exaltation of Adam and the Fall of Satan." *Journal of Jewish Thought
  and Philosophy* 6 (1997): 105–43.

———. "Is Eve the Problem?" In *Theological Exegesis: Essays in Honor of Brevard S.
  Childs,* edited by Christopher Seit and Kathryn Greene-McCreight. Grand
  Rapids, Mich.: Wm. B. Eerdmans Publishing Co., 1998.

———. "The Status of the Torah in the Pre-Sinaitic Period: St. Paul's Epistle to
  the Romans." In *Biblical Perspectives: Early Use and Interpretation of the Bible in
  Light of the Dead Sea Scrolls. Proceedings of the First International Symposium of the
  Orion Center, 12–14 May, 1996,* edited by M. Stone and E. Chazon. Leiden: Brill,
  1998.

———. "Adam and Eve in the 'Life of Adam and Eve.'" In *Biblical Figures Outside of
  the Bible,* edited by T. Bergren and M. Stone. Harrisburg, Penn.: Trinity Press,
  1999.

———. "Necessarium Adae Peccatum: An Essay on Original Sin." *Pro Ecclesia* 8
  (1999): 319–337.

———. "The Fall of Satan in the Thought of St. Ephrem and John Milton." *Hugoye:
  Journal of Syriac Studies* 3 (2000), *http://syrcom.cua.edu/Hugoye/*Vol3No1/HV3N1-
  Anderson.html.

———. "The Original Form of the *Life of Adam and Eve*: A Proposal." In *Literature
  on Adam and Eve,* edited by G. Anderson, M. Stone, and J. Tromp. Leiden: Brill,
  2000.

———. "What is Man that Thou Hast Mentioned Him? Psalm 8 and the Nature
  of the Human Person." *Logos: Journal of Catholic Thought and Culture* 3 (2000):
  80–92.

———. "Garments of Skin in Apocryphal Narrative and Biblical Commentary." In
  Studies in Ancient Midrash, edited by James Kugel. Cambridge: Harvard University Press, 2001.

———. "Biblical Origins and the Problem of the Fall." *Pro Ecclesia* 10 (2001): 1–14.

Anderson, Gary and Michael Stone, eds., *A Synopsis of the Book of Adam and Eve,* 2nd
  ed. Atlanta: Scholars Press, 1999.

Anderson, Gary, Michael Stone, and Johannes Tromp. *Literature on Adam and Eve:
  Collected Essays.* Leiden: Brill, 2000.

Aulén, Gustav. *Christus Victor.* New York: Macmillan, 1968.

Awn, Peter. *Satan's Tragedy and Redemption: Iblis in Sufi Psychology.* Leiden: Brill, 1983.

Balthasar, Hans Urs von. *Mysterium Paschale: The Mystery of Easter.* Grand Rapids, Mich.: Wm. B. Eerdmans Publishing Co., 1990.

Bagatti, Bellarmino. "L'iconografia della tentazione di adamo ed eva." *Liber Annus: Studium Biblicum Franciscanum* 31 (1981): 217–230.

Bamberger, Bernard. *Fallen Angels.* Philadelphia: Jewish Publication Society, 1952.

Bammel, Carolyn P. "Adam in Origen." In *The Making of Orthodoxy: Essays in Honor of Henry Chadwick,* edited by R. Williams. Cambridge: Cambridge University Press, 1989.

Barr, James. *The Garden of Eden and the Hope of Immortality.* Minneapolis: Fortress Press, 1993.

Bassler, Jouette. "Adam, Eve, and the Pastor: The Use of Genesis 2–3 in the Pastoral Epistles." In *Genesis 1–3 in the History of Exegesis: Intrigue in the Garden,* edited by Gregory Robbins. Toronto: Edwin Mellen Press, 1988.

Beck, Edmund. *Ephraems Hymnen über Paradies: Übersetzung und Kommentar.* Studia Anselmiana, 26; Rome: Orbis Catholicus/Herder, 1951.

———. "Ein Beitrag zur Terminologie des ältesten syrischen Mönchtums." In *Antonius Magnus Eremita St. Ans.* 38; Rome, 1956.

———. "Asketentum und Mönchtum bei Ephraem." *Orientalia christiana analecta* 153 (1958): 341–62.

Bellis, Alice, and Joel Kaminsky. *Jews, Christians, and the Theology of Hebrew Scriptures.* Atlanta, Ga.: Society of Biblical Literature, 2000.

Best, E. *An Historical Study of the Exegesis of Colossians 2:14.* Rome: Pontificia Universitas Gregorian, 1956.

Børresen, Kari E. *Subordination and Equivalence: The Nature and Role of Woman in Augustine and Thomas Aquinas.* Trans. Charles Talbot. Washington, D.C.: University Press of America, 1981.

Blenkinsopp, Joseph. *Prophecy and Canon.* Notre Dame: Notre Dame Press, 1977.

———. *The Pentateuch: An Introduction to the First Five Books of the Bible.* New York: Doubleday, 1992.

Blowers, Paul. "The *Regula Fidei* and the Narrative Character of Christian Faith." *Pro Ecclesia* 6 (1997): 199–228.

Bonner, Gerald. *Augustine of Hippo: Life and Controversies.* London: SCM Press, 1963.

Boyarin, Daniel. *Carnal Israel: Reading Sex in Talmudic Culture.* Berkeley: University of California Press, 1993.

Brésard, Luc, and Henri Crouzel. *Origine: Commentaire sur le Cantique des Cantiques.* SC, 375, 1991.

Brock, Sebastian. "Early Syrian Asceticism." *Numen* 20 (1973): 1–19.

———. "Jewish Traditions in Syriac Sources" *Journal of Jewish Studies* 30 (1979): 212–232.

———. "Clothing Metaphors as a Means of Theological Expression in Syriac Tradition." In *Typus, Symbol, Allegorie bei den östlichen Vätern und ihren Parallelen im Mittelalter,* edited by M. Schmidt and C. Geyer. Regensburg: Friedrich Pustet, 1982.

———. *The Luminous Eye: The Spiritual World of St. Ephrem.* Kalamazoo, Mich.: Cistercian Press, 1990.

———. "A Brief Guide to the Main Editions and Translations of the Works of St. Ephrem." *The Harp* 3 (1990): 7–25.

Bronner, Leila Leah. *From Eve to Esther: rabbinic Reconstructions of Biblical Women.* Louisville: John Knox Press, 1994.

Brooks, Peter. *Reading for the Plot: Design and Intention in Narrative.* Oxford: Clarendon, 1984.

Brown, Peter. *Augustine of Hippo: A Biography.* London: Faber, 1967.

———. "The Rise and Function of the Holy Man in Late Antiquity." *Journal of Roman Studies* 61 (1971): 80–101.

———. *The Body and Society: Men, Women and Sexual Renunciation in Early Christianity.* New York: Columbia University, 1988.

Burns, J. Patout. "The Fall of Humanity according to Augustine." forthcoming article.

Clark, Elizabeth. " 'Adam's Only Companion': Augustine and the Early Christian Debate on Marriage." *Recherches Augustiniennes* 21 (1986): 139–62.

———. "Heresy, Asceticism, Adam and Eve: Interpretation of Genesis 1–3 in the Later Latin Fathers." In *Genesis 1–3 in the History of Exegesis: Intrigue in the Garden,* edited by Gregory Robbins.

———, ed. *St. Augustine on Marriage and Sexuality.* Washington, D.C.: Catholic University of America Press, 1996. Toronto: Edwin Mellen Press, 1988.

Constas, Nicholas. "The *Conceptio per Aurem* in Late Antiquity: Observations on Eve, the Serpent, and Mary's Ear." Unpublished manuscript.

———. "Weaving the Body of God: Proclus of Constantinople, the Theotokos, and the Loom of the Flesh." *Journal of Early Christian Studies* 3 (1995): 169–94.

Damrosch, David. *The Narrative Covenant: Transformations of Genre in the Growth of Biblical Literature.* San Francisco: Harper and Row, 1987.

Daniélou, Jean. "Terre et Paradis chez les Pères de l'Eglise." *Eranos-Jahrbuch* 1953, 433–72.

———. *The Angels and their Mission; According to the Fathers of the Church.* Westminster, Md.: Newman Press, 1957.

———. *The Theology of Jewish Christianity.* London: Longman, 1964.

———. "Les tuniques de peau chez Grégoire de Nysse." In *Glaube, Geist, Geschichte,* edited by G. Müller and W. Zeller. Leiden: Brill, 1967.

Di Vito, Robert. "The Demarcation of Divine and Human Realms." In *Creation in Biblical Traditions,* edited by R. Clifford and J. Collins. Washington: Catholic Biblical Association, 1992.

Dodaro, Robert, and George Lawless, eds. *Augustine and His Critics: Essays in Honour of Gerald Bonner.* New York: Routledge, 2000.

Dotson, Esther. "An Augustian Interpretation of Michelangelo's Sistine Ceiling." *Art Bulletin* 61 (1979): 223–256, 405–429.

Douglas, Mary. *Purity and Danger: An Analysis of the Concepts of Pollution and Taboo.* New York: Praeger, 1966.

Evans, J. Martin. *Paradise Lost and the Genesis Traditions.* Oxford: Clarendon Press, 1968.

Feldman, David. *Birth Control in Jewish Law.* New York: NYU Press, 1968.

Fraade, Steven. "Ascetical Aspects of Ancient Judaism." In *Jewish Spirituality from the Bible through the Middle Ages,* edited by A. Green. New York: Crossroads, 1986.

Fredriksen, Paula. "Beyond the Body/Soul Dichotomy." *Recherches Augustiniennes* 23 (1988): 87–114.

Frei, Hans. *The Eclipse of Biblical Narrative.* New Haven: Yale University Press, 1974.

Gaventa, Beverly. *Mary: Glimpses of the Mother of Jesus.* Minneapolis, Minn.: Fortress Press, 1999.

Gilbert, Creighton. *Michelangelo, On and Off the Sistine Ceiling. Selected Essays.* New York: Braziller, 1994.

Gottstein, Alon Goshen. "The Body as Image of God in rabbinic Literature." *Harvard Theological Review* 87 (1994): 171–95.

Greenfield, Jonas. "A Touch of Eden." In *Orientalia J. Duchesne-Guillemin emirito oblata.* Leiden: Brill, 1984.

Greenstein, Edward. "The Formation of the Biblical Narrative Corpus." *Association for Jewish Studies Review* 15 (1990).

Griffith, Sidney. "Images of Ephraem: The Syrian Holy man and his Church." *Traditio* 45 (1989–90): 7–33.

———. "Julian Saba, 'Father of the Monks' of Syria. "*Journal of Early Christian Studies* 2 (1994): 185–216.

Guillaumont, Antoine. "Monachisme et éthique judéo-chrétienne." In *Judéo-Christianisme: Recherches historiques et théologiques offertes en hommage au Cardinal Jean Daniélou.* Paris: Recherches de Science Religieuse, 1972.

Haran, Menahem. *Temples and Temple-Service in Ancient Israel: An Inquiry into Biblical Cult Phenomena and the Historical Setting of the Priestly School.* Oxford: Clarendon Press, 1977.

Harl, Marguerite. "La prise de conscience de la 'nudité' d'Adam: une interprétation de Gen 3,7 chez les Péres grecs." *Studia Patristica* 7 (1966): 486–95.

Hart, Mark D. "Reconciliation of Body and Soul: Gregory of Nyssa's Deeper Theology of Marriage." *Theological Studies* 51 (1990): 450–478.

Hartman, Geoffrey. "Struggle for the Text." In *Midrash and Literature*, edited by G. Hartman and S. Budick. New Haven: Yale University Press, 1986.

Hays, Richard B. *The Moral Vision of the New Testament: Community Cross, New Creation.* San Francisco: HarperCollin, 1996.

Henze, Matthias. *The Madness of King Nebuchadnezzar : The Ancient Near Eastern Origins and Early History of Interpretation of Daniel 4.* Leiden: Brill, 1999.

Henry, Paul. *Les Eglises de la Moldavie du Nord des origines à la fin du XVIe siècle.* Paris: Leroux, 1930.

Hunter, William B. "The War in Heaven: The Exaltation of the Son." In *Bright Essence*, edited by W. Hunter, C. Patrides, and J. Adamson. Salt Lake City: University of Utah Press, 1971.

Hurowitz, Avigdor. *I Have Built You an Exalted House: Temple Building in the Bible in the Light of Mesopotamian and North-West Semitic Writings.* Sheffield: JSOT Press, 1992.

Jenson, Robert. "How the World Lost Its Story," *First Things* 36 (1993): 19–24.

Jervell, Jacob. *Imago Dei: Gen 1,26ff im Spätjudentum, in der Gnosis and in den paulinischen Briefen* FRLANT 76; Göttingen: Vandenhoeck & Ruprecht, 1960.

Jolly, Penny Howell. *Made in God's Image? Eve and Adam in the Genesis Mosaics at San Marco, Venice.* Berkeley: University of California Press, 1997.

Jonge, Marinus de, and Johannes Tromp. *The Life of Adam and Eve and Related Literature.* Sheffield: Sheffield Academic Press, 1997.

Kaminsky, Joel. "Paradise Regained: Rabbinic Reflections on Israel at Sinai." In *Jews, Christians, and the Theology of Hebrew Scriptures*, edited by Alice Bellis and Joel Kaminsky.

Kartsonis, Anna. *Anastasis : The Making of an Image*. Princeton: Princeton University Press, 1986.

Kearney, Peter J. "Creation and Liturgy: The P Redaction of Ex 25–40." *Zeitschrift für die Alttestamentliche Wissenschaft* 89 (1977): 375–387.

Kelly, Henry A. *The Devil at Baptism*. Ithaca, N.Y.: Cornell University Press, 1985.

Kimmelman, Reuven. "The Seduction of Eve and Feminist Readings of the Garden of Eden." *Women in Judaism: A Multidisciplinary Journal* 1 (1998): 2. *http://www.utoronto.ca/wjudaism/journal/previous/vol1n2/eve.html*

Kinzer, Mark. "All Things Under His Feet: Psalm 8 in the New Testament and in Other Jewish Literature of Late Antiquity." Dissertation, University of Michigan, 1995.

Klawans, Jonathan. *Impurity and Sin In Ancient Judaism*. Oxford: Oxford University Press, 2000.

Kowalski, A. "Rivesti di gloria. Adamo ed Eva nel commento di sant'Efrem a Gen 2,25. Ricerca sulle fonti dell'esegesi siriaca." *Cristianesimo nella storia* 3 (1982): 41–60.

Kraft, Robert. "The Pseudepigrapha in Christianity." In *Tracing the Threads*, edited by J. Reeves. Atlanta: Scholars Press, 1994.

Kretschmar, Georg. "Ein Beitrag zur Frage nach dem Ursprung frühchristlicher Askese." *Zeitschrift für Theologie und Kirche* 61 (1964): 27–67.

Kretzenbacher, L. "Hunger treibt Urvater Adam zum pakt mit dem Teufel." In *Teufelsbünder und faustgestalten im abendlande*. Klagenfurt: Rudolf Habelt Verlag, 1968.

———. "Jordantaufe auf dem Satansstein." In *Bilder und Legenden*. Klagenfurt: Rudolf Habelt Verlag, 1971.

Kronholm, T. *Motifs from Genesis 1–11 in the Genuine Hymns of Ephrem the Syrian with Particular Reference to the Influence of Jewish Exegetical Tradition*. Coniectanea Biblica Old Testament Series, 11. Lund: Gleerup, 1978.

Kugel, James L. *The Bible as It Was*. Cambridge, Mass.: Harvard University Press, 1997.

Kuhn, Rudolph. *Michelangelo: Die Sixtinische Decke: Beiträge über ihre Quellen und ihre Auslegung*. Berlin: De Gruyter, 1975.

Lambden, Stephen. "From Fig Leaves to Fingernails: Some Notes on the Garments of Adam and Eve in the Hebrew Bible and Select Early Post-Biblical Jewish Writings." In *A Walk in the Garden: Biblical, Iconographical and Literary Images of Eden*. Journal for the Study of the Old Testament Supplement, Series 136; edited by P. Morris and D. Sawyer. Sheffield: JSOT Press, 1992.

Lash, Nicholas. *Believing Three Ways in One God : A Reading of the Apostles' Creed*. London: SCM Press, 1992.

Lask, I. M. *Tehilla and Other Israeli Tales*. New York: Abelard-Schuman, 1956.

Laurentin, René. "L'interprétation de Genèse 3,15, dans la tradition jusqu'au début du xiiie siècle." *Bulletin de la Société française d'Etudes mariales* 12 (1954): 77–156.

Levenson, Jon. *Sinai and Zion*. San Francisco: HarperCollins, 1985.

———. "The Eighth Principle of Judaism and the Literary Simultaneity of Scripture." *Journal of Religion* 68 (1988): 205–225.

———. *The Hebrew Bible, The Old Testament, and Historical Criticism.* Louisville, Ky.: Westminster John Knox Press, 1993.

———. *The Death and Resurrection of the Beloved Son.* New Haven: Yale University Press, 1993.

Levison, James R. *Portraits of Adam in Early Judaism. From Sirach to 2 Baruch.* JSOT Suppl. Series 1. Sheffield: JSOT Press, 1988.

Lewis, C. S. *A Preface to Paradise Lost.* Oxford: Oxford University Press, 1942.

Lipscomb, William Lowndes. *The Armenian Apocryphal Adam Literature.* University of Pennsylvania Armenian Texts and Studies 8. Atlanta: Scholars Press, 1990.

MacCulloch, John Arnott. *The Harrowing of Hell: A Comparative Study of an Early Christian Doctrine.* Edinburgh: T. & T. Clark, 1930.

Maguire, Henry. "Adam and the Animals: Allegory and Literal Sense in Early Christian Art." *Dumbarton Oaks Papers* 41 (1987): 363–373.

Meeks, Wayne. "The Image of the Androgyne: Some Uses of a Symbol in Earliest Christianity." *History of Religions* 13 (1974): 165–208.

———. "'And Rose Up to Play': Midrash and Paraenesis in 1 Cor. 10:1–22." *Journal for the Study of the New Testament* 16 (1982): 64–78.

Meyers, Carol. *Discovering Eve: Ancient Israelite Women in Context.* New York: Oxford University Press, 1988.

Milgrom, Jacob. *Leviticus 1–16.* Anchor Bible 3. New York: Doubleday, 1991.

Moberley, Walter. "Did the Serpent Get it Right?" *Journal of Theological Studies* 39 (1988): 1–27.

Morris, Paul. "Exiled from Eden: Jewish Interpretations of Genesis." In *A Walk in the Garden: Biblical, Iconographical and Literary Images of Eden,* edited by Paul Morris and Deborah Sawyer. Sheffield: JSOT Press, 1992.

Muffs, Yohanan. *Love and Joy: Law, Language, and Religion in Ancient Israel.* Cambridge: Harvard University Press, 1992.

Murdoch, Brian. "The Garments of Paradise." *Euphorion* 61 (1967): 375–82.

Murphy, Cullen. *The Word According to Eve.* New York: Houghton Mifflin, 1998.

Murray, Robert. "Mary, the Second Eve in the Early Syriac Fathers." *Eastern Churches Review* 3 (1971): 372–84.

———. "The Lance Which Re-opened Paradise." *Orientalia Christiana Periodica* 39 (1973): 224–34.

———. "The Exhortation to Candidates for Ascetical Vows at Baptism in the Ancient Syriac Church." *New Testament Studies* 21 (1974–75): 60–70.

———. *Symbols of Church and Kingdom.* Cambridge: Cambridge University Press, 1975.

O'Malley, John. "The Theology Behind Michelangelo's Ceiling." In *The Sistine Chapel. The Art, the History, and the Restoration.* New York: Harmony Books, 1986.

Nellas, Panayiotis. *Deification in Christ: Orthodox Perspectives on the Nature of the Human Person.* Crestwood, N.J.: St. Vladimir's Press, 1987.

Nagel, Peter. *Die Motivierung der Askese in der alten Kirche und der Ursprung des Mönchtums.* Texte und Untersuchungen zur Geschichte der altchristlichen Literatur 95. Berlin: Akademie Verlag, 1966.

Nohrenberg, James. *Like Unto Moses: The Constituting of an Interruption.* Bloomington Ind.: Indiana University Press, 1995.

Pagels, Elaine. *Adam, Eve, and the Serpent.* New York: Random House, 1988.

————. *The Origin of Satan.* New York: Random House, 1995.

Partridge, Loren. *Michelangelo. The Sistine Chapel Ceiling, Rome.* New York, Braziller, 1996.

Patrides, C. A. *Milton and the Christian Tradition,* Oxford: Clarendon Press, 1966.

Pelikan, Jaroslav. *Mary Through the Centuries: Her Place in the History of Culture.* New Haven, Conn.: Yale University Press, 1996.

Peterson, Eric. "Theologie des Kleides." *Benediktinische Monatsschrift* 16 (1934): 347–56.

Poorthuis, Marcel. "Who Is to Blame: Adam or Eve? A Possible Jewish Source for Ambrose's *De Paradiso* 12,56." *Vigiliae Christianae* 50 (1996): 125–135.

Poschmann, Bernhard. *Penance and the Anointing of the Sick.* New York: Herder & Herder, 1964.

Quinn, Esther C. *The Quest of Seth for the Oil of Life.* Chicago, University of Chicago Press, 1962.

Rahner, Karl. *Penance in the Early Church. Theological Investigations,* vol. 15. New York: Crossroad, 1982.

Robbins, Gregory, ed., *Genesis 1–3 in the History of Exegesis.* Lewiston, N.Y.: Edwin Mellen Press, 1988.

Rosenstiehl, Jean-Marc. "La chute de l'Ange, Origines et développement d'une légende, ses attestations dans la littérature copte." In *Écritures et traditions dans la littérature Copte.* Louvain: Peeters, 1983.

Safran, Bezalel. "Rabbi Azriel and Nahmanides: Two View of the Fall of Man." In *Rabbi Moses Nahmanides: Explorations in His Religious Virtuosity,* edited by I. Twersky. Cambridge: Harvard University Press, 1983.

Satran, David. "Early Jewish and Christian Interpretation of the Fourth Chapter of the Book of Daniel." Dissertation, Hebrew University of Jerusalem, 1985.

————. *Biblical Prophets in Byzantine Palestine: Reassessing the Lives of the Prophets.* Leiden: Brill, 1995.

Séd, Nicolas. "Les hymnes sur le Paradis de Saint Ephrem et les traditions juives," *Le Muséon* 81 (1968): 455–501.

Seters, John van. "The Creation of Man and the Creation of the King." *Zeitschrift für die alttestamentliche Wissenschaft* 101 (1989): 333–342.

Shäfer, Peter. "Tempel und Schöpfung." *Kairos* 16 (1974).

————. *Rivalität zwischen Engeln und Menschen: Untersuchungen zur rabbinischen Engelvorstellung.* Berlin: De Gruyter, 1975.

————. "Adam in jüdischen Überlieferung." In *Vom alten zum neuen Adam: Urzeitmythos und Heilsgeschichte,* edited by W. Strolz. Freiburg: Herder, 1986.

Schwartz, Baruch. "The Bearing of Sin in the Priestly Literature." In *Pomegranates and Golden Bells,* edited by D. Wright et al. Winona Lake, Ind.: Eisenbrauns, 1995.

Sieger, Joanne. "Visual Metaphor as Theology: Leo the Great's Sermons on the Incarnation and the Arch Mosaics at S. Maria Maggiore." *Gesta* 26 (1987): 83–92.

Simonetti, Manlio. "Alcune osservazioni sull'interpretazione origeniana di Genesi 2,7 e 3,21." *Aevum* 36 (1962): 370–81.

Smith, Jonathan Z. "The Garments of Shame." *History of Religions* 5 (1965/66): 217–38.

Smith, Morton. "On the Shape of God and the Humanity of the Gentiles." In *Religions in Antiquity,* edited by Jacob Neusner. Leiden: Brill, 1970.

Sommer, Benjamin. "Expulsion as Intitiation: Displacement, Divine Presence, and Divine Exile in the Torah." In *Beginning a Reading/Reading Beginnings: Towards a Hermeneutic of Jewish Texts*, edited by S. Magid and A. Cohen. New York: Seven Bridges Press, 1999.

Stager, Lawrence. "Jerusalem and the Garden of Eden." In *Eretz Israel* 26 (1998): 83–88.

Steinberg, Leo. "The Line of Fate in Michelangelo's Painting." *Critical Inquiry* 6 (1980): 411–454.

Stichel, Rainer. "Die Verführung der Stammeltern durch Satanael nach der Kurzfassung der slavischen Baruch-Apokalypse." In *Kulturelle Traditionen in Bulgarien*, edited by R. Lauer and P. Schreiner. Göttingen: Vandenhoeck und Ruprecht, 1989.

Stone, Michael E. *The Penitence of Adam. CSCO*, 1981, 429–30.

———. *Armenian Apocrypha Relating to Patriarchs and Prophets.* Jerusalem: Israel Academy of Sciences, 1982.

———. *A History of the Literature of Adam and Eve.* Early Judaism and its Literature 3. Atlanta: Scholars Press, 1992.

———. *Adam's Contract with Satan: The Legend of the Cheirograph of Adam.* Bloomington, Ind.: Indiana University Press, 2001.

Trible, Phyllis. *God and the Rhetoric of Sexuality.* Philadelphia: Fortress Press, 1978.

Urbaniak-Walczak, Katarzyna. *Die "Conceptio per aurem." Untersuchungen zum Marien-bild in Ägypten unter besonderer Berücksichtigung der Malereien in El-Bagawat.* Altenberge: Oror Verlag, 1992.

Virgo, Hugo. *Eva-Virgo Maria. Neue Untersuchungen über die Lehre von der Jungfrauenschaft und Ehe Mariens in der ältesten Kirche.* Berlin-Leipzig: de Gruyter, 1937.

Weinfeld, Moshe. "Sabbath, Temple and the Enthronement of the Lord." In *Mélanges bibliques et orientaux en l'honneur de M. H. Cazelles*, AOAT 212, edited by A. Caquot and M. Delcor. Neukirchen-Vluyn: Neukirchener Verlag, 1981.

Wills, Garry. *Saint Augustine.* New York: Viking, 1999.

Wright, David P. "Holiness, Sex and Death in the Garden of Eden." *Biblica* 77 (1996): 324–327.

Wyschogrod, Michael. "Incarnation." *Pro Ecclesia* 2 (1993): 208–215.

Young, Francis. "Insight or Incoherence: The Greek Fathers on Good and Evil." *Journal of Ecclesiastical History* 24 (1973): 113–26.

Textual References

General Index